Current Research Trends in Commerce and Management

Current Research Trends in Commerce and Management:
A Survey, 2022

(B: Management)

Dr K. L. Narasimha Murty
Chief Editor

GYAN

ISBN: 978-81-212-6475-4

Published, 2022

Published by

Gyan Publishing House
5, Ansari Road
Daryaganj, New Delhi-110002
Phone: 011-47034999, 9811692060
www.gyanbooks.com
E-mail: books@gyanbooks.com

Printed at: Gyan Press, Delhi.

Dedicated to My Teachers

Sri Nanduri Subbarayudu Garu, M. Com.
Seniormost Lecturer in Commerce,
D.N.R. College, Bhimavaram.

Sri Vangapandu Upendra Rao Garu,
"Sahitya Ratna" M. Com. F.C.A., F.I. C.W.A. B.G.L.
"V. R. Upendra & Co."
Senior Lecturer in Commerce
D.N.R. College, Bhimavaram.

Contents

Preface

The present volume presents 12 chapters relating to the description analysis of Current Research Trends (CRT), in Commerce and Management volume two relates to research in management in Indian environmental scenario to the extent of interrelated subjects covered the uncovered subjects such as Commerce, Geography and Management so far.

In the first chapter, the above three subjects have a common platform i.e. environment with the other two subjects and earlier studies, covered so far and the uncovered subjects and themes were systematically and scientifically organised with thematic presentation. Second chapter is related to the theme i.e. evolving scenario for Commerce and Management in India besides corporate survival struggle during pandemic era "Impact of Sustainability Dimension of Corporate Governance on select companies" by the author in the 4th chapter. The author has presented the Gender responsive Budgeting emerging paradigm in Management in Chapter 5.

Technological factors, such as Geospatial applications in Disaster Management is an important thought provoking and scientific oriented paper in Chapter 6. Role of Blockchain technology in 7th chapter and Role of Board of Directors in policy formulation and decision making have been presented in 7th and 8th chapters respectively. In chapter 9, Rao presented the importance and utility of quantitative techniques in Commerce and Management research. In chapter 10, Dr. Rayudu has presented the scenario relating to Management of Tribal's produce in Andhra Pradesh (Marketing Management).

Dr. Padmamalini has presented the recent techniques, factors and its impact on society (consumers) i.e. the process of Digitalisation Banking in banking sector identified the difference basically in Government and private banks in Andhra Pradesh.

Summative analysis (S.A), New Areas of Research (NAR) Ph.D. Thesis in Management and U.G.C. project proposals were presented in the 12th chapter. At the end, Annexure I & II were added to knowledge.

K.L. Narasimha Murty

305, Manikanta Saisudha Appts,
Meena Cafe Lane,
Warasiguda,
Hyderabad-500 061,
Telangana State, India.
Cell No. 7207337962

Hyderabad,
18th January 2022

List of Contributors of the Present Volume

1. **Dr K. L. Narasimha Murty,** Principal (R), Government P.G. and U.G. College (M), Srikakulam, Andhra Pradesh and formerly Research Consultant, RCUES, Osmania University, Hyderabad, T.S.
2. **Professor V. Madhava Rao,** Research Professor, GIET University, Odisha, India.
3. **S. Nagamani,** Assistant Professor of Commerce, Vivekananda Government Degree College, Vidyanagar, Hyderabad, T.S.
4. **Dr K. Anjaneyulu,** Associate Professor of Commerce, Vivekananda Government Degree College, Hyderabad, T.S.
5. **Sri G.E. Lesilie,** Research Officer, Regional Centre for Urban and Environment Studies, Osmania University, Hyderabad, T.S.
6. **Dr Ch. Kishore Kumar,** Assistant Professor of Commerce, Vivekananda Government Degree College, Vidyanagar, Hyderabad, T.S.
7. **Ms. M. Sangeetha,** Assistant Professor of Commerce, Vivekananda Government Degree College, Vidyanagar, Hyderabad, T.S.
8. **Dr C.S.S.R.L. Hanumantha Rao**, Senior Assistant Professor of Statistics, M.R.A. College, Vizianagaram, Andhra Pradesh.
9. **Dr P. Padmamalini,** Former Reserach Scholar, Department of Commerce, Rayalaseema University, Kurnool, Andhra Pradesh.
10. **Dr A. Venkata Rayudu,** Joint Director (R), A.P. Tribal Development, Hyderabad.
11. **Smt. T.V. Jagadamba,** Former P.G. Student, Department of Commerce, A.U.P.G. Centre, Etcherla, Srikakulam, Andhra Pradesh, and also @ Masterminds, Guntur, Andhra Pradesh.
12. **Sri N. Subbarayudu,** Senior Lecturer in Commerce

List of Contributors of the Present Volume

A. Environment and Development

1

Introduction

Dr K. L. Narasimha Murty
(Annexture-2)

'Search' and 'Research' are two important aspects and these should be taken up for active, reactive and interactive phenomena in inter-disciplinary and multi-disciplinary search both intensively and extensively attempts to identify and recognize the on-going scientific and technological research. Modern research is considered as multidimensional one which is highly competitive but not complementary. Economics, Commerce including modern business management, business organisation and business administration are having common approach with special treatment of organising the space (Geographic space). For the above subjects to understand crystal clearly the aspects of locating of an industry is quite important. Keeping in view of the geographic factors (Geographic determination), there should be a scientific approach for its application, adoption and process.

1. EARLIER STUDIES: LITERATURE SURVEY

Environmental Economics, business environment, environmental organisation including environmental administration are important aspects totally with a totality in Human efforts are to be infused in order to attain and achieve sustainable development through innovations and entrepreneurship. Corporate social responsibility and its role in community development, C.S.R. expenditure in education sector, Role of NGOs in corporate Social Responsibility (CSR), innovation entrepreneurship and sustainable development, C.S.R. policy and practices and evaluating Pradhan Mantri Gramin digital Sakshrta Abhiyan (PM DISHA) for sustainable expansion are important contributions to the modern research in commerce and Management till 201 8-2021. (Reference: Annexure - 1)

2. GAPS IN RESEARCH

Keeping in view of the earlier studies the following are certain gaps in the past research:

1. To identify key components which are going to impact commerce and management for present decade and decades to come.
2. G.D.P. decline: causes and its impact.
3. Impact of sustainable governance, management responsibility and oversight for sustainability activities and performance besides catalysing sustainability through corporate governance's influence on the society.
4. Environmental influence i.e. impact of the corporation in the geophysical geographical environment, such as water waste, paper waste and energy waste (4ch).
5. Millennium Development Goals (M.D.Gs) and the sustainable Development Goals (SDGs), 5th out of 17th goals in Gender Equality.

   To identify women's equity, promotion of gender equality and the empowerment (steps so far taken by G.O.I).
6. Role of geospatial technology in disaster management.
7. Role of Blockchain Technology.
8. To Study the policy Formulation and decision making besides best practices.
9. Role of quantitative techniques for analysing the data, (input/ Application of research methods), and
10. To identify the alternative banking system in the existing banking system and its impact.

3. OBJECTIVES

1. Keeping in view of the above aspects in mind, there's every need to bring out the volume of work relating to management research (Current Research Trends in Commerce and Management).
2. To evolve research methodologies in Management search.
3. To identify the new areas of research in Management; and
4. Project proposal (A blue print).

4. METHODOLOGY

Mathematical and economic statistical methods have to be adopted for the data analysis.

Title: "Current Research Trends in Commerce and Management": A Survey (Volume two) (1-300 pages)

Chapterisation:

1. Introduction.
2. Evolving scenario for commerce and management in India.
3. Corporate survival struggle during pandemic era.
4. Impact of sustainability dimension of corporate governance on select companies.
5. Gender Responsive budgeting, emerging paradaigm in Management.
6. Geospatial Technology Applications in Disaster Management.
7. Role of Blockchain Technology - A case study in Banking sector.
8. Role of Board of Director's in policy formulation and decision making.
9. Quantitative Techniques in Management Research
10. Digitalisation Banking.
11. Design and structure of tribal product marketing: A strategy; and
12. 12.1 Analysis, 12.2 Summative analysis, 12.3 New areas of research, 12.3 Detailed project proposal and 12.4 Conclusions. Annexure - I and Annexure-II.

An attempt is made to present the entitled work to understand further for the furtherance of commerce and management scenario in chapter-2.

2

Evolving Scenario for Commerce and Management in India

Prof V. Madhava Rao

Over the years from traditional to professional modern management, commercial practices, small trading to big business houses, imports to exports, dependence to self reliance, scattered market to global markets, single product to multi product, selected product and service range to wide product range, small retail stores to super markets and malls, India has evolved the process over period of time and has been established as a fast growing economy in the world.

The post Covid-19 pandemic has brought a sea change in commerce and management practices not only in India but across the world. The critical aspects of the post pandemic scenario, in the evolving process have been the adaptation of New Normal approach, Circular Economy, Industry 4.0 and the wide use of Artificial Intelligence applications, which have been an integral part of the present happenings and are going to be dominant players in foreseeable future.

An attempt has been made to provide an overview of the four key components which are going to impact commerce and management for present decade and decades to come.

I. NEW NORMAL

The COVID-19 pandemic has brought in a New Normal Standard being adopted in all sectors at all levels, in programmes and policies, in day to day lives, in education, health care, agriculture, industry, services, mobility, and all areas, which no one ever imagined, since last one and half years and has brought in large scale ramifications for India. The lockdown, restrictions in movements, restricted to homes, hospitals and quarantine centres, made people to settle to live with the 'new normal' due to Covid-19 cases and deaths, wearing face masks, maintaining social distance, proper sanitisation, and tried to manage life, career, work, studies, with technology and by managing with basic necessities and bare minimum requirements.

The Union and State Governments, Local Bodies, Government and Non Govt Agencies, National and International Agencies, Civil Societies, Youth Associations, Citizens, and practically all evolved ways to adjust with the requirements to contain Covid-19. The work from home, Online Classes, digital contactless payments, e-supply of medicines, groceries, food and other essential items, through e-commerce networks, e-grievance redressal with Police, Banks, Government Departments, medicare and all activities in e-mode.

The New Normal during Pandemic was social distancing, wearing masks, supply chain disruptions, public health and sanitation. The Pandemic has led to gather all data on infected people, contact tracing, almost at each place, which was a massive exercise, where Data Analytics and Artificial Intelligence, was used to facilitate monitoring on realtime mode. The data collection was on virtual data collection mode, on evidence based, through surveys or interviews or group calls location based services, for formulating action plans to mitigate the Pandemic Situation and provision of effective healthcare, vaccination, support services, ambulance, oxygen and other vital health facilities.

The data and analysis reports, from qualitative to quantitative, Covid-19 impacted communities; utilisation of risk communication massages from pandemic managing agencies; social economic hardship faced by the migrant labour and displaced population; and various aspects of human rights of pandemic response stakeholders.

Satellite Remote Sensing, GIS, GNSS, Data Analytics, Artificial Intelligence based Virtual Surveys to capture field Data, analysis, mapping, providing Dash Boards, Decision Support Systems are all, is a part of the New Normal, for urgent disaster mitigation, in an humanitarian system.

This now led to Virtual data collection will be more common, and acceptable, to make data more authentic and credible, helping in cost effective, realtime, precise and accurate data, reflecting field realities on the ground, for helping resolve the situations more effectively.

There were significant improvements in environment, pollution reduction, clear sky, drastic reduction in noise pollution, reduction in the anthropogenic pressure, which are really learning lessons for planning and managing global environment.

New normal has attracted people towards organic kitchen garden and organic products viz. vegetables, lintels, food crops, fruits etc and even animal products without exposed to chemical feed and maintaining in natural atmosphere, for which great demand has been generated across the globe.

The adaptation of New Normal for the Indian Economy is getting internalised, to changing scenarios due to Covid-19 Pandemic and reemerging with different mutations and variants, with a signal that pandemic will remain across countries for some more time.

The New Normal scenario for the Indian Economy will bring visible results sooner or later, even though growth rates are estimated slower, wherein structural reforms such as these two and other reforms would take some time to bear fruits and hence, it is better to be prepared for a prolonged slowdown.

Digital Cashless Payments and Aadhaar and PIN based transactions with Tax Compliance, and GST, is transforming India from an Informal to the Formal Economy, in the New Normal Scenario. Primarily the State and Union Governments provide all fund flows digitally with Direct Benefit Transfer to eligible common citizen under different categories, on real time mode, with Dash Board and Pop Up monitoring and tracking.

Regulations in Small and Medium Enterprises and labour laws, bring a sea change in the management, operation and functioning of business, economy and industry and other sectors, under the New Normal.

Circular economy, Industry 4.0 and Artificial Intelligence, including IoT is necessitating adoption of New Normal to forge ahead to ensure sustainability and generate optimum success in growth, returns, innovations, environmental compliance, reduction in carbon dependency and popularise waste to wealth.

There is a perceptional attitudinal change among people after having experienced the risks and measures for protection, for health and well being and these will go a long way for adopting to New Normal environment and practices.

The COVID-19 pandemic has given the world to reflect, reassess and rethink, for bringing resilience and adoptability in economy, employment, human life and well being, and broughtin tremendous alternatives for managing situations of livelihood, healthcare, basic provisions, and rolling on the economic, social and development activities, on different paces to normalise the situations.

Even though there was risk and uncertainties in the air about the Covid-19 Pandemic blues, the government, people, businesses and industry synergistically faced the virus out break situation and largely on the path to recovery, learning from the fact that agility and resilience as the key to survival, and brought in flexible and adoptability, in changing times and prompted to rethink economy, business, organisation, Government, to strategies and prepare for adjustments to structural changes.

Communities, citizens, Government, Local Bodies, Women Groups, Youth, CBOs, Farmers, learn to be more resilient, healthy, productive, sustainable, and be creative during difficult times, under the New Normal situations. The construction sector embracing ecofriendly construction techniques and introducing an array of wellness features in self-sustained townships, ability of homes to enable deeper emotional connection with oneself and foster a sense of community, and with preference towards amenities that lead to overall well-being.

The health and wellness concerns have led to an evolution in project design and architecture to design, structure, location, the ecosystem, facilities, and state-of-the art amenities. The significance of a lifestyle in harmonious coexistence with nature, with adequate light, air and natural views, emanated from Pandemic experience.

Carbon neutral, reduction in the use of energy consumption, renewable and reusable resources, green building features and energy-efficient technologies, water harvesting, conservation and recycling, vegetation, alternative building materials, and disaster resilient structure are priorities in building technologies now, a new normal features of appreciation, jubilation and happiness among the community, with spaces that bring them together through common experiences within the safety and comfort of their own neighbourhood.

Tomorrow's building structures and infrastructure designs will encourage touchless tech features, theme-based residences uniquely tailored to citizen, Government, Communities, Local Bodies, Industry, business, preferences, that will become the New Normal.

Work from home has become the New Normal and people will start preferring faster contact and communication network to connect with surrounding and the world, for business, livelihood, innovation, trading, commerce and industry. Suburbs of metropolitan cities, Tier 2 and 3 cities preference for living in peripheral areas, and hinterland, will emerge as the new locus for real estate development, thus will evolve as fast spaces for infrastructural development and enabling policy framework to accentuate the prospects in these areas, under New Normal.

The world has witnessed all, common citizens, industry, NGOs, CBOs, Corporates and Industry, Civil Society, Local Bodies, and Government, come together for working towards tackling the healthcare challenges, in these unprecedented times. The infrastructure and construction industry, through collaboration and innovation, in spite of shortage of labour at construction sites, tried to forge ahead, with possibilities.

II. CIRCULAR ECONOMY

According to Paul Ekins, the circular economy is relating to the flow of materials through an economy, and concerned with thinking about the economic conditions that might bring about such a flow, postulated during 1960s and 1970s and established a symbiotic relationship among the two aspects. However, in 1940s, the term Industrial Symbiosis was used in economic geography, which referred to the location of industries in order to make efficient utilisation of resources and avoid waste. The system necessitated the optimized consumption of energy and materials, with minimum generation of waste, which was conceptualised by Frosch and Gallopoulos in 1989. Geissdoerfer, Erkman, Boulding, Stahel and Reday-Mulvey, Stahel, Kerry Turner Pearce, Ellen MacArthur, Kirchherr, Blomsma and Brennan, and Pietrulla, contributed substantially for Circular Economy concepts, approaches and applications, emphasizing cleaner production systems, conservation, recycling and sustainability.

Boulding's paper opens with a discussion of the difference between open and closed systems, particularly in respect of the three essential elements of existence, namely materials, energy, and information/ knowledge, called as Econosphere, a material process involving the discovery and mining of fossil fuels, ores, etc., and effluents of the system passed out into noneconomic reservoirs. Boulding explains entropy, giving a description of the thermodynamics of a circular economy, stressing the importance of both energy and information, based on physical system condition, philosophical, ethical and economic dimensions, within the cyclical ecological system.

Stahel explained that the use of goods, will have a transition towards a sustainable society in which progress is made consistent with the world's finite resource base, and coined spiral loop system which is expected to minimise matter, energy-flow and environmental deterioration without restricting economic growth or social and technical progress, with processes of reuse, repair, recondition and recycle.

Boulding established that the economy and environment are not characterised by linear interlinkages, but by a circular relationship, that is everything is an input into everything else.

Pearce and Turner (1990) asserted that the environment has the capacity to be reabsorbed into the environment, namely the emissions to air and biologically degradable wastes, in the natural environment, within reasonable limits, and identified the exhaustible and renewable resources.

Braungart, Stahel and Benyus and Roland Clift, aggressively promoted the concept of circular economy in 2013, which were experimented by the European Commission and other International Agencies.

Ellen MacArthur Foundation defines a Circular Economy, as an industrial system that is restorative or regenerative by intention and design, and replaces the End-of-Life concept with restoration, shifts towards the use of renewable energy, eliminates the use of toxic chemicals, which impair reuse, and aims for the elimination of waste through the superior design of materials, products, systems, and business models (2013).

Recycling is the core of a circular economy, with 3 Rs as Reduce, Reuse and Recycle and 4 Rs as Reduce, Reuse, Recycle and Recover, 5 Rs as Reduce, Reuse, Recycle, Recover and Residual Management, 7 Rs as Rethink, Reuse, Reduce, Repurpose, Refuse, Recycle, and Rot, while the 12 Rs are Remember, Respect, Refuse, Reduce, Reuse, Return, Refill, Rot, Restore, Repurpose, Repair, and Recycle.

Kirchherr (2017) described the circular economy as an economic system that is based on business models which replace the 'end-of-life' concept with reducing, alternatively reusing, recycling and recovering materials in production/distribution and consumption processes, thus operating at the micro level (products, companies, consumers), meso level (eco-industrial parks) and macro level (city, region, nation and beyond), with the aim to accomplish sustainable development, which implies creating environmental quality, economic prosperity and social equity, to the benefit of current and future generations.

The EMF defines Circular Economy based on restorative and regenerative, ecology and symbiosis, identifying renewable energy, elimination of toxic chemicals and waste, superior design and business models, as key elements.

Blomsma and Brennan (2017) refer to the circular economy as an Umbrella Concept, rooted in and around resource and waste management, with circular economy strategies, called resource life-extending strategies, to extend resource life, through reuse, recycling, remanufacturing, servitisation, repair, waste-to-energy, product longevity approaches, and the cascading of substances and articulated the capacity to extend the productive life of resources as a means to create value and reduce value destruction.

The characteristics of Circular Economy are environment, efficiency, waste reduction, and end-of-life disposal. Thus, the circular economy is one that has low environmental impacts and that makes good use of natural resources, through high resource efficiency and waste prevention, especially in the manufacturing sector, and minimal end-of-life disposal of materials.

The relationship between the circular economy and sustainability is the overall development of economic, social and environmental, creating social justice and equitable distribution. Non-economic factors may also be significant both as drivers and barriers. Institutional conditions such as material management regulations could either enable or inhibit recycling or remanufacturing. Technological and infrastructure factors can enable or limit the options available to industry, business and services to operate within the circular economy.

As per the EMF Delivering the Circular Economy: A Toolkit for Policymakers (2015), for policymakers at all levels, from local to municipal to national level, policy intervention, namely regulatory, fiscal, education, public procurement, innovation, infrastructure, etc.

Under the Solid Waste Management Rules (SWM), 2016, explicitly mandates source segregation of waste for value addition and promote recovery, reuse and recycle, with local bodies allowed to levy charges, spot fine, for littering and non-segregation. The policy calls for increased production of compost and mandates the department of fertiliser for increased marketing of these products, and promotion of waste to energy plant.

Under the Construction and Demolition Waste Management Rules (2016), the responsibility to waste generators for their storage and transportation to collection centre are assigned to local bodies or to be handed over to authorised processing facilities.

The government of India notified the construction and demolition waste management rule in 2016. The rule assigns responsibility to waste generators for their storage and transportation to collection centre as provided by local bodies or to be handed over to authorised processing facilities. The rule suggests administrative and other logistic supports from the State Governments to the business in the C& D Waste Management Sectors (MoEF&CC, 2016).

For E-Waste treatment and resource recovery, the E-Waste Management Rules were formulated in 2016, rules were notified in 2016, emphasizing setting of collection centres and use of innovative technologies, for environmentally sound recycling and recovery.

The MoEF&CC, Government of India formulated the Plastic Waste Management Rules in 2016, fixing responsibilities in system of collecting back plastic wastes, use of plastic waste for road construction as per Indian Road Congress guidelines or energy recovery, or waste to oil etc. for gainful utilisation of waste.

The Ministry of Environment & Forestry, Climate Change (MoEF& CC), developed detail guidelines for recovery and reuse of materials from hazardous and other waste materials, in 2016.

The GST Council significantly reduced the rates on electronic waste from 28% to 5% plastic wastes as well as other waste or scrap of glass and rubber waste, reduced from 18% to 5%, to incentivize the waste management.

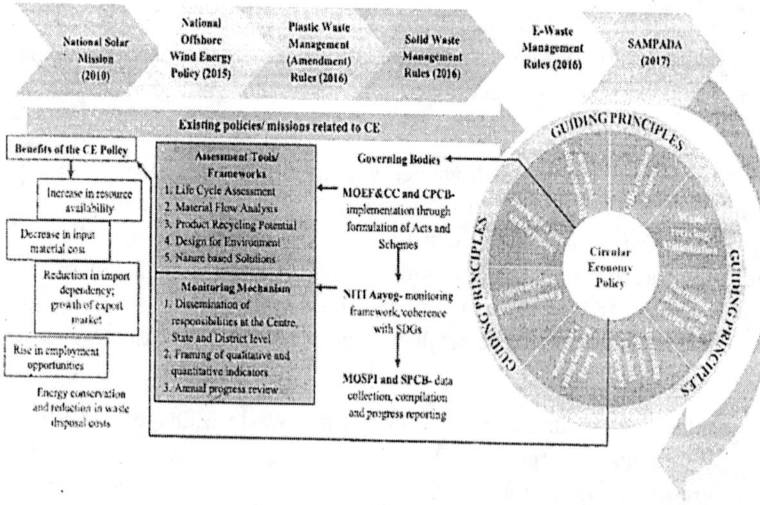

Fig. 1

The Fig. 1 illustrates the various National Policies of Government of India to streamline the Circular Economy operation in India.

The circular economy aim at enhancing product life cycle, bring in innovativeness, promoting carbon trading, ensuring profitability, and improving return on investment. In the environmental aspects the waste to wealth by adopting 5 R concept, promoting biodegradable materials, waste minimisation, neutralising carbon foot print, energy conservation, and promotion clean development mechanism. Societal aspects like development of housing and service infrastructure, health and education, enhancement of job opportunities, promotion of social capital, and legislation and enforcement.

The Circular Economy has it's own challenges, which are organisational, technical, managerial and social. The proactive role of State and Union Governments, bring ' turnaround and propel growth and optimum returns. The 5 Rs of Waste to Wealth, viz, reduce, reuse, recycle, recover and residual management, bring in immense opportunities in innovations, start ups, business and industry promotion, protection of environment, and integrate all stake holders, up to the last mile.

The Waste Electrical and Electronic Equipment recycling generate technology creation, extraction of useful commercial components for reuse, socially acceptable, environment friendly and economically viable. This sector is coming up great opportunities for start ups and innovations, as there are increasing generation of electrical and electronic waste in the country.

Public Private Partnership enhances investment and technology infusion in the waste collection, segregation, recycling, and disposal, following environmental regulations and minimal or zero adverse impact.

There needs greater awareness of all stake holders, among Local Bodies, Municipalities, Citizens, Industry, Farmers, youth, students, women groups and all associated bodies.

The Circular Economy promotes a healthy economy, environment, business and industry. The Swatch Bharat had generated mindset change and taken off and numerous technology innovations are adopted across the country, for effective collection, segregation, recycling, reuse and disposal methods, and generated integrated logistics activities.

The universal demand for the energy efficiency lighting, heating and electric utility product s like washing machines, fridge, air conditioners, kitchen items, industrial equipments and systems, etc, shows growing awareness for practice of circular economy principles.

Government officials, non-profits, social scientists and technology experts need to be on board to plan and design circular economies for various sectors, to bring in both environmental benefits as well as huge economic benefits.

The Indian Industry has started interest in adaptation of circular economy principles, to adhere to environmental compliance and optimising returns on investment, for growth, profitability, expansion, diversification, technology infusion and bring circular economy order in the regions and the country.

III. INDUSTRY 4.0

The Industrial Revolution refers to 17th to 20th centuries developments in the world of manufacturing and technology and witnessed the Information Technology, internet, renewable energy, communication technologies, mobile and other connected devices.

With the present technological development, in the areas of advanced analytics, Big Data, Robotics & Automation, Artificial Intelligence, Internet of Things (IoT) and Process Digitisation across the business value chain, the Industry 4.0 has evolved.

The Department of Heavy Industries, Ministry of Heavy Industries & Public Enterprises, has launched the India's Smart Advanced Manufacturing and Rapid Transformation Hubs (Samarth Udyog Bharat 4.0), under Industry 4.0, to propagate technological solutions to Indian manufacturing, business and service sector.

The primary objective of adopting to Industry 4.0, for India through Samarth Udyog Bharat 4.0, primarily to use advanced analytics to enhance production capacity and its quality, Robotics and automation to shorten production cycle, reduce time-to-market and bring inefficient utilisation of resources, use of digitisation in all sectors and at all levels, to save cost render better service to customer and employees, use of IoT and connectivity of machines, for efficient supply chain and lead time reduction.

India plans to increase manufacturing sector to 25% of GDP by 2025, and establish itself as a global competitor through Make in India programme and through Smart Manufacturing. The PSU and Industry Sector are facilitating the establishment of four centres in the country to help SMEs implement Industry 4.0. India has established the first Smart factory at Bengaluru, using data exchange in manufacturing and the Internet of Things (IoT), developed at the Indian Institute of Science's (IISc) Centre for Product Design and Manufacturing (CPDM).

State Governments like Andhra Pradesh, Telangana, Kerala, are aiming to develop IoT Hubs on a PPP Mode with Industry Sector, which is expected to create 50,000 direct employment in various IoT verticals.

India must embrace Industry 4.0, and has started making inroads in Indian manufacturing and other sectors, with adopting Smart manufacturing, analytics and IoT, evidence and data-based decision for faster enhancement of smart technologies, internalising innovations, automation, robotics, AI, etc to create more jobs, in emerging areas and upskill the present employees in the various sectors, to cope up with the industry, business, economy requirements.

Industry 4.0 primarily aim at promoting Industrial Resurgence, innovations and bring in faster growth and economic development, not only empower business and industry but country as well.

Thrust on new technologies, innovations, digital technologies like IoT, Sensors, Artificial Intelligence, Machine Learning, Augmented Reality and a host of precision technologies.

Big Data Analytics, as part of Industry 4.0, comes as an intelligent Data Analytics processing system, providing current scenarios and future predictions, for optimum decision making.

Data Storage solutions through Cloud Computing is coming as a boon to business, commerce and industry, for storage, retrieval, updation, realtime tracking, dash boards, monitoring and evaluation process.

Internet of Things (IoT) integrates all functions and systems in an organisation, business, industry and provides interface without face to face communication between man to man or man to machine, namely multifunctional electronics gadgets, widely used in almost in all sectors viz. health, transportation, agriculture, energy, communication, and other sectors of the economy.

Simulation has gained importance for generation of real life situations, scenarios and decision alternatives, which give wide opportunities for taking optimum decisions for growth and development of various sectors of business and industry, thus the economy.

Industry 4.0 necessities automation through production methods across various sectors and facilitate devices, systems and machines to interact with each other in real-time, proving cost effective, time saving and error free processes.

Realtime information and decision making has become an essential part of any business or industry, social and economic systems and thrust on Augmented Reality systems, for real-time information, with multitude of benefits and efficiency of functional aspects in an industry or in an economy.

With the digital age products and transactions, there is a necessity of Cyber Security systems and processes, to ensure safety and functionality, on a sustained basis, for which there are inbuilt fool proof security systems are in place and are evolved, to make the Industry 4.0 as a happening thing.

For ensuring flexibility, performance, and cost-effectiveness, Additive Manufacturing is promoted in an operating environment in industry or in business, and other sectors of the economy, small batch individual parts or personalised products, directly impacting clients, customer, suppliers.

Under Industry 4.0, industries, and departments, facilitate knowledge integration and allow the industrialisation through the Vertical and Horizontal System Integration.

As Industry 4.0, gyrates around the capabilities of machines and technologies, connections between people, data, machines and systems, as integral part of manufacturing, service, product and innovations, will develop into a robust system, for sustained operation.

Industry 4.0 is a new standards of productivity, efficiency and dependability and is evolving, which will enshape the business, industry, economy, with a new thinking and new normal practice, that the world will experience for quite some time.

The fourth industrial revolution, Industry 4.0, a global phenomena, thrusts on automation of manufacturing processes to a new level by linking the cyber and physical, incorporating AI and enabling customized and flexible mass production technologies, and creates a Smart Factory, where cyber physical systems monitor physical processes, create a virtual copy of the physical world and make decentralised optimum decisions, communicate and cooperate with each other and with humans in real time over Internet of Things.

Industry 4.0 ensures minimising wasteful processes, optimizing use of energy, by using real time data, analysis, and big data, physical production and operations with smart digital technology, machine learning, to create a more holistic and better connected ecosystem for industry, organisations, business, commerce and economy, and focus on manufacturing and supply chain management and improved decision alternatives.

Industry 4.0 thrusts on transformational effect, on the way your entire business operates and grows, including infusing new technology and tools to improve manufacturing efficiency, with emphasis on digital technology, interconnectivity through the Internet of Things (IoT), access to real-time data, and by cyber physical systems, reflecting the concept of holistic manufacturing, and connects physical with digital, and allows for better collaboration and access across departments, partners, vendors, product, and people, leveraging instant data to boost productivity, improve processes, and drive growth.

Tools like Enterprise Resource Planning (ERP), is used to manage information across an organisation. The Internet of Things (IoT) refers to connections between physical objects like sensors or machines and the Internet. The Industrial Internet of Things (IIoT), refers to the connections between people, data, and machines and relate to manufacturing.

The Big data refers to large sets of structured or unstructured data that can be compiled, stored, organised, and analyzed to reveal patterns, trends, associations, and opportunities. The Artificial intelligence (AI), refers to a computer's ability to perform tasks and make decisions that would otherwise require human intelligence.

The machine-to-machine, refers to the communication that happens between two separate machines through wireless or wired networks, digitisation process facilitates collecting and converting different types of information into a digital format. In a Smart Factory, technology, solutions, and approaches, are emphasised. The Smart Factory imbibe tenets of Industry 4.0. The Machine learning refers to the ability that computers have to learn and improve on their own through artificial intelligence, without being explicitly told or programmed to do so.

The Cloud computing refers to the practice of using interconnected remote servers hosted on the Internet to store, manage, and process information. The Real-time data processing refers to the abilities of computer systems and machines to continuously and automatically process data and provide real-time or near-time outputs and insights.

An ecosystem, in terms of manufacturing, refers to the potential connectedness of your entire operation, inventory and planning, financial, customer relationships, supply chain management, and manufacturing execution. The Cyber physical systems (CPS), namely cyber manufacturing, refers to manufacturing environment that offers real time data collection, analysis, and transparency across every aspect of a manufacturing operation, thus ushering greater business insight, control, and data visibility across their entire supply chain, delivers products and services faster, cost effective, and qualitative.

Industry 4.0 provides organisations and business the ability to monitor, predict, evaluate, various scenarios, promote preventive maintenance, automated and streamlined, thus provide Predictive analytics allowing industry and business, to generate current, ongoing, future and streamline any untoward situations very effectively, following a process of Operational Report, Descriptive Analytics, Diagnostic Analytics, and Predictive Analytics.

The Asset tracking and optimisation operations under the Industry 4.0, facilitate efficient operation with assets at each stage of the supply chain, keep a better monitoring of inventory, quality, optimise logistics, and streamline in real time.

The outcome envisaged under the Industry 4.0 have significant and transformational benefits ranging from optimisation of logistics and supply chain management, adaptation of innovative technologies, increase efficiency, boost collaboration between departments, enable predictive and prescriptive analytics, and allow people including operators, managers, and executives to more fully leverage real-time data and intelligence to make better decisions, real-time data, internet-connected machinery, and automation, reduce costs, boost profitability and economy, energy efficiency, growth and development thrust.

The automation and application of digitisation, IoT-enabled supply chains, advanced analytics, AI and ML techniques, are transforming the manufacturing sector with flexibility and operational efficiency, through structured scenario analysis, inventory optimisation, predictive maintenance, effective monitoring and auto-correction of processes; for maximum outputs.

Maintaining quality standards and ensuring zero defects are one of the primary objectives of Industry 4.0. Wide scale of AI based Systems, robotic systems, automated warehouses, reduction in cost of manufacturing, IoT enabled machine to machine (M2M) communication, High-bandwidth industrial communication networks that enable machines, robots, wearables, sensors and actuators to exchange data at high speed, allowing realtime monitoring and updates, faster and more streamlined workflow from ideation to approval for testing and deployment of novel technologies such as autonomous vehicles and collaborative robots, brings in Industry 4.0 framework and environment, promoting business, industry, commerce and management across the country, on par with industrial revolution in the world scenario.

Industry 4.0 in the transportation system, generates data on geo location, traffic, road network, weather, mobility of people and vehicular traffic, for smart scheduling, and enabling real time driver assistance, autonomous fleets for ride sharing, engine monitoring and predictive maintenance of vehicles. Supply chains expert decision systems, facilitate computer vision based transport goods more efficiently, reduce the risk and vulnerabilities of a supply chain caused on account of weather, traffic or unnatural events.

According to CIA Fact book, sector-wise Indian GDP composition in 2017 was 15.4% in Agriculture sector, with the production of agriculture of $375.61 billion and India was 2nd larger producer of agriculture products.

The agriculture, dairy and fisheries are primary sectors of Indian rural economy, and absorb over 50% of the workforce. The agriculture sector has challenges of inadequate demand prediction, lack of assured irrigation, soil degradation, overuse/misuse of pesticides and fertilisers, availability of capital for farmers, and unorganised and low-tech practices, which is evolving for ICT, Satellite based, scientific and technological practices.

In Industry 4.0, AI-powered intelligent solutions for smarter production, processing, storage, distribution and consumption of agricultural products, site-specific and timely data about crops for appropriate inputs of fertilisers and chemicals, monitoring of crop health and disease, spreads, monitoring health of farm animals, and intelligent farm mechanisation through autonomous machines such as harvesters, which propel yield per square unit of land, commodity packaging and storage with lower wastage and spoilage.

Large farm holds use Industry 4.0 AI based multi-variant agro-commodity price forecasting model on the cloud, satellite imaging, drone, mobile, sensor technologies and help providing decision support and expert decisions at various levels.

Industry 4.0 facilitate mechanising farms through a combination of a semi-autonomous vehicle with robotic arms, 3D location and vision. Further Fruits, Orchards, cotton picking machines used with minimum manual labour, repetitive efforts, loading and unloading etc.

Industry 4.0 use automate and streamline workflows, chatbots for automated conversational flows and efficient customer service, intelligent personalised financial planning, and fraud detection and prevention of money laundering, cognitive solutions that combine robotics and optical character recognition (OCR) to increase the safety and efficiency of trades.

Automated Systems help insurance sector in areas such as improving underwriting efficiency and automated handling of claims. Automated Systems also handle ATM withdrawals, credit card payments, and e-commerce transactions. Intelligent Technologies help cashless transactions, handle large volume of transactions in a transparent and secure manner.

Indian start-ups are successfully using AI to improve the quality of education under Industry 4.0, help personalised teaching, minimizing mistakes, improved student scores, provide differential pace of student learning, identifying areas where students lack clarity, rectify the gaps and improve knowledge levels of students.

Robotic teaching assistants connected over the cloud may alleviate the inaccessibility of experienced knowledge practitioners in remote locations by emulating their teaching style, either on a standalone basis or in real-time collaboration with human teachers.

Digital assistants, customer service bots, and engines for e-commerce and entertainment portals coming up as start-ups to improve user experience by providing personalised suggestions, preference-based browsing and image-based product search.

Industry 4.0 AI applications promote personalised design and production, deep learning, assessing customer demand and efficient inventory and delivery management.

In the retail store setting, shopper-friendly robots can help assist shoppers by directing them towards the appropriate product stocked in a particular section of the store, including payments, unique customer identification, personalised exchanges and supply chain automation.

In energy sector, the Industry 4.0, the use of smart metering, real-time information on energy usage, reduction on wastage and loss, efficient grid operation, and storage and predictive infrastructure maintenance, cost effective supply and usage of energy and leading to more secure supplies and fewer outages.

Industry 4.0 promotes smart cities and smart industrial zones, in terms of information, mass transportation, sensors, pavements, airports, malls, tax information, regulation, safe transportation, and ensuring quality of services for citizens. In addition parking, accident, crime, filling stations, public facilities power, heat, water, smart urban lighting, waste management, smart city maintenance, telecare, citizen safety, smart grid, smart energy and water and drainage management.

Industry 4.0 ensures strengthening of public infrastructure such as railways, civil aviation, nuclear plants, telecommunication towers and power stations. Predictive maintenance using advanced analytical models can help improve the availability of such infrastructure and reduce safety incidents associated with them. Among public sector and utilities, communication networks with sensors, health infrastructure, natural resource availability, location-based geotagged data are captures through GNSS using IRNSS.

Industry 4.0 necessitate technological support system for differently able persons, through smart phones, equipment to assist visual, speech, hearing, person centric movements, with ease. Smart Prosthetics with 3 D printing is coming up a great support system for the differently abled people.

Renewable energy based solar power, lighting and heating systems, reducing emissions, energy efficiency, use of smart sensors, smart homes, smart transportation systems, eco driving, autonomous drones, help evolve the operational aspects under Industry 4.0.

The cognition and natural language processing expected to generate creative and innovative tech jobs for humans.

The central and state governments promote AI, ML, robotics, IoT, the cloud, and virtual reality (VR) and augmented reality (AR), and offshoot of SMEs and start-ups, Industry 4.0 business process.

Step 1: Identified all relevant stakeholders

Macro Level	Meso Level	Firm Level
1. Government Departments	**1. Institutes**	**1. Service providers**
1. NITI Aayog	1. SAMARTH Udyog	1. Hardware manufacturers
2. DHI	Industry 4.0 Centres	2. Systems integrators
3. DIPP	of Excellence	
4. DST	1. IIT Delhi	
5. DSIR	2. HSc, Bangalore, etc.	
6. MSME	2. IIM, Bangalore	2. Early implementers
7. MeitY	3. IIT Kharagpur	
8. HRD	4. HIT, Hyderabad	3. Large enterprises

9. Skills Ministry	5. CDOT	
10. DoT	**2. Organisations**	4. MSMEs
	1. IMTMA	
	2. SIAM	5. Thought leaders
	3. ACMA	
	4. CG associations	
	5. IMF	
	6. Fraunhofer	
	7. VDMA	
	8. TIFAC	
	9. World Bank	
	10. NASSCOM	
	11. NPC	
	12. WEF	

Source: CII.

Fig. 2

Fig. 2 depict the implementation of Industry 4.0 at various levels and the Ministries, Departments and Agencies promoting the same.

IV. ARTIFICIAL INTELLIGENCE (AI)

India's journey towards embracing technology for digital transformation has come a long way. The foundation to leapfrog with the new wave of emerging technologies has been well-laid in terms of flagship programmes such as Digital India, Make in India, Smart Cities, Jan Dhan Yojana, Startup India and Skill India. Every stakeholder group can be proud of the efforts and achievements around the creation of the world's largest rural broadband network, largest direct benefit transfer system, largest digital identity system and the citizen engagement platform MyGov. These initiatives, coupled with the push to skilling and entrepreneurship, are providing the foundation for the infusion of the next wave of technology solutions around artificial intelligence (AI), the Internet of things, cyber security, blockchain, etc.

Various studies have highlighted the potential positive impact of AI on economic growth. AI will help address critical societal challenges and yield tangible benefits for citizens. It is expected to address challenges in priority areas such as healthcare, public security and disaster management. There is very clearly an opportunity for India to emerge as a leader in the development of products and services in this space. At the same time, AI offers the opportunity for businesses and governments to radically reform and redesign service delivery through intelligent systems. Globally, reference cases and applications have already emerged wherein substantive cost reduction and revenue enhancements have been projected. Indian entrepreneurs are already working and delivering products and solutions in this area.

Artificial intelligence (AI) is fast becoming the most significant general purpose technology of our era. Manufacturing, financial services, agriculture, and defence and the dominant challenges plaguing each of these sectors.

AI is fast moving with increasingly modern software and applications, for wide variety of commerce, business, industries, banking, health, social development, with location specific, evidence based, shortest distance, decision alternatives, optimum decisions, analysis of present scenario and forecasting future trends and scenarios, and facilitate human-AI collaborative workflows.

The AI has integrated with sectors like Manufacturing and Supply Chain, Healthcare, Agriculture, Financial Services, Education, Consumer and Retail, Accessibility technology for the differently abled, security and defence, Public and utility services, and Environment.

The Digital India and Make in India promote a big boost to AI evolved in India in the recent past promote investment in AI based technologies. The success of AI and robotics in the manufacturing and supply chain sector supported by standards for data transformation and exchange for the large volumes of data generated by IoT-enabled machine-to-machine (M2M) communication, high-bandwidth industrial communication networks that enable machines, robots, wearables, sensors and actuators to exchange data at high speed, allowing realtime monitoring and updates, faster and more streamlined workflow from ideation to approval for testing and deployment of novel technologies such as autonomous vehicles and collaborative robots.

In the transportation sector, data on geo location, traffic and weather are used for smart scheduling so as to overcome jams and allow for real-time route adjustments, enabling semiautonomous driver assistance, autonomous fleets for ride sharing, engine monitoring and predictive maintenance of vehicles.

During Covid-19 Pandemic and post-Pandemic time, the healthcare sector in India used extensively the AI based intelligent technologies, and ensured to serve more patients, improved health delivery and facilitating live saving facilities. Sensors based smartphones and wearable devices, remotely extracting information from patient records for monitoring health, supporting diagnosis, enabling health trackers and predicting onset of symptoms, and powering patient connectivity with specialists, made remarkable mark on possibilities of AI applications in health sector, early identification of potential pandemics and tracking disease incidence to contain spread, and image processing and diagnostics for radiology and pathology. AI enabled surgical robots practice expert systems, for diagnosis of diseases like cancer, and recommending treatments, with assistive and augmentative applications in healthcare delivery.

AI powered intelligent Precision Agriculture, enable smarter production, processing, storage, distribution and consumption of agricultural products, with site specific and timely data about crops. Crop suitability, productivity, forecasting, use of appropriate inputs on fertilisers and chemicals, crop health and disease, spreads, monitoring health of farm animals, and intelligent farm mechanisation through autonomous machines, improving the yield per square unit of land, with effective, low wastage and spoilage.

The FinTech firms have started using AI, ML and robotics for financial services, with use of chatbots to facilitate automated conversational flows and efficient customer service, intelligent agents such as Robo advisors for personalised financial planning, and advanced algorithms to facilitate fraud detection and prevention of money laundering, keep a track on information on ATM withdrawals, credit card payments, and e-commerce transactions, to monitor transactions as potentially fraudulent at the time of occurrence and hence contain the damage as early as possible.

The AI based intelligent technologies helping Government promote financial inclusion for Schemes like Jan Dhan and Cashless India, ensuring transparency, speed and efficiency and regulatory compliance. Banking and non-banking financial institutions use AI for preventing malpractices, lapses in human judgement, risk assessment, improve capital access, better customer service, providing more personalised services and improving the back-office efficiencies.

During Covid-19 Pandemic, online education system have kept the education on move and changed the approach to education with technological alternatives. AI based education not only disseminate knowledge effectively but also capture feedback, and rectify gaps. Indian start-ups are successfully using AI to improve the quality of education. Robotic teaching assistants for accessing remote locations by emulating their teaching style, either on a standalone basis or in real-time collaboration with human teachers.

Digital assistants, customer service bots, and algorithms for e-commerce and entertainment portals, as AI-powered products and services, for improving user experience by providing personalised suggestions, preference-based browsing and image based product search, personalised design and production, deep learning for predicting customer demand and orders, and efficient inventory and delivery management. Shopper-friendly robots can help assist shoppers by directing them towards the appropriate product stocked in a particular section of the Mall, Store, shop etc.

With AI applications in defence, robots are used to recover explosives, detecting mines, space exploration, deep water probes, scanning hostile territories and capturing video feed, use in unmanned aerial vehicles (UAVs) and unmanned ground systems (UGS) guided bombs and missiles.

AI based smart metering, real-time information on energy usage which reduces wastage and loss, efficient grid operation, and storage and predictive infrastructure maintenance, benefit companies and consumers through cost effective supply and usage of energy and leading to more secure supplies and fewer outages.

The Smart cities, Smart industrial zones, Industrial Corridors, Fab Cities, where the realtime information is captured through various sources mass transportation tickets, cameras and sensors on roads, pavements, airports, malls, tax information, police filings, etc. create endless possibilities for improving the quality of services for citizens.

Public spaces over a timeline, peak loads of vehicles and parking lots, incidence of crime at locations, monitoring real-time resource usage of public facilities power, heat, water, fuel, etc and autonomously adjusting inputs based on usage patterns, thus leading to significant savings.

The 2015 Draft Policy on IoT (revised), published by the Department of Electronics & Information Technology (DeitY), emphasised the government's plan of developing 100 smart cities under the Digital India programme, where smart parking, intelligent transport systems, smart urban lighting, waste management, smart city maintenance, telecare, citizen safety, smart grid, smart energy and water management.

AI applications strengthen the operations and functioning of public infrastructure such as railways, civil aviation, nuclear plants, telecommunication towers and power stations. With the use of predictive maintenance help infrastructure operation and maintain fool proof safety.

Provisions for large-scale communication networks with sensors capturing information like infrastructure health, natural resource availability, chemical properties, geotagged data providing precise locational intelligence and increased use of ISRO Satellite Imageries and IRNSS Navigation data, significantly improve the infrastructure management.

India is one of the affordable prosthetics manufacturer in the world. With AI applications, in combination with other emerging technologies like 3D printing and IoT, there is great potential to promote widespread availability, affordability and feasibility of innovations in smart prosthetics, for the differently abled people. Further AI and Ml based natural language processing, perceptual interfaces computer aided vision, speech and language help people to understand people with autism and dementia.

AI based smart energy grids, increased efficiency, power balance, storage of renewable energy through intelligent grids, smart lighting and heating systems, improve reliability of solar energy, etc changing the energy economics, environment and ecology, for sustained future.

AI reduces the impact of risks such as fire, floods and earthquakes ,maximise energy and building design and improve energy efficiency, Big data, IoT and cloud-enabled vehicles communicate with transport infrastructure, which helps in managing vehicle flows, eco-driving and effective traffic control.Al-enabled autonomous drones and sensors linked to IoT platforms can offer real-time traffic and logistics information for optimised routing.

The AI/ML Landscape: Globally

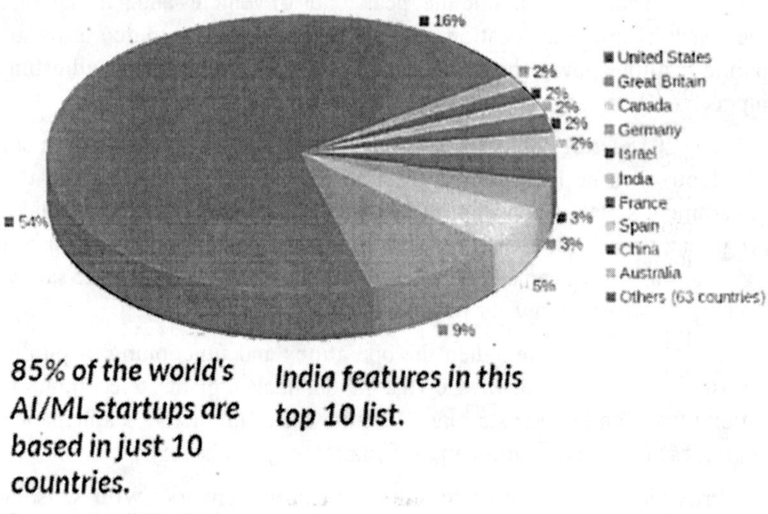

Source: MeiTY, GOI.

Fig. 3

Fig. 3 illustrates the AI/ML scenario globally with India's position within the first ten countries.

The Government of India started using wide range of AI applications through facial recognition and hotspot analysis, biometric identification, criminal investigation, traffic and crowd management, wearables to empower women safety, real time monitoring, tracking of Covid-19 cases, decision support, scenario generation, forecasting, and along with Big Data Analytics, generate real time Dash Boards and data dissemination.

The Indian government has launched a dedicated artificial intelligence (AI) portal, designed to support the country's AI development capabilities and to boost its standing as an emerging tech innovation hub, developed by the Ministry of Electronics and IT (MeitY) and NASSCOM, as a one stop platform for AI related advancements in India.

It provides resources such as case studies, research reports and investment funding news, details of AI start ups and AI education institutions, and job opportunities in the field. The platform also promotes collaboration between Departments, including MeitY, NITI Aayog and State Governments, and with the Corporate Sector, Industries, and other sectors of the economy.

The AI Portal primarily aim at inclusion and empowerment of human beings by supplementing growth and development rather than making human beings less relevant. Further the Government of India, has launched the "Responsible AI for Youth' programme, aims to encourage students in India to develop their careers in AI innovations and application development, by MeitY, Intel India, and HRD Ministry, India uses artificial intelligence for data protection, processing, technology agnosticism, data controller accountability, data minimisation, holistic application, like Cyber Security, Defence, Agriculture, Law Enforcement, Legal System, Decision Support, monitoring, analysis of situations, forecasting, scenario generation, helping inclusive and empowered governance.

The Centre for Development of Advanced Computing (CDAC) and IIT-Patna are working on developing the cyber forensic tools driven by AI for law enforcement, the government, and other intelligence agencies, in addition to the engagement of industry to analyse data, from intelligence agencies to evaluate threat patterns and predict future outcomes.

AI in the agricultural sector uses predictive analytics, weather and climatic conditions forecasting, disaster prediction, crop analysis, rainfall analysis, and disease cycling. The International Crops Research Institute for the Semi-Arid Tropics(ICRISAT), use machine learning and AI with mobile application, provides advisories to farmers information on the optimal date to sow through text messages on their phones. The Government of India, has launched AI-based Kisan Suvidha, IFCO Kisan Agriculture, and RML Farmer, in agriculture sector.

The AI help surveillance systems to track people's movement, potential crime incidents, and general security of the residents, public safety, and predict potential activities that could disrupt public peace.

The Government has developed the Court Case Information, Computerised Districts and Subordinate Courts in the country accessible through e-Courts. An AI-based technology, converts into editable documents, after scanning, and used to extract the data, summarises it, and analyses the contract.

CONCLUDING REMARKS

The 21st Century has faced insurmountable human challenges and technology excellence. The AI, Industry 4.0, New Normal and Circular Economy, as a composite transforming economy, environment, business, industry, manufacturing and technology. The evolving scenario for commerce and management in India necessitate the adoption of Industry 4.0 and internalising the evolving concepts of circular economy, AI and New Normal practices. Technology and economy is interwoven and bringing great opportunities for growth, with sustainable production and consumption patterns, and improved waste management. Industry 4.0 is the result of a tipping point in technology innovation, poised to change the new way of business and economy redefined, automated, and optimised value chain. Artificial Intelligence facilitate could think and perform tasks just as humans do, with cognitive expressions and provide new Learning systems, for growth, development and innovations, in commerce, business and industry.

REFERENCES

1. Paul, Ekins, Teresa, Domenech, Paul, Drummond, Raimund, Bleischwitz, Nick Hughes, Lorenzo Lotti. UCL Institute for Sustainable Resources, University College London.
2. Ekins, P., Domenech, T., Drummond, P., Bleischwitz, R., Hughes, N. and Lotti, L. (2019). "The Circular Economy: What, Why, How and Where", Background paper for an OECD/EC Workshop on 5 July 2019 within the workshop series "Managing environmental and energy transitions for regions and cities", Paris.
3. EMF (2013). *Towards The Circular Economy*, Vol. 1, (Ellen MacArthur Foundation), Cowes, Isle of Wight.

4. Gessdoerfer, M., Savaget, P., Bocken, N. and Hultink, EJ. (2017). 'The Circular Economy - A new sustainability paradigm?' *Journal of Cleaner Production*. Vol. 143.
5. Blomsma, F. and G. Brennan (2017). The emergence of circular economy: a new framing around prolonging resource productivity', *Journal of Industrial Ecology*, Vol. 21, No. 3, pp. 603-614, http://doi.wiley.com/10.llll/iiec.12603.
6. OECD (2019). Business Models for the Circular Economy: Opportunities and Challenges for Policy, OECD Publishing, Paris, https://doi.orq/10.1787/q2g9dd62-en.
7. Mihir R. Bhatt. COVID-19 Impact in India, *Humanitarian Actions*, Issue No. 190, November 2020.
8. ANI. (26 February 2018) AI to the rescue: 6 startups that are redefining healthcare market in India. *Business Standard*. Retrieved from http://www.business-standard.com/artide/companies/ai-to-the-rescue-6-startups-that-are-redefining- healthcare-market-in-india-118022500706_l.html
9. CB Insights (2018). Artificial intelligence trends to watch in 2018. Retrieved from https://www.cbinsights.com/ research/report/artificial-intelligence-trends-2018.
10. Gupta, B. (19 June 2017). Analytics and Data Science India Jobs Study 2017 - by Edvancer & AIM. *Analytics India Magazine*. Retrieved from https://analyticsindiamag.com/analytics-and-data-science-india-jobs-study-2017-by- edvancer-aim/
11. NASSCOM Knowledge Center, (n.d.). AI, beyond the myth & the hype. Retrieved from http://www.nasscom.in/ knowledge-center/publications/ai-beyond-myth-hype.
12. NDTV Profit Team, (9 July 2017). Demand for analytics professionals surges, 2 lakh shortage likely in US. NDTV. Retrieved from https://www. ndtv.com/india-news/demand-for-analytics-professionals-rises-2-lakh-shortage-likely-in-us-1721815
13. Saha, T. (6 June 2017). 12 artificial intelligence based healthcare startups in India. Medgenera. Retrieved from https://news.medgenera.com/12-artificial-intelligence-healthcare-startups-india-ai/
14. Thomas, A. (1 February 2018). Budget 2018: Niti Aayog to establish National Programme on Artificial Intelligence. Retrieved from https://economictimes.indiatimes.com/small-biz/startups/newsbuzz/budget-2018-niti-aayog-to-establish-national-programme-on-artificial-intelligence/articleshow/62738713.cms
15. ANI, (26 February 2018). AI to the rescue: 6 startups that are redefining health-care market in India. Business Standard. Retrieved from http://www.business-standard.com/artide/companies/ai-to-the-rescue-6-startups-that-are-redefining-healthcare-market-in-india-118022500706_l.html
16. CB Insights (2018). Artificial intelligence trends to watch in 2018. Retrieved from https://www.cbinsights.com/ research/report/artificial-intelligence-trends-2018/

17. Gupta, B. (19 June 2017). Analytics and Data Science India Jobs Study 2017 - by Edvancer& AIM. Analytics India Magazine. Retrieved from https://analyticsindiamag.com/analytics-and-data-science-india-jobs-study-2017-by- edvancer-aim/
18. NASSCOM Knowledge Center, (n.d.). AI, beyond the myth & the hype. Retrieved from http://www.nasscom.in/knowledge-center/publications/ai-beyond-myth-hype
19. NDTV Profit Team. (9 July 2017). Demand for analytics professionals surges, 2 lakh shortage likely in US. NDTV. Retrieved from https://www.ndtv.com/india-news/demand-for-analytics-professionals-rises-2-lakh-shortage-likely-in-us-1721815
20. Saha, T. (6 June 2017). 12 artificial intelligence based healthcare startups in India. Medgenera. Retrieved from https:// news.medgenera.com/12-artificial-intelligence-healthcare-startups-india-ai/
21. Thomas, A. (1 February 2018). Budget 2018: Niti Aayog to establish National Programme on Artificial Intelligence. Retrieved from https://economictimes.indiatimes.com/small-biz/startups/newsbuzz/budget-2018-niti-aayog-to-establish-national-programme-on-artificial-intelligence/articleshow/62738713.cms
22. Joseph Fiksel, Praveena Sanjay, Kavya Raman, "Steps toward a resilient circular economy in India", 2020 © Springer-Verlag GmbH Germany, Springer Nature 2020.

3

Corporate Survival Struggle During Pandemic Era

S. Nagamani

To those on the front lines of the coronavirus crisis, is ultimately above fear. "People are terrified", says Kathryn Lott, executive director of Houston's Southern Smoke Foundation, a crisis relief organisation for people in the food and beverage industry. "All are afraid they will lose their homes, end the terror in their voices is something I have never experienced. I have done case work for years, during natural disasters, people who have been gunned down, new mothers on the streets with infants during winter. I have never heard of this."

No one has ever heard this, the pleas for help from so many Americans rendered jobless withstanding suddenness- more than 16 million and counting as of early April. For them, the covid-19 pandemic has triggered a intertwined crisis of personal health and personal finance, threatening disaster for them individually and, in the aggregate for the country. The great challenge facing each person- and the nation overall- is overcoming the two crises together. In the modern economy there is no playbook for how to do it.

More than any past economic collapse, US consumers are at the heart of this one. Not only do they face the threat of getting sick, but they are also getting fired or furloughed by the millions because their workplaces are being shut down to prevent others from being infected. As a result, they can't spend, forcing more businesses to close, and so on - "an aggregate demand doom loop" says Glenn Hubbard, chairman of White House council of economic advisers from 2001 to 2003. "The problem is radiating from consumption demand by households", says Matthew slaughter, a CEA member from 2005 to 2007. "It's unprecedented - an involuntary shock to consumption demand. The magnitude of it is huge."

For consumers, the cosmic injustice of it all is head - spinning. The US economy has long been consumer driven, and over the first five years consumers have powered economic growth even more than usual, expanding America's economy faster than those of most other big, developed economies. Consumers' share of GDP reached a towering 68% in last year's fourth-quarter, higher than it got even in the 2006 to 2008 shopping festival that preceded the financial crisis and recession. Yet unlike then, consumers in the recent years have increased their buying responsibly. Shaving a prudent 8% of their disposable personal income on average vs. near 0% back then. Household debt reached 99% of GDP in the last boom; at the end of 2019, it was just 76%.

And now, having kept the economy cruising along, consumers are suddenly under intense financial pressure. Of those who still have jobs, millions cannot work from home and must choose between risking their health (and potentially their lives) by working in grocery stores, warehouses post offices, hospitals and other high contact settings, or not working.

The top of it all is a crowning irony: because the US is still fundamentally a consumer driven economy - land can't transform overnight - consumers as a group will have to get in themselves and the whole economy out of this.

No one knows how deep hole they will have to climb out of; everything is happening too fast for official statistics to keep up. But we know this is the steepest economic plunge in modern history. More people lost their jobs in 2 weeks in March than in the entire 2008-2009 recession.

The great depression caused real GDP decline for 43 months, eventually shrinking by 30%. This time, Morgan Stanley forecast a 30% decline in the second quarter; Goldman Sachs says 34%; and Saint Louis Fed President James Bullard says 50%. For now, the most important indicators to watch are not economic ones. They are the weekly trends in new covid-19 cases, number of deaths, and governors making isolation order more stringent or lenient.

BREAKING THE "DOOM LOOP"

Consumers can bring back the economy without help. Reviving consumption is a major goal of the coronavirus Aid, Relief, and Economic Security Act and the many other actions by federal agencies, states, and the Fed to put more cash in consumers' hands. But darling out money is not enough. "There is the immediate loss of jobs, but the bigger issue is uncertainty," says Hubbard, who advised Senate Republicans on the CARES Act. Getting a $1200 check, augmented unemployment benefits, and tax relief may offer some respite, but consumers won't spend much and employers want to hire if they are braced for still worse to come.

That's why the Paycheck Protection Programme, an innovative element of the CARES Act that got off to a rocky start, is especially worth watching. It offers small businesses (up to 500 employees) small business administration loans equaling about 20 weeks of major expenses, including payroll, mortgage and rent. If a business gets a loan by June 30 and restores staffing and pay to pre-Feb. 15 levels, while also meeting the other tests, the loan can be forgiven. The effect could be significant: Firms with 500 or fewer workers account for over half of US employment. In theory it's a sensible policy response, helping to break the doom loop by giving businesses and workers certainty. Employees will know they can keep paying employees, even if there is no work to do, confident that it won't cost them a thing; employees will know their employer has a strong incentive to keep paying them, so they will be more inclined to spend. At least it's a certainty until June 30th, by which time the policymakers hope the pandemic will be in decline, and the economy will have turned up. But at least initially the programme has spawned massive uncertainty among prospective borrowers and the banks through which loans are being made. The hastily written law only outlined the programme, leaving the treasury to write, at warp speed, 31 pages of regulations. The SBA was entirely unprepared to lend 10 times as much money in a few weeks as it normally lends in a year, and the amount appropriated for lending, $ 299.4 billion, was clearly far too little. Larger risk: Maybe the pandemic won't be under control by June 30th; either the economy will sink back into the depths when the programme ends, or Congress will extend it at a cost of still more hundreds of billions.

LONG TERM "SCARS" FOR CONSUMERS

For the moment that's unknowable. But we can say with some confidence how tills already traumatic experience will change the behaviour of shaken consumers. In the near term, those who have income will save more of it if they possibly can. The dominant feeling of consumers in an economic meltdown is loss of control, and having money put away even just a little, gives them a feeling of more control. Of the money they spend, they will spend more of it on necessities again because they feel more control when their necessities are on hand. The NPD group, a retail research firm, has observed this shift already and says that "wrestling with necessities vs discretionary products will play a huge role" in how retailers adjust through the pandemic.

In the longer term the pandemic experience will change consumers for decades, "we will be different", says economist Ulrike Malmendier of the University of California at Berkeley. "We will make different product choices, consumption choices, human capital choices." This is beyond economics; it's neuroscience. A crisis experience *is* deeply emotional, and "stronger emotions get anchored more strongly in our memories", said Ulrike Malmendier. "Our handwriting changes."

We will buy differently. "Macroeconomic crisis appear to leave long-term 'scars' consumer behaviour," Malmendier and coauthor Leslie sheng Shen in a pioneering 2018 study. They found, for example, that regardless of income, households that experience high unemployment personally or in the macroeconomy consume less, including less food, than other households. They use significantly more coupons when they shop and buy more sale items and products of lower quality again regardless of their income. Such households also save more. Those effects fade over time but are still measurable years later. It's a similar story with investing. In a separate study, Malmendier and coauthor Stephen Nagel found that households financial risk taking is strongly related to how well or poorly markets have performed during their lives, and again, the effects are long lasting. "Even returns experience certificates earlier still have some impact," they report.

One more key finding: In addition to recent experiences being most influential among all age groups they are most powerful by far among the young, who increased consumption more during booms and cut back more during busts, they may be living on way, way less for some time.

For two groups of young people-those graduating from high school or college this spring-that's just the beginning of the disappointing news. College students who graduated into the labour force during a recession suffer reduced earnings for 10 years on an average and for those with the lowest predicted earnings (based on college and major), the earnings penalty may last much longer, it gets worse. Some research finds that in midlife, recession graduates on average work more and earn less, are less likely to be married and more likely to be childless and suffer higher death rates.

One research on this topic, Northern Western University's Marines Schwandt, sums up the findings thus: "the bad luck of living in schools during hard times can lead to higher rates of early death and permanent differences in life circumstances".

In past trends from serious recessions hold true, the pandemic might alter the economy's structure, diminishing the earning power of the labour force - potentially for years. Lack of funds will force some prospective college students to postpone or abandon their plans. If the recession is long, many of the newly unemployed may remain jobless for many months or even years, during which their skill might deteriorate and become outdated, as happened in the last recession. Even if they get jobs eventually, they may well be less valuable workers.

Apart from its effects on workers' earnings, the pandemic may do other lasting damage to the labour force as well. If the unlikely worst-case scenarios play out and Covid-19 kills over 100,000 Americans plus millions more worldwide, the simple shrinkage of the labour force would reduce output for years. Even without that extreme circumstance, the same factors that have caused the schools to close will significantly curtail early childhood education, a prover, factor in better educational achievement later in life.

Researchers have also uncovered an unexpected effect of the 1918 flu pandemic that could potentially recur: it reduced educational attainment by people who had not been born yet. Americans who were born in the months after the pandemic, and thus were in utero during it, were less likely to graduate from high school than the cohorts immediately before and after them. In any long term economic recovery plan Congress and the White House hammer out, policymakers would be wise to invest in incentives that help young people finish school.

PLANNING FOR THE NEXT CATASTROPHE

As businesses respond to this grand scale recording of their world, some implications are already clear. Remote work will become mainstream, if only because so many people will have an online meeting app and know how to use it. Companies are Slashing capital spending as they scramble for cash, weakening the foundation of future economic growth while also fuelling a B2B Doom loop in the present. They will diversity supply chains beyond China when demand returns, further slowing that country's decelerating economy.

As in all recessions, companies will learn to do more with fewer people, so the already spiking unemployment rate may well continue to rise at least briefly after this recession ends. It's a safe bet that many companies will compile pandemic plans for the future- surely a wise move, but if that's all they do, they will be missing a crucial lesson of this experience. A global pandemic is the most predicted disaster since hurricane Katrina, yet, now as then, business and government work caught flat-footed. When the urgency of this calamity abates, it will be time to start thinking through other plausible catastrophes - a major earthquake strikes California; some group or nation detonates a; nuclear bomb; a large electrical grid gets hacked and shut down. You will never foresee exactly what happens, but the experience of working out the second - and third - order effects will put you miles ahead of competitors if one of these events occurs. It's a lot of work. But remember the conclusion of Mohammed El-Erian, CEO of bond trading firm Pimco during the financial crisis: "it's better to be prepared for events that don't happen than unprepared for events that do".

As we look ahead to days that will probably remain challenging, what can be offered to the supremely important, terrified consumer, the hero and victim of this saga? Only hope -based on history. For cash multiplying deaths and unprecedented economic collapse comes with percentages and decimal points. Human ingenuity, passion, and energy are beyond any economist's ability to predict, and those are what get us through times of trial. It's unsatisfying to say that a better future awaits us because of forces and factors that we can't exactly describe. But we must not forget that it is true.

THREE KEYS TO LIVING IN A CRISIS

This crucial experience will be career defining for many leaders. In any crisis-especially a historical Global Catastrophe in which the main factor is uncertainty- people want leaders to give them information, reassurance and the plan. Yet this is exactly when all of those are maddeningly difficult to deliver. History says leaders will benefit by following a few principles:

1. *Remember that people want to be led:* We understand in our bones the simple efficiency of it that no group accomplishes much if no one is in charge. In a life-threatening historical crisis, we want direction more than ever. We also need a leader to be, in effect, a repository for our fears, someone who has the power to do what we cannot. The leader assumes a part of our burden and helps as sleep at night. If you are in charge be in charge.
2. *Be decisive:* In a crisis, even people who would normally be at one another's throats accept that major decisions must be made

quickly. These decisions will be debated- but after they are made, not before. That's a valuable opportunity for leaders. The difficulty is that just when decisions are most easily accepted, they are hardest to make. Every leadership decision is made with incomplete information, in a crisis the problem is worse and the stakes are higher. Don't let that fact stop you from making firm decisions.

3. *Define reality and give hope:* People hunger for the unvarnished truth about their organisation and its prospects, and they can sense evasion a mile away. The news in a crisis is really good. The leader's art is outlining reality unflinchingly and framing it as a challenge that can be met, not as a disaster that must be endured. Effective leaders never make a promise that can't be kept with 110% certainty, they do offer realistic reasons for hope.

   Even these principles will be of limited value to any leader who has not built trust and credibility. You can't change the past, out a crisis is an excellent time to start changing the future.

THE DEBT STRESS

Another struggling area for corporates is *Debt stress* experienced by all corporate companies irrespective of size, sector, asset base and consumer attraction towards their products.

The only man who sticks closer to you in adversity than a friend is a creditor, 62 year old Harsh Goenka, chairman of RPG Enterprise quotes a famous line to describe the current predicament of corporate India whose debt in stressed sectors amounts to Rs 37.72 lakh crore, nearly 38 % if all loans given by the banking sector.

The magnitude of stress is akin to Black Swan events such as the global financial crisis of 2008 or the Great Depression of 1929 when thousands of companies had to file for bankruptcy.

India Inc., already under pressure due to several quarters of falling GDP growth, and dealt a severe blow by recent lockdowns starting at massive ratings downgrades and loan defaults. The reason, its capacity to service debt is weakening due to low capacity utilisation and falling revenues and profits, triggering a flurry of actions ranging from sale of assets, stakes shutting down of stressed businesses, frenetic fund-raising and sharp, almost brutal, reduction in costs. This will particularly hurt firms with high debt and low interest coverage ratios or ICR which measures how many times a company's earnings can cover current interest payments.

Those with low ICR include giants such as Anil Agarwal's Vedanta Ltd., Gautam Adani's Adani Power and Sunil Mittal's Bharti Airtel. Many of them can tide over the crisis with support from other group of companies and assets.

HOWEVER, FURTHER WORSENING OF THE ECONOMIC ENVIRONMENT COULD SPELL TROUBLE FOR THE GIANTS TOO

Take Tata Motors, the company's ICR turned negative in March. In a post-Covid review, in June, Moody's downgraded its debt by a few notches. The automotive division is saddled with Rs 67,800 crore debt, its net debt to equity ratio rose from 0.84 in June last year to 1.44 in June this year. Tata Group Chairman N. Chandrasekaran has targeted making the company net debt free in three years. Credit rating agencies are not convinced. The downgrade reflects sustained deterioration in the automaker's credit profile Moody's Vice President and Senior Credit Officer Kaustubh Chaubal said in his report.

Subodh Rai, Senior Director at CRISIL, expects more rating downgrades than upgrades to continue for more quarters due to economic slowdown. However, there are a host of sectors where recovery is likely to take much longer. These include construction and real estate, telecom. Steel and power which were under stress in the Pre Covid period too. Over Rs 22.20 lakh crore debt is parsed in such sectors.

One of the biggest pain points is construction and real estate bank loans of Rs.3.32 lakh crore, Niranjan Hiranandani, Co-Founder and MD Hiranandani Group, says debt is just one part of the problem. The second is continued access to credit for growth and working capital. The volume of corporate defaults looming over real estate sector can best be a guesstimate but the numbers will be huge, he says. The economy has been impacted and buyer sentiment hit. Sales have been down and ability to service debt has been impacted. Things can become really challenging for some balance sheets, says Hiranandani.

Lenders to real estate are also impacted, Piramal Enterprises will have to support its financial services business as it has a large real estate portfolio. It will not be easy as companies are giving up office space due to poor demand and the growing trend of work from home.

In steel, the big companies with cash buffers continue to maintain cash flow to meet fixed costs through exports even to China. But medium and small companies are struggling as they became financially weak while competing with the five-six big players in the market which itself has shrunk considerably says Seshagiri Rao, Joint Managing Director and Group Chief Financial Officer JSW Steel. Bank uses to the steel sector are in the region of Rs 2.66 1akh crore.

The four power majors; in the list of the 20 most indebted companies have a combined gross debt of Rs 1.63 lakh crore with Adani Power topping the list. The current crisis has delayed the commissioning of its 1,600 MW ultra supercritical, coal based thermal power project in Jharkhand. The company has evoked Force Majeure clauses under the Power Purchase Agreement. An Adani Power spokesperson says they have significant unrealised claims on various Discoms towards compensatory tariff claims. Adani Power aims to reduce its leverage and improve liquidity with the help of funds from resolution of claims and pending dues from Discoms, he said.

Auto is another area facing rough weather. R.C. Bhargava, Chairman, Maruti Suzuki India, says the industry is improving every month but is not normal yet. We are still not where we were two - three years ago, says Bhargava, whose company does not have significant financial liabilities. But some industry' flayers could be affected. It will be difficult for everyone as nobody knows the demand scenario after the festival season. It is fine now but is not clear whether it will sustain and grow post December. That will decide the industry's health, says Bhargava.

Going forward, capital intensive sectors that were struggling prior to Covid and where the situation got exacerbated due to the pandemic would face bigger challenges. These sectors may necessitate long term solutions, says Valecha of India Ratings.

ASSETS SALES TO THE RESCUE

GVK Reddy the Chairman of GVK Group and face of India's infrastructure revolution, had been facing debt issues for years. Post-Covid, financials of its marquee asset, the Mumbai International Airport got hit due to flight ban. The six month loan moratorium did help but the 83 years old first generation entrepreneur had no option but to onboard a financial investor the Adanis in the airport.

Adanis will provide the much needed liquidity to Mumbai International Airport to meet debt and other obligations. This will also help the company achieve financial closure for the Navi Mumbai International Airport Project.

It is under these circumstances that we agreed to cooperate with Adani so as to achieve these twin objectives, says Reddy.

For the past decade or so, old economy sectors such as infrastructure, steel and power were facing the most stress. But now; due to Covid it is the turn of new sectors such as hospitality, travel and tourism, airports, entertainment and retail. Arvind Fashions Ltd, Ahmedabad based Lalbhai Group's retail arm had to keep stores shut in the initial phase of the lockdown. The impact on cash flow forced the company with brands such as Arrow, Tommy Hilfiger and Calvin Klein to opt for the loan moratorium. While 80 percent of its stores are now open, its sales in August were only 46 percent of usual. India Ratings has predicted 40-45 percent revenue dip for the apparel retail sector this year.

In the last two months, Arvind Fashions has managed to strengthen its balance sheet by selling a stake to Walmart owned Flipkart and raising Rs 400 crore through a rights issue. It has also transferred the wholesale trading business of the Flying Machine brand to wholly owned subsidiary Arvind Youth Brands which will generate Rs 62 Crore for the company. Arvind Fashions did net respond to the query on whether it is approaching banks for loan restructuring.

Similarly, drugmaker Wockhardt has sold a part of its domestic branded formulations division along with a manufacturing facility at Baddi in Himachal Pradesh, to Dr. Reddy's Laboratories Ltd for Rs 1.850 Crore. The company which went through corporate debt restructuring in 2012 has a debt of Rs 1,875 crore in March. The deal will deleverage its balance sheet.

Just before the virus outbreak, GMR Infrastructure was looking at options to pare its over Rs 32,000 crore consolidated debt. But the lockdown seriously hit its airport business. Consolidated net loss for quarter ended June 30 more than doubled to nearly Rs 834 crore. The company has now announced divestment of the group's entire stake Kakinada SEZ Ltd to Aurobindo Realty and Infrastructure Private Ltd The equity stake including the sub-debt in KSEZ has been valued at Rs 2,610 crore. GMR had in February also agreed to divest a 49 percent stake in GMR Airports Ltd to French company Groupe ADP for Rs 10,780 crore in two stages. But in July it modified the second stage of the deal in the wake of the plummeting airport traffic.

SHUTDOWNS AND EXITS

Kishore Biyani's mantra has always been rapid expansion. It got him the title of India's retail king; it has also been the source of his debt troubles.

He sold his flagship Pantaloons Retail to Aditya Birla Retail a few years ago to save Future Group's retail business. The journey too, hit a roadblock in March, when shares of Future Group companies lost significant value leading to ratings downgrade of the promoter holding company and invocation of pledged shares by lenders. The virus outbreak farther worsened the cash position of group of companies Future Retail defaulted on interest payments in July.

Recently, Future Consume defaulted followed to Future Enterprises default on interest payment on non-convertible debentures. Biyani had no option but to sell his food and fashion retailing business including Big Bazaar, tbb Foodball easy bay, Nilgiris, Central and Brand factory besides the logistics and warehousing business to Reliance Retail Ventures (RRV) for Rs 24,713 crore. Reliance will also take over certain loans and liabilities.

After the deal, RRVL will hold a 13.4% stake in Biyani's Future Enterprises Ltd. (FEL) RRVL will enter into a long term agreement with FEL for sourcing branded fashion and FMCG produces, FEL will have the freedom to sell to other retailers.

Experts says, RRVL's pace of growth both organic and inorganic can cause more stress in the retail sector, just like in telecom where entry of Reliance Jio created huge pressures for the other two big players, Vodafone and Bharti Telecom. The retail sector will also face stress from digital models. Slowdown and low footfalls in markets and malls. The last one has already proved to be the nemesis of eight years old gaming and entertainment provider Smaash Entertainment which was under financial stress earlier also. But could not survive Covid, cash flow dried up as its business with 45 branches across India offering activities such as indoor cricket and go karting was closely linked to malls. Smaaash did poor respond to BT is queries.

FIRE FIGHTING AND BIG LESSONS

The 139 year long Thomas Cook India Ltd which has been many business cycles, focussed on payroll cost marketing spends rental payments affixed costs and better debtor management to survive the lockdown. The travel industry has global linkages that is why there is little hope of recovery any time soon. Moody's has said that it does not expect a return to pre-Covid volumes until 2023 at the earliest. The bigger worry is the Rs 50,000 crore bank debt in tourism, hotel and restaurant sectors. Biggies have also been feeling the heat. Reliance Industries Ltd had to cut the salary of its employees and executives in the oil and gas division by 10-50 percent.

The cash rich Tata Sons, the holding company for the Tata Group too, initiated cost cutting measures. Tata Steel increased liquidity levels to Rs 20,000 crore plus as a buffer. Tobacco to FMCG major ITC Plans to sell businesses such as consumer lifestyle in case they do not align with strategic objectives of the group.

Corporates are relooking at real estate infrastructure cost model says Abizer Diwanji, National Head, Financial Services EY India. Some are cutting down on capex. A large number have managed to beef up liquidity funding wherever feasible, says Rakesh Valecha, Senior Director, India Ratings.

PVR Ltd a market leader in terms of screen count, has raised confidence capital of Rs 300 crore through a rights issue. We have seen some companies looking at rights issues. This prevents dilution of promoter stake. I think raising equity will be the last resort for companies, says S. Venkataraghavan, Managing Director and Head, Equity Capital Markets, Equitus Capital. There will be more IPOs and QIP is in the next half of the year. There are estimates that Rs 50,000 crore worth of equity could be raised by March next year he adds.

In the debt market only AA rated paper is in demand. The top 100 companies have not seen much damage in market capitalisation but they also don't need capital immediately. In the case of companies after the top LOG the market cap hasn't recovered to pre Covid levels. These companies are a bit hesitant in raising capital as it will result in higher dilution given that their share prices have not Covid sell off says Deepak Jasani Head of Retail Research at HDFC Securities. Internally we continue to focus on optimising our expenses and conserving cash constantly looking for auras to reduce costs and take up only critical spends. Amit Syngle, Managing Director and CEO of Asian Paints said during a recent interaction with analysis.

Rao of JSW Steel however, says credit flow was a problem even pre-Covid. But there were other sources of financing such as mutual funds, insurance companies foreign portfolio investors and non-banking financial companies. Commercial papers were majorly funded by mutual funds. When credit flow has stopped from other sources banks are also not lending. This logjam has to be cleared he says. The industry is also complaining that low interest rates are available to only those with triple A rating. In the last 18 month the RBI has reduced the repo rate by 2-5 percent. But SBI's MCLR has come down only by 1-15 percent. This means not even 50 percent of the cut has been passed on to consumers, says Rao.

Experts have predicted a V-shaped recovery for services sectors such as hospitality and tourism when the situation normalises. The services sector which contributes over 50 percent to the country's GDP is likely to grow the fastest if the economy revives. But we don't know when our economy will start drafting the V, says Diwanji of FY India. A big fear is the second wave of Covid infections for example is toying with the idea of going for a second lockdown. Segments most impacted by social distancing such as tourism, travel, theatres or malls and restaurants are likely to take months to get back to normalcy.

Till a year ago, companies, banks and global investors were preparing for the economy to double to $ 5 trillion with 8-9 percent growth over the next five years. That hope is gone with Covid. It as further accentuated corporate stress, says Diwanji of EY India.

With the threat of downgrades and default rising the corporate sector is tightening its belt and so are risk averse hanks and creditors. Banks are keen to lend to corporate India but with a caveat. There is absolutely no point pumping in money into assets expecting that the bank will be able to recover the money in future, says S.K. Ramachandran, Executive Director at Indian Bank. Only a steadfast focus on economic growth and adequate liquidity can get India Inc out of this mess.

B. Governance and Budgeting

4

Impact of Sustainability Dimension of Corporate Governance on Select Companies

Dr K Anjaneyulu

In the last few years, the emphasis of governance has started extending from "Share holders" to "Stakeholders" and consequently from mere "profitability" now to "Sustainability". Growing companies have realised that it is necessary to govern themselves focussing on sustainability with long term sustainability which calls for strengthening and re-orienting the business strategies and the governance framework in harmony with sustainable development goals.

Despite economic growth in the era of neoliberal globalisation, the first round of the neoliberal reforms failed to reduce global poverty and inequality which led to economic and political instability. This approach did not recognize the challenges which such development policy creates in terms of results. Growing concern about environmental degradation, disappointment with development efforts to reduce poverty and inequality on a global scale together with economic and socio-political instability has shifted focus from the model of economic and growth to the new model of sustainable development. There are changes in society, the thinking and behaviour of people is changing, business environment is changing. New trends and concepts being developed to which enterprises should respond appropriately if they have to ensure their success in the long run on a sustainable basis.

It is an undisputable fact that the concern for sustainable development has entered our life and caused quite a lot of things to changes may be one the most important changes that should be mentioned is the way the business would begins to think, work and act. The companies, especially the big transnational corporations have started taking the sustainable development issues seriously. What has changed is that the management boards and the executives have begun bearing actions. The mindset of the business leaders, of the people with money has begun to change and getting profits and more money is no longer the only leading principle in the corporate governance world. The sustainable development ideas have entered there as well and have the potential to improve this world for the better.

CORPORATE GOVERNANCE

At a fundamental level the word governance comes from the Latin root "Gubernare", meaning to steer or to pilot. Corporate governance as first defined by the UK Cadbury Committee in 1992 is the system by which companies are directed and controlled. However, corporate governance is more than the system of specific checks and balances that contribute to the responsible oversight of a company. Corporate governance is concerned with achieving a balance between social and economic objectives, and between the objectives of individuals and the company. The corporate governance matrix exists to encourage the efficient use of resources and also to ensure that someone is held to account for the way in which these resources are used. The goal is to align as closely as possible the interest of individuals, corporations and society. It's the all encompassing mechanism that, when implemented effectively imparts integrity, ethics, transparency accountability and culture across the company. Corporate governance is a combination of structures and processes. While the structures refer to all the bodies responsible for the firm's direction and control, the processes consist in the activities developed to satisfy the stakeholder's expectation. Good governance is not only important for corporations, it's important for society. Corporations that recognize that their business impacts the environment around them create an innate sense of accountability to their societies. Sustainability governance is a part of the overall governance structure in which an organisation defines its management responsibility and oversight for sustainability activities and performance.

SUSTAINABILITY AND SUSTAINABLE DEVELOPMENT (SD)

Corporate sustainability means that companies should consider the future as well as the present in their decision-making and actions, with the aim of using their resources for creating value in the long run. Sustainability is a long term vision that characterizes socially responsible companies and that refers to a concept of global corporate responsibility including legal, economic, social and environmental aspects. This approach implies the balance of interests of all those who contribute to the current and future company's success, by means of sustainable value creation that satisfies both shareholders and other stakeholders in the long term.

The principles of sustainable development include stable and long term economic growth proportionate and balanced economic and social development. Active employment policies reduction of regional differences, growth of personal income and consumption preservation of the environment for future generations and efficient usage and allocation. The Dow Jones sustainability index is an opportunity for companies to differentiate themselves. This index considers sustainability as a business model that allows companies which take economic, social and environmental risks and opportunities into consideration in their management decisions to be identified.

CATALYSING SUSTAINABILITY THROUGH CORPORATE GOVERNANCE

In today's economy companies are facing intense pressure and scrutiny around their corporate behaviour apart from their own jurisdictions, also from communities, investors and customers across the globe. Corporate governance is a structure that boards and senior managers rely on to help them manage the company responsibility and according to sound ethics and accountability. The principles of corporate governance are based on transparency, accountability responsibility and the company's corporate social responsibility and fairness. The corporate governance begins to pay more and more attention not only to the return rate of the investments but also to the footprint that the company has on the society. Corporations are also taking a look at how they can incorporate sustainability into their strategic planning. In taking this approach companies need to take four key aspects into account. These aspects have equal importance:

1. *Societal influence:* this refers to how society impacts the corporations including the influence on stakeholders.
2. *Environmental influence:* this refers to the impact of the corporations in the geophysical environment, such as water waste, paper waste and energy waste.
3. *Organisational influence:* this refers to the relationship between the corporation including its managers and its internal stakeholders, particularly employees and all that those relationships entail.

4. *Finance:* this refers to the impact of the corporation's financial return in relation to the potential for risk and the level of risk.

THE GOVERNANCE OF SUSTAINABILITY

Good governance is widely acknowledged as a foundation for sustainable development, including sustained and inclusive economic growth, social development environmental protection and the eradication of poverty and hunger. The relevance of sustainability for the business activities of organisations has led to the need to include sustainability management as a direct formal responsibility of the Board of Directors.

In order to carry out the role of supervising sustainability the Board of Directors must:

1. Implement a Governance model that can evaluate and advise executive management of the company about the principles, policies, commitments and actions that need to be taken to meet the expectations of shareholders and of society in relation to Sustainable development and corporate responsibility.
2. Have a sufficient number of non-executive directors with the knowledge and experience to evaluate and challenge executive management regarding the implementation of all actions in the area of sustainability.
3. Set up mechanisms and communications channels which make sufficient and necessary information available to Non-executive Directors to evaluate sustainability management in the organisation.
4. Separate the powers of supervision and execution at all hierarchical levels of the organisation in order to provide relevant and independent information about the company's results

SUSTAINABILITY GOVERNANCE BEST PRACTICES

1. *Strategy and Culture:* The board ensures material environmental, social and governance risks and opportunities are addressed by the company's strategy.
2. *Oversight and CEO relations:* The board establishes a governance structure to enable oversight of the company's management of ESG issues, risks and opportunities and includes ESG in CEO relations.
3. *Risk management and major decisions:* The board ensures ESG related risks and opportunities are integrated into the company's management of enterprise risk and major corporate decisions.

4. *Board composition and competency:* The board builds ESG into board renewal, education and evaluation systems.
5. *Disclosure and shareholders relations:* The board provides oversight of the company's disclosure of its ESG performance and position and ensures shareholders have appropriate ESG information.

FACTORING CORPORATE GOVERNANCE IN SUSTAINABILITY EFFORTS

Sustainable governance considers not only the board's role in ensuring the long term and enduring success of the company but also includes the steps the board takes to ensure it performs an effective oversight function of the organisation's social and environmental performance. Boards must question the effectiveness of their internal controls and evaluate their governance processes by asking in depth and challenging questions such as:

How well does the board understand the pressing new risks that are affecting their company? To what extent is the board considering and actively discussing ESG related risks and opportunities? What does the communication and oversight look like between sustainability and other relevant business functions? Are there specific key performance metrics and indicators around ESG related issues that are being supervised by top level management? Is the board composed of directors with the company's strategy that promotes long term growth?

Corporate Governance and Sustainability- Action Agenda

A critical question is how will sustainable development be implemented? It must be understood that sustainable development does not just happen in an automatic or preordained way. It needs to be carefully discussed, openly debated and possibly even centrally planned.

Theme questions

1. A clear understanding of sustainable development is the concept of SD sufficiently clear and understood by all employees and other related parties. Clear commitment and leadership is required.
2. Specific organisational mechanism for management of sustainability considerations is a catalyst. Effective stakeholder involvement is another question and how to handle it.

3. Efficient knowledge management mechanism in place for managing knowledge is also required.

TOP DOWN INTEGRATION

Since the board of directors is at the apex of a corporation, governance plays a central role in the implementation of a sustainable strategy. Boards can better integrate sustainability throughout the systems and process:

1. By establishing clear lines of responsibility between executives, committees managers and regional business functions. In doing so a company can encourage accountability towards certain targets and goals.
2. By establishing oversight and monitoring mechanisms such as frequent assessments. Evaluations or reports to the board or committee responsible.
3. By dedicating a Board level committee to ESG Issues. Sustainability education, skills and expertise at board level.
4. ESG related issues in enterprise risk management and internal control processes.
5. Executive remuneration pay for sustainability performance.
6. Culture ethics and values.

ASSOCIATION WITH RESPONSIBLE SUPPLIERS IS DIVIDED UNDER THREE MAJOR HEADS,

(i) Sustainable practices
(ii) Sustainability reporting
(iii) Total thoughts on corporate governance sustainability

Here an attempt is made to present the successful stories of Hindustan Unilever (HUL) and HDFC Ltd.

Can HUL win in the next Decade

It is among the most admired companies in India. Not only for constantly grooming leaders for India Inc, and for being an outstanding marketer, but also for its sincere effort with social responsibility and environmental matters - something that is becoming an important part of any corporate legacy.

That's not all. The story looks even better when you look at how the stock market has showered its adulation on Hindustan Unilever over the and March 31, 2020, adding Rs 4.5 trillion to its market cap. Over the past five years alone, the stock price compounded at 21%, amid irrational exuberance in the sector. Trading at a price - earnings (P/E) multiple of 67x trailing earnings, the company will have to grow a minimum of 10% every year for the next 35 years and about 5% thereafter to justify the current valuation, according to research done by Abakkus Asset Manager founder Sunil Singhania, a year ago.

That seems like a tall order going by its past performance. The best period of business growth for HUL in this millennium was between FY05 - FY15 when sales compounded at 11.67% and net profit at 13.79% as against nominal GDP growth of 15.86%. Thereafter, its growth has been more muted. Over the past five years, its sales grew a modest 4.47%, lagging real GDP growth of 6.61% and nominal GDP growth of 10.69% for the same period. Its earnings growth of 9.08%, while double the sales growth, was still lower than the nominal growth in GDP.

Even though India continues to be a consumption - led economy, with 60% of GDP driven by consumption expenditure, HUL's portfolio is increasing not capturing a considerable share of consumer spending. While consumers tend to allocate a higher share of their wallet to durables and other indulgences such as travel and entertainment as per capita income rises, a trend that has been established over the past decade with rising household credit spurring penetration in several consumer segments, HUL has not adequately captured new segments in the staples space either, say analysts.

HUL's product portfolio covers a wide range of products in personal care straddling all price points and a narrow range of foods too, but that hasn't proved enough to track India's growth. To lift its sales growth curve, the company will have to add significant new high growth categories to its portfolio. Although HUL has premiumised its portfolio over the years and added new categories that have better growth runway, its portfolio is still dominated by product categories that have attained high penetration and that poses a limitation to growth going forward, according to analysts. "The best case for HUL would be to match GDP growth," says Singhania.

A relatively easier way to fix the growth deficit will be to snatch market share from competitors or enter newer sub-segments through acquisitions, and then gun for disproportionately high bottom line growth by doing a great job of extracting synergies from these acquisitions, something the current management has been doing with high degree of success. Even then, the 10% growth that the market expects may be a tough task.

"Acquisitions will be the best route, but given their elephantine size, it will need a very aggressive strategy to better the past track record", points out Singhania.

The market has a way of tempering unrealistic expectations, but that process could be long and painful. For 10 long years, between 2000 and 2010, the HUL stock remained flat as the company managed a 4.95% growth in sales and 6.6% growth in net profit.

After a decade of relentless optimism which kept the stock climbing, the sentiment towards the HUL stock is finally changing. The flat growth of last year and fear about COVID-19 impact on consumer sentiment has dragged down consumer stocks including HUL. The more serious question now is, in the face of an economic slowdown can the industry leader prevent its growth from declining. The very fact that the company was able to better its operating margin from around 15.82% in FY20-21 and 17.64% in FY15 to nearly 22.92% in FY20 raises doubts over further efficiency gains that the company can pocket. This makes sales growth even more imperative.

Post-covid, HUL, like several others in the sector saw a strong business recovery in June. Its production and supply bounced back to 90% of what they were before the Pandemic. Rural demand, new product launchers and focus on new distribution channels, analysts say, will fuel growth over the near term. Meanwhile the company is confident that 90% of the portfolio, which constitutes essentials, will continue to post a strong performance. Even if there is down trading by consumers, HUL with its portfolio across various price points is confident of garnering a good share of volume growth.

While synergistic benefits from GSK consumers acquisition may contribute to operating margin growth in coming quarters, the company might need more such big ticket acquisition that can bring growth in sales as well as bump up its bottom line. CEO Sanjiv Mehtha and CFO Srinivas Phatak talked about the company's strategy for growth, COVID-19 impact and more.

In an interview with OutLook Business, Sanjiv Mehtha has expressed his views over down trading in consumer goods:

(i) In the opinion of Sanjiv Mehtha, mustering of resources won't be easy, but then there is plenty of money going around in the world. Money is not the constraint, if you make attractive pics and if people believe in the long story of India, investors will come forward.

(ii) According to Mehtha, growth in India will come back in the latter Half of 2020-21 and definitely 2022 shall witness consumption revival.

(iii) He further opined that as an FMCG company, HUL will be recession resistant, not recession proof. So there are products people would consume even when the times are tough, though they may down trade to a lower price brand or may go down to a smaller unit price pack. But, those essential habits, people don't give them up completely. For example categories like Detergents, soaps and shampoos are highly resistant.

(iv) Post-COVID, there are some categories where the consumption levels are very high. These product categories are what I call "obsessive" such as sanitizers and hand washes. We used to spend crores of Rupees every year, trying to inculcate the right habits, even the basic habit of washing hands with soap and water. But COVID-19 has raised the consciousness of hygiene to a whole new level, and we believe this heightened awareness will remain even after the Pandemic is over.

(v) COVID-19 has also increased the focus on health and wellness. People have suddenly realised that boosting their immunity critical that the marriage with the GSK is made in heaven. It came at the most appropriate times. Hygiene and nutrition from his perspective are going to be the key drivers even beyond the Pandemic.

(vi) In response to the question why HUL clocked 4.5% annual sales growth over the past 5 years, trailing GDP growth during the same period?

(vii) He responded that, this period witnessed Demonetisation and GST disruption and big rural slow down in 2015. Over the past 9-10 years, HUL has grown at 9% CAGR, of which about 60% has come from volume growth. The EBIDT which has grown handsomely around 890 basis points, and return on capital employed which has been 3 digits, has increased. From a value creation perspective, HUL was about $17 Billion in 2013 and now it is about $68 billion. With this capitalisation, HUL acquired GSK consumer.

HUL's historic performance shows it will need an aggressive strategy to mimic even GDP growth. (%)

Table - 1

Years	Sales	PAT	Nominal GDP
3 years	6.16	14.59	9.86
5 years	4.47	9.08	10.69
10 years	8.40	12.37	12.65
20 years	6.66	8.77	13.10
10 years*	4.96	6.65	12.64
10 years**	11.67	13.79	15.36

* Worst 10 years performance for HUL Dec, 1999 to Mar, 2010, for GDP FY10 - FY20.

**best 10 years performance for HUL and GDP FY05 to FY15

Source: Published Reports of HUL.

(viii) In response to the acquisition strategy adopted by HUL, Mehtha said that HUL acquired Indulekha, Adithya Ice creams and Vwash and now GSK, the largest acquisition in the FMCG space to fit in with HUL strategy. Their focus will be on market development, which is growing the nascent categories, renovating their big brands in the core categories to keep them contemporary and premiumising their portfolio with higher order benefits.

(ix) Elaborating on sales channel shift perspective, Mehtha said, there are two channels that have really stood out during Pandemic one is E-commerce, which constituted 3% to 4% of total categories. It is going to gallop at a much faster pace. The other is the humble grocer, because people have suddenly realised the benefit of neighbourhood store. The share of Kiran's may go down from 75% to 60-65% over the next 10 years. But they will remain the most prominent channel. If the grocers adopt the technology, then this channel can not only survive but thrive. Their Shikhar app is being adopted by 2 lakhs stores.

(x) Mehtha opined on ESG (environmental, social and governance) goals as follows. HUL has three fundamental beliefs, that brands with purpose grow companies with purpose last and people with purpose thrive. These are the three fundamental beliefs which drive us. HUL adopted a classic multi - stakeholder model by giving preference to consumers, employees, society and the Planet, shareholder value gets created.

(xi) The HUL goal for water conservation was adopted to solve the water shortage problem in a couple of decades by working in about 5000 villages and creating a water potential of 1 trillion litres in the past but also in the next five years.

(xii) Similarly, HUL has a target by 2025 to get all the plastic reusable, recyclable or composable. By 2020, recyclable sachets would be 60% and it will reach 100% in another 2 years. HUL is recollecting the 50% of total plastic used by them and reprocess-ing or recycling it by the end of 2020.

(xiii) Responding to the last question about surviving in the lockdown period, he said that to get success companies should adopt the Leadership qualities and be resilient and adoptable. Further he said that COVID-19 brought about behaviour change at scale never seen before, that companies should keep a close watch on the consumer behaviour patterns that are emerging. Being a cash rich, Zero debt company, they need to have a laser focus on cash and cost by not ignoring the people and community.

SUCCESS STORY OF HDFC

In his 26 years long illustrious stint, at the helm of the country's premier private sector bank, Aditya Puri innumerable accolades. They came not just from India, but from across the world. The economist in its November 2020 edition acknowledged Puri as the "world's best banker" for "creating something from nothing and delivering long term shareholder return while supporting the economy".

HDFC Bank was incorporated in 1994 under a strategic alliance between HDFC and the UK based Nat west markets. In March 1995 it went public racing Rs 50 millions, through an at par IPO, which was oversubscribed 55x. The something from nothing remark can be gauged from this one statistic since May 1995 Croma the stock has delivered a wolfing 33.6 4th% CAGR. Simply put, Rs 10000 invested then, would be Rs 14.1 million today. Not to mention the Rs 457,950 worth of dividend. At it's listing price of Rs 40 in 1995, on equity of 2 billion shares, the bank was worth Rs 8 billion. Today it is worth Rs 7.91 trillion! The bank has the highest weightage in the Nifty 50, at 11.21%. Just as it seemed to be reaching another Pinnacle the bank began being weighed down. First, there were market whispers when the outgoing CEO cashed out his entire holding. Then, the market began getting antsy about top level executives resigning in significant numbers and finally, the RBI came down hard on HDFC Bank when the latter's digital services stalled a few times. And all of this was happening against, the backdrop of the pandemic, which has given rise to concerns over the possibility of retail loans turning bad.

It is a difficult time for a new CEO to take charge. But Puri handed over the reins to the Shashidhar Jagadishan, who was heading the HR and finance functions at the bank. The new chief is not unfamiliar to the investment community, and he is well liked and is known to get things done. Sounds good. But, are these enough to carry forward the intimidating legacy of Puri. Will Jagadishan create one of his own ?

The simmering cauldron

For the compounding machine that Puri had created, it was surprising to see the outgoing CEO cashing out of his holdings. Of the 7.796 million shares between July 21st and July 24 and his recently vested options on October 21st and November 3rd. However, Puri played it down in a media interview stating that it was part of an asset allocation advice given by his colleagues that he should diversify a bit. "It was actually thinking too much about the bank", he said. Interestingly, Jagadishan was one of the advisors behind the sale. He told analysts in August 3 con call: "For a person who is reaching 70 years of age, we need to advise; him on lessening the proportion of equity…that is why the balance 30% he is going to de-risk and put it in lesser riskier financial assets".

As per the details of ESOP scheme, shared by the bank with the US SEC, when an employee including a director to whom the options are granted retires, the employee concerned has to exercise their options within six months from the date of retirement, failing which the options would lapse. Part of selling was attributed to the requirement for funds for the ESOPs. Jagdishan told analysts over the call, "when retirement happens there is a scheme under which a lot of options would vest at the time of retirement. So, you need to provide a fair amount of liquidity for this. In Mr Puri's case, this was going to be a substantial amount of liquidity, which needed to be there to exercise these options." The HDFC Bank management did not respond to queries from *Outlook Business.*

Sterling track record

Over the past 25 years, HDFC Bank has become the second -largest bank in India by deposits.

Table - 2

Rs billion	March 1995	March 2020
Deposits & other borrowings	6.82	12921.30
Advances	0.98	9937.02
Total Income	0.14	1380.73
Net profit	0.08	262.57

Source: company.

Putting the sale into context, Suresh Ganapati analyst at Macquarie capital securities explains the sale is not like cutting the umbilical cord. "70% of the money is going to come back into the bank. As per the terms and conditions of employment, whenever the CEO retires his options must immediately. When the options West immediately, you need a massive sum of money to buy those options. So for that 70% of the money is going to come back, depending on the schedule."

Even as the management played down the sale, Puri, in his parting mail to the bank employees in August, wrote: "our best is yet to come suffice to say that in him (Jagadishan) you have the best person to lead and I have the worthiest person to hand over the baton to Jagadishan had joined the bank in 1996 as manager finance and went on to become the chief financial officer in 2008. In 2019, Srinivasan Vaidyanathan took over as the CFO, while Jagadishann was promoted as additional director and head of finance and HR.

In the run-up to succession, however, the Bank saw an exodus of several old hands, prominent among them was Paresh Sukthankar, the deputy managing director who was seen as a likely successor. In fact, a report by Ambit capital highlighted the talent drain: since 2017, the bank had seen 18 senior level exits. This included group heads - Munish, Mittal (IT), Ashok Khanna (auto loans), Abhay Aima (private banking), Nitin Chugh (digital banking), Rajesh Kumar Ratna Chand (retail credit and risk) - all of whom had spent anywhere between 18 and 25 years in the bank. In the Q1FY21 earnings call, Puri tried to assuage concerns by stating that while Mittal had left for further studies to Oxford, Aima wanted to pursue a different path. "We have a clearly defined succession plan," said Puri.

The street, too, is keeping its faith in the bank. Raamdeo Agarwal of Motilal Oswal financial services believes the next HDFC Bank can only be HDFC bank given it is fairly institutionalised. "there is a discipline, processes...... It's not a one person dependent Bank." Even though the name of the successive was revealed only early this year. For analysts, the name was quite evident. Nitin Agarwal, analyst at Motilal Oswal securities, says: "For more than a year now, Sashi used to lead the calls, she would call out names of group heads to answer some questions.... It was clear to us that Sashi was being groomed to take over," Ganapati adds, "He is an excellent taskmaster with great execution ability. He is not brash but a people's guy and gels with a lot of people very well...more amenable and that's a positive thing."

Puri, in his parting email, sought the same love and affection that he was showered with for Sashi. But, it was not to be.

Welcome Punch!

Jagdishan began his innings with an apology to the bank's customers. The banking regulator has pulled up HDFC Bank, on a first search stricture, for a snag that disrupted the latter's digital services. Incidentally, Shyamala Gopinath, former deputy governor of RBI, is the chairperson of the bank, and also a member of the bank's IT strategy committee.

While HDFC Bank is the second largest bank in India by deposits, it leads in terms of digital transactions processed. In FY20, about 95% of banks retail transactions were conducted digitally, up from about 85% in financial year 2018. How critical digital has been for the bank in gaining distribution efficiency can be gauged by the fact that over the past decade, the cost to Income ratio has improved by 900 basis points 36.8%(Q2 FY21) as against 43.48% for ICICI Bank and 59.44% for Kotak Bank. But, in the process, it appears that the bank has struggled in building adequate capabilities to strengthen its digital footprint.

Digital leverage

HDFC bank has effectively used digital payments to eke out distribution efficiency

Table - 3

Year	FY18	FY19	FY20	Q2FY21
Cost to Income ratio%	41	39.7	36.6	36.8

Source: company's published reports.

The regulator has barred tie bank frcm launching its digital 2.0 initiative, under which the bank is trying to bring all customers digital transactions, including payments, savings, investments, shopping, trade, insurance and advisory services, onto one 21 platform. The RBI has barred the bank Ram Sur Singh new credit card customers and any revenue accruing digital initiatives. HDFC Bank was looking to migrate the origination of two and four wheeler loans to the digital platform and since these loans account for 18% of its retail portfolio, a Delay will impact growth.

Yet, analysts don't seem too worried about the turn of events. Santanu Chakrabarty of edelweiss securities believes the incident is not a reflection on the bank's new leadership but the fact that their IT systems were old. But the clampdown of sourcmg new business is what analysts feel is a bit harsh, considering that technical glitches have been a way of life for customers. "The problem is not just about HDFC Bank, we have several instances where ATMs 70 public sector banks are out of order for days. So, while the intent of the regulator is right, the punishment is severe," feels Agarwal.

Rating agency Modi's believes the episode could result in an increase in spending to improve the bank's digital infrastructure, which would stran its profitability. However, analysts feel the moon is a blessing in disguise for the bank. "It also puts HDFC tech plan on a non-discretionary accelerated time frame. If the bank uses this opportunity to go ahead with all its near-term planned fixes and not just restrict itself to merely the regulator's mandate, it could, on balance, gain from this incident," mentions Chakrabarty in his report.

While Motilal Oswal's Agarwal says growth will be impacted for a quarter or two, structurally nothing changes for the bank. "Once they plug the gap and RBI does a digital audit, growth will be back on track" Agarwal, too, believes the bank will overcome the challenge." It could be that the RBI wants to send an ernest message to the entire banking sector to take digital disruption, seriously. But in digital, you do not know how soon and how last you will grow, so you need that extra buffer...my sense is that it's a surmountable problem. I would have been worried only if the earlier leadership had left behind a bad book."

While over business cycles the bank has never seen NPAs to go beyond 2%, a section of the market feels things could be different. Even as FY20 saw overall credit growth at an over five decade low of 6.14%, the bank outgrew the industry at 21%. Its better performance was largely led by corporate banking (29% year on year growth), while retail loan growth was soft at 15%. A report by Bernstein in March raised a Red flag over the bank having the highest exposure to unsecured retail credit compared with ICICI Bank and Axis Bank (9% of loan mix).

"While Axis Bank and ICICI Bank have also changed their growth strategy towards unsecured consumer segments, they have a much smaller book and, thus, their growth has been recent and off a lower base, "the brokerage stated. Bernstein points out that since the bank is a consumer finance market leader, it has greater sensitivity to its bottom line with 24% earnings and 36% earnings growth coming from unsecured loans.

What's in the book?

Though the pandemic has raised questions over the impact on unsecured loans, HDFC Bank seems to be sitting pretty for now. Of its total unsecured portfolio of 16% , 6% comprises cards and 10% personal loans. However, 75% of the personal loans are to salaried employees of A - rated top tier clients. "HDFC Bank always said they cater to the top 20 to 25% customers in various markets that they operate.......They are not going to cater to the customer that Bajaj finance caters to. They really cater to cream-de-la-cream customers, who dearly are far more resilient," says Ganapati.

Similarly in the case of wholesale lending, 80% is to AA and above clients, while 80% of the small and medium enterprises are covered by additional collateral.

In fact, Q2 has seen a greater drawdown by highly rated entities and an increased demand for working capital, in wholesale SME, Bank added 1550 new customers in Q2FY21, which is 3x of the first quarter.

As of Q2FY21, the advances book stood at Rs 10,383 billion, of which 47% was from retail advances (Rs 5534 billion). Kotak institutional equities believes, as the loan took shifts towards a less aggressive portfolio (mostly state owned entities), margin contraction may be inevitable.

In the earnings call the management mentioned that the weighted average rating of the book-on an internal scale that ranges from 1 to 10, with 1 being highest rated corporate and 7 corresponding to an external A rating-is currently at 4.4.

The great divide

Compared with HDFC Bank, other private banks exhibit considerable variance with respect to gross/net NPAs

Table - 4

Company	Gross NPA in %	Net NPA in %
HDFC	1.08	0.17
ICICI	5.20	1.0
Axis	4.18	1.0
Kotak	2.60	0.64

Source: Published sources of different Reports.

Post denomination, the bank has been showing higher than usual corporate book growth, as it utilised the excess liquidity and the low cost of funds environment in building the corporate book. "In fact, much before Covid, the bank had already started going slow in rctail, specially auto loans," says Agarwal.

Even in a worst fiscal like the current one, the bank has continued to stay conservative. The bank has made contingent provisions of Rs 23.04 billion, including Rs 11.3 billion for specific accounts and Rs 11.73 billion to strengthen the balance sheet in Q2FY21. While the Supreme Court has passed an interim order stating that those accounts that had not been declared NPA till August 31st 2020 should not be declared as bad loans until further orders, and the bank has complied with the orders, it has used analytical models to estimate potential NPA on a proforma basis. A pro forma financial statement is based on certain assumptions and projections and not actual numbers. As of Q2FY21, the bank's gross NPA (proforma; stands at 1.37%). "It takes guts for a fellow taking over to do it", Puri told analysts during the Q2FY21 earnings call. The bank's collection efficiency on the non moratorium book stood at 95%.

In fact, among private banks, HDFC does not have a NPA (gross/net) variance (1.08%/0.17%) to the extern that ICICI, Axis and Kotak have at (5.2%/1.0,%), (4.18%/1.0%) and (2.6%/0.64%), respectively. Avinash Tanawade of Dalai and Broacha mentions in his report that the banks loan book quality across segments is significantly stronger then the rest of the industry, you should hold it in a comparatively better stead. Even if the NPA numbers turn out to be higher, analysts believe the bank is much better placed than its peers. "Uncertain times put a premium on resilience, which is what HDFC bank offers-strong balance sheet and likely higher residual capital than most," mentions Chakrabarty of edelweiss.

In fact, Ganapati believes the competitive landscape by far is the best-ever for HDFC Bank. "You have extremely weak public sector banks, only a handful of private banks, the old private sector barks are dying; we have NBFCs failing. So, why not take it this way that it's the best time for the CEO to do even better?"

The bank has also been gaining on the liabilities side, added by the flight to safety sentiment, specially from PSUs and corporates. In Q2FY21, total deposits increased 20.3% (Rs 2.08 trillion) year on Year to Rs12.29 trillion, of which current account comprises Rs 7.1 trillion savings accounts Rs 3.4 trillion. Siji Philip, analyst. Axis securities, points out the competitive environment remains weak due to Covid-19, which will ensure that the bank continues to gain market share. "Recent episodes with Yes Bank and PMC Bank for the implied savers are more comfortable choosing larger banks such as HDFC," she says. The focus *on* strong deposits franchise has resulted in Healthy liquidity coverage ratio at 153%, well above the regulator requirement. Though the excess liquidity has impacted net interest margin by 15 basis points, analysts believe with higher capital adequacy and strong provisioning buffer, the bank is in a better position to withstand any upcoming economic upheavals.

The bank has a quarter of new credit in India since 2017. Going ahead, the bank is only looking at a higher pie. In December 2019, Puri stated that, globally, the top three banks get 80% of business. "Our aim is to be the number one bank in your wallet, but as long as we are in the top three banks for you, we will get enough business," said Puri. But the big difference is that unlike in the past, the bank will have to battle the growing clout of fin-tech firms.

Competitive Landscape- A Conclusion

HDFC Bank is a market leader in payments and has plans to further double its merchant reach. It has reached 1 million touch points since demonetisation and plans to touch 4 million by FY21. Through digital mode, the bank has already acquired 6.5 million new customers. Though the competitive intensity from fintech firms is rising, Ganapati believes the bank is in a different League altogether.

"Fintechs are just disintermediating the payment business, which anyway doesn't make any money. Look at Paytm's P and L explains Ganapathy. Further, the analyst believes that though fintechs will grow, they will still need to Ally with Banks. If someone wants an auto loan, will they go to PayTM? If you want my housing loan over Rs 10 million, will any fintech have that? Google pay has market share but I need HDFC bank account to have G Pay. Tomorrow, if Google pay wants to cross sell to customers when they are at 40% market share, to whom they cross-sell? They will have to come to a bank", opines Ganapathy.

Agarwal, too, believes that the bank is best positioned to make the most of the growth in the coming years. "As we go from a $ 3 trillion economy to $5 trillion, credit intensity will double. At present, total credit is Rs 150 trillion for Rs 200 trillion GDP, that is a credit to GDP ratio of 73%. Be assured that it will minimum go to 100% if not 150% for the next

$2 trillion. For the next 6 years, you will have to write Rs 150 trillion of credit, there are only 5 players who can do it: SBI, HDFC Bank, ICICI Bank, Axis Bank and Kotak Bank."

Going ahead though Ganapathy believes the immediate challenge for the Jagadishan will be to build scale as the bank is already on a very high market share. "Building scale is everything HDFC Bank was taken from market share of 1% to 10% by Puri, but from 10 % to 20%, it's going to be a more difficult task," he says.

Thus, far the Bank's growth has largely been organic, barring the merger with Times Bank in 2000 and acquisition of Centurion Bank in 2008. So, would an acquisition get it heft? Ganpathy believes otherwise. "To begin with, there is no large player in the market and anyway they are gaining 1 to 2% market share every year.

However, the possibility of a merger-with its own parent-could prove to be a rather challenging one for Jagadishan. Every once in a while, talks about a potential merger of HDFC bank with HDFC comes up because of the vulnerable position non-banks find themselves in because of lack of access to low cost deposits. Agarwal believes the merger will depend on swap ratio and how investors perceive the impact on financials. Currently, while FII holding is scattered, LIC holds 3.79 percent in the bank and 5.52% in the parent. "A larger share of mortgage will mean lower RoA,but higher Rose as housing gets the benefit of lower risk rate. Any such transaction will raise caution levels and will put pressure on the stock price of both," feels Aggarwal. If a merger goes through, the new entity will have to set aside higher reserves applicable for banks for the whole entity, something HDFC does not have to as a non-bank. Ganapati feels a merger can happen only if there is a statutory relaxation. "Otherwise, it will be debilitating on the profitability for both the institutions and negative for shareholders," he says. Seconds Agarwal, "A lot depends on the regulator's approach. You either create a condition for voluntary conversion or there is a regulatory push......*samay batayega kya hoga*".

Not only with respect to a merger with its parent, but in all respects how Jagadishan plays his cards will be vital. "Mr. Puri was two steps ahead of everyone on the latest trend, is Jagadishan like Puri in having the vision? I don't know. You have to give him at least five years to take a call on his ability to deliver," says Ganapathy. And the delivery that is expected is no easy ask-Puri got 26 years but Jagadishan's time starts now.

5

GENDER RESPONSIVE BUDGETING- Emerging Paradigm in Management

Sri G.E. Lesilie

ABOUT THIS SECTION

Management in the world today has taken altogether new connotations in scope and style. With respect to the former. Management as an area, has increasingly gained relevance in the service sector as much as in the realm of business and entrepreneurship which was the forte till recently. Today the application of Management practices in hospitals, hospitality and similar industries as well as in the area of rural and urban administration and provision of amenities to the people has increasingly been felt, bearing down on the sustainability of the initiative as much as the institution responsible for providing the said service or infrastructural facility. This has significantly transformed the management style which is now characterised by a significant shift to include a wide range of stakeholders including the user and the interface individuals and focusing on sustainability in the larger context, including conservation of the environment, focusing on the well-being of the user and the initiative, whether business or public service, triggered by the urge to fulfil some of the most pressing needs of the community or a category within it.

Gender Sensitivity is one perspective that has taken a very huge place in the realm of management in administration and governance, the world over. Giving due credibility of the vulnerability of the female gender in all aspects of life through the entire lifecycle, has brought into the forefront the wide ramifications of lack of gender sensitivity in the quality of services and facilities provided that is responsible for their continuing vulnerability. The immediacy of the problem is reflected in the Millennium Development

Goals (MDGs) and the Sustainable Development Goals (SDGs) of which the 5th out of 17 Goals is Gender Equality. The indicators under this goal include in the realm of woman's equity, the following: women's full and effective participation and equal opportunities for leadership at all levels of decision-making in political, economic and public life; legal frameworks in place to promote, enforce and monitor equality and non-discrimination on the basis of sex; Proportion of seats held by women in (a) national parliaments and (b) local governments; Proportion of women in managerial positions; sound policies and enforceable legislation for the promotion of gender equality and the empowerment of all women and girls at all levels with systems to track and make public allocations for gender equality and women's empowerment.

With this as the backdrop, Gender responsive Budgeting (GRB) has gained lot of ground in the past decade, continuing. Ongoing parleys on defining the exact connotation of GRB as to what is does, and does not stand for, institution of Gender Budgeting Cells by many Ministries and Departments, in-depth studies on gender sensitisation, gender equity and equality issues, various initiatives taken up in institutionalising gender responsiveness etc., bring home the great need to add this to the metamorphosing paradigm in Management.

This section attempts to provide near exhaustive information on some of the issues mentioned above to inform, inspire and instigate individuals from the Management fraternity to pursue and steer this subject into mainstream Management framework, apply the existing Management related tenets into this area and develop a robust framework for its inclusion into Management practices in the long term into the future.

1. INTRODUCTION

The Development debate has taken the term Women Empowerment as an integral aspect of its focus and approach. Seldom is there any contemporary concept of development in vogue which does not have women as the major stakeholders. In the third world countries especially, the primary focus is on women who, though constituting a half approximately of its demography, are recognised as twice disadvantaged, based on gender in addition to other socio-economic deprivations. In India, which is known its myriad cultural weave and the recognition of women as the primary force (Aadi Shakti) and which deified her and gave her a higher place in mythology and history, the current impacts are perceptible in some pockets whereas in others, glaring discrimination leading to inhuman incidents rise up constantly to show that a more lasting address is necessary. Women centric and women related legislations have been enacted to safeguard the rights and interest of women, currently adding up current imminent issues like discrimination, violence, and atrocities and also to prevent socially undesirable practices. All these incorporations of women's issues have been done from the five year plans of the government of India. The focus, however has changed to give a more comprehensive place to the women in various realms of societal life. A brief run-through of the different Five Year Plans of the government of India reflects this:

- Development of women in the First Five Year Plan (1951-56) was clubbed with the welfare of disadvantaged group like destitute, disabled, aged, etc.
- The Second to Fifth Plan (1956-79) continued to reflect the same welfare approach, besides giving priority to women's education and launching measures to improve maternal and child health services, supplementary feeding for children, and expectant and nursing mothers.
- Sixth Plan (1980-85) has marked a clear shift in its approach, from welfare to development oriented plans towards women.
- Seventh Plan (1985-90) aimed at raising women's economic and social status and bringing them into the mainstream of the national development.
- Eighth Plan (1992-97) focused on human development with special reference to women.
- Ninth Plan (1997-2002) made significant changes in the conceptual strategy of planning for women development.
- Tenth Plan (2002-07) continued with its strategy of empowering women as agents of social change and development.
- Eleventh Plan (2007-12) focus is on tackling the multifaceted exclusions faced by women through their mainstreaming and play decisive role in the family and social context.
- Twelfth Plan (2012-17) takes the perspective further, stressing on economic empowerment to ensure that every woman is able to develop her full potential and share the benefits of the economic growth and prosperity.

Over the last two decades, India's planning process has increasingly recognised the need to address gender inequalities. Formal earmarking of funds for women began with Women's Component Plans in 1997-98, however, gender sensitivity in allocation of resources started with the Seventh Plan. The plan documents have over the years reflected the evolving trends in gender matters.

- The Seventh Plan introduced the concept of monitoring of 27 beneficiary oriented schemes for women by DWCD. The exercise continues and number of schemes covered is being expanded.
- The Eighth Plan (1992-97) highlighted for the first time a gender perspective and the need to ensure a definite flow of funds from the general developmental sectors to women. The Plan document made an express statement that "…the benefits to development from different sectors should not bypass women and special programmes on women should be complementing the general development programmes. The later, in turn, should reflect great gender sensitivity".
- The Ninth Plan (1997-2002) adopted "Women Component Plan" as one of the major strategies and directed both the Central and State Governments to ensure "not less than 30 percent of the funds/benefits are earmarked in all the women's related sectors. Special vigil advocated on the flow of the earmarked funds/ benefits through an effective mechanism to ensure that the proposed strategy brings forth a holistic approach towards empowering women.
- The National Policy for Empowerment of Women 2001 envisaged introduction of a gender perspective in the budgeting process as an operational strategy.
- Tenth Plan reinforced commitment to gender budgeting to establish its gender-differential impact and to translate gender commitments into budgetary commitments.
- Eleventh Plan has recognised women not just as equal citizen but as agents of economic and social growth. The approach to gender equity is based on the recognition that intervention in favour of women must be multi-pronged and they must: (i) provide women with basic entitlements, (ii) address the reality of globalisation and its impact on women by prioritising economic empowerment, (iii) ensure an environment free from all forms of violence against women, (iv) ensure the participation and adequate representation of women at the highest policy levels, and (v) strengthen existing institutional mechanism and create new ones for gender mainstreaming and effective policy implementation.

2. BACKGROUND OF GENDER BUDGETING

Gender Equality in the Post-2015 Development Agenda

Similar to the MDGs, the new international norms for development expected to be decided in 2015 will guide the setting of priority goals, the mobilisation of global resources towards shared objectives, and enhanced accountability for realising a common vision of sustainable development. The lead-up to the adoption of a post-2015 agenda, together with other global developments such as the Rio+20 outcome, the review of the ICPD Programme of Action Beyond 2014, the 15th anniversary of Security Council Resolution 1325 (2000) on women and peace and security, as well as the 20th anniversary of the Fourth World Conference on Women (Beijing+20), offer a unique collective opportunity for underscoring both the intrinsic centrality and the instrumental value of gender equality and women's empowerment.

Following the Rio+20 outcome document, a proposal for a set of sustainable development goals to replace the MDGs was submitted in September 2014 to the 68th session of the General Assembly for negotiation. The definition of the post-2015 development agenda will culminate during the General Assembly's 69th session in 2015. Both the sustainable development goals and the post-2015 agenda will provide frameworks for eradicating poverty; creating sustainable consumption and production patterns; ensuring sustainable water and energy access while protecting the environment; promoting transparent and accountable governance; achieving equality including gender equality and human rights; and ensuring access to high quality education and healthcare, and essential laws, services and infrastructure.

In the context of this global policy debate, gender equality advocates, including UN Women, 10 are calling for an explicit commitment to achieving gender equality, women's rights and women's empowerment. Within the United Nations system, there is a general consensus that in the post-2015 agenda, gender equality and the empowerment of women are pivotal as intrinsic human rights principles, and as catalysts for achieving all human development goals, good 10 See UN Women 2013. Governance, economic growth, sustained peace and security, and sound relationships between people and the environment.

To be transformative, the commitment to gender equality should be universal; address the structural foundations of gender-based inequality, including in the three dimensions of sustainable development—social, economic and environmental; and ensure accountability.

Building on the experiences and lessons learned from the MDGs, gender equality thus needs to be addressed both as a stand-alone goal and as an issue cutting across all other parts of the agenda, in order to address gender-based discrimination specific to each development sector, and to ensure the meaningful achievement of all other goals.

According to UN Women and many other development partners, a stand-alone gender equality goal should be retained in parallel to the mainstreaming of gender equality in all other goals because gender equality is a prerequisite for achieving progress in other development goals, and achieving gender equality is an important human rights goal in itself.

Three critical target areas have been identified for a stand-alone gender equality goal: freedom from violence against women and girls; gender equality in the distribution of capabilities; and gender equality in decision-making in all spheres of public and private life. This proposal is grounded in global commitments by UN Member States to gender equality and women's rights, and enshrined in international treaties and agreements.

Gender Equality Goal in the Post-2015 Development Agenda

Post-2015 development framework:

- Recognizes the active roles of women as leaders and agents of change in the development, humanitarian and peace-building processes;
- Reflects an understanding that poverty is, in part, a result of women's socially enforced gender roles and relations, and that, without specifically addressing the causes of gender inequality, poverty cannot be fundamentally resolved; and
- Focuses on the most disempowered people in society, including people of various abilities, races, classes, sexual and gender identities, etc.

Mainstreaming of the gender perspective into the framework is achieved through the following:

- Agreeing to specific development targets under each goal that reflect explicit efforts to tackle the gender-related barriers women and girls face;
- Developing gender-sensitive indicators reflecting the kind of information needed rather than merely the availability of data;
- Providing incentives within targets and indicators to reach the poorest and most marginalised people in societies, explicitly including women from socially excluded groups;

- Ensuring all indicators are disaggregated by sex and other relevant determinants of gender disparities at societal level, in daily life and in all spheres; and
- Substantially increasing the availability of data disaggregated by sex at societal level, in daily life and in all spheres.

A stand-alone goal or domain on gender equality embeds the following factors:

- Prioritises the poorest and most disempowered women and girls;
- Takes into considerations the vulnerabilities of men and boys;
- Reflects priorities defined by the poorest and most disempowered women;
- Meets women's and girls' long-term strategic interests by tackling the roots of gender inequality and discrimination;
- Provides politically feasible targets and indicators that will contribute towards the transformative goal; and
- Complements the other goals.

Source: Adapted from Smee and Woodroffe 2013 *(Additional Views from Civil Society Think Tanks)*

3. DIMENSIONS OF GENDER DEVELOPMENT

There are several dimensions of gender development. These mainly include social, economic, political and legal. Women's development has come a long way from the earlier welfare orientation. In the welfare approach, women were taken as vulnerable sections of the population, whose situation could be ameliorated through the provision of support services like health, nutrition and childcare. Women's development has been looked at variously from perspectives that have followed the welfare approach. The present approach of empowerment looks at unequal gender and power relations and use conscientisation, mobilisation, solidarity and collective action as solution (Chart-1).

Chart - 1: Different Aspects of Gender Development

CULTURAL	LEGAL	POLITICAL	ECONOMIC	SOCIAL
Respect of rights of indigenous and traditional people	Awareness rights Decentralisation Mainstreaming gender perspectives Decision making	Gender justice for elimination of forms of gender discrimination	Poverty Eradication Micro-credit Women and Economy Globalisation	Education Health Nutrition Drinking water Sanitation

(Contd...)

Participation in local resource management Inclusion indigenous knowledge			Women and Agriculture Women and Industry Support services	Housing and Shelter Environment

Chart-2: Different Perspectives to Women's Development

Type of Project	Concepts		Type of developmental interventions
	Concept of the problem	Concept of the solution	
Welfare	Women's poverty, women special needs, women as vulnerable groups, women lower socio-economic status	Provision of support services health, nutrition, childcare	Build maternity clinics, health clinics, immunisation, health education, nutrition education
Economic sector reliance	Women as underemploy unproductive, dependents lacking in productive skills	Promote self reliance and interdependence, provide product skills, encourage women productive enterprises	Income generating projects women, women's clubs, so making, school uniform making etc.
Efficiency	Women as previous overlooked resource development planning, women as under-developed human capital	Identify actual productive role of women, support women with skills, training and improve technology, invest in previous overlooked resource	Integration of women development planning main-streaming of women development, exten-sion adv for women farmers, appropriate technology for women, increase women's access to factors production
Equality	Structure of inequality discrimination against women in schooling, credit, access land	Equality of opportu-nities women in schooling, access factors of production	Affirmative action to promote Equal opportunity revenue development planning so the women are equal partners beneficiaries in development process.
Empowerment	Unequal gender pro relations, the patriarchal resistance	Awareness generation, mobilisation solidarity, collective action	Grass roots projects, support women's collective action project concerned with democratisation and political action

Source: UNICEF based on Moser, in ICECD (undated) Making Development Gender Sensitive, a Guide for Trainers, Ahmedabad, ICECD.

India being a socio-culturally and ethnologically diverse society bound in complex traditional microcosm, a host of social, economic and political factors impact the status and development of women. According to a 2005 study on gender development, Kerala, Tamil Nadu, Punjab, Gujarat, Karnataka and Maharashtra are the leading states as far as achievement of overall gender development indicators are concerned.

A look at India's development indicators based on 2011 census reports shows marked demographic contrast between the northern, eastern and central parts of India on the one hand and the rest of the country on the other. The educational backwardness has been reported high in Bihar, West Bengal and Rajasthan while health indicators show that Bihar, Assam, Uttar Pradesh and Madhya Pradesh are backward states. The social status of women has also found to be poor in Andhra Pradesh, Assam, Rajasthan and Bihar. Similarly, the economic status of women is found to be poor in Maharashtra, Orissa, Kerala and Rajasthan. As far as the leadership is concerned, Uttar Pradesh is ahead of state like Kerala. However, SHG's per lakh females were reported high in Andhra Pradesh, Tamil Nadu, Karnataka, Kerala and Orissa.

Indian women are at the crossroads of their destiny. There is a great upsurge in consciousness about their rights among all sections and classes of society in the country. There has been tremendous increase in developmental activity for women since the 1980s with a great leap forward in the 1990s. Women constitute 48.2 percent of the country's population. However, development process has bypassed women. Their holistic development in terms of materials, resources, programmes and policies is the broad mandate of working of Ministry of Women & Child Development, Govt. of India.

Department of Women and Child Development was setup in the year 1985 as the national machinery for advancement of the women in the country. In the view of increasing importance of women empowerment, Government of India has converted the department into full-fledged Ministry in the year 2006. Government of India has implemented a number of programmes for women empowerment.

Government of India has also adopted National Policy for Empowerment of Women, 2001 which aimed at bringing about the advancement, development and empowerment of women and to eliminate all forms of discrimination against women and to ensure their active participation in all space of public life and activities. The gender budgeting is also widely accepted as a powerful tool for empowerment of women. The Government of India is focusing on mainstreaming gender budgeting initiatives and bringing the subject center stage. The detailed guidelines for gender budgeting have been issued for budgetary allocation and reviewing the policy and implementation of schemes.

For the first time, there was a sub-group on gender budgeting, as part of the working group of empowerment of women. The sub-group recommended the setting up of a Gender Budgeting Bureau in the Ministry, establishment of Regional Resource and Training Centre for Gender Budgeting and preparation of gender budgeting training manuals. Strategic framework of the activities pertaining to gender budgeting is shown in Box-1.

Box-I: Strategic Framework of Activities

- Quantification of allocation of resources for women in the Union, States and Local Administration budgets and expenditure thereof.
- Refining and standardizing methodology and development of tool Trend analysis.

Analysis of change in pattern, shift in priorities in allocation across clusters of services etc.

Variations in allocation of resources and actual expenditure.

Adherence to physical targets.

Gender audit of policies of the Government- monetary, fiscal, trade etc., at the Centre and State levels.

Research and micro studies to guide macro policies like credit policy, taxes etc.

Identification of gender impact of policies/interventions viewed as gender neutral.

Micro studies to identify need for affirmative action in favour of women towards correcting gender imbalances.

Impact assessment of various schemes in the Union and State budgets.

Micro studies on incidence of benefits.

- Analyzing programmes, strategies, interventions and policy initiatives from the perspective of their impact on status of women as reflected in important indicators like literacy, maternal mortality rate (MMR), participation in work-force.

e.g. analysis of substance and content of various interventions directed at health and women and correlate the same with indicators like MMR to establish need for corrective action in formulation of schemes/approach.

- Institutionalising the generation and collection of gender disaggregated data

Developing management information system (MIS) for feedback from implementing agencies.

Inclusion of new parameters in data collection in Census and surveys by National Statistics Organisation (NSO). Census Statistics Organisation (CSO) etc.

- Consultations and capacity building

Collation of research and exchange of best practices.

Developing methodologies and tools for dissemination.

Forums and partnerships amongst experts and stakeholders.

Review of decision-making processes to establish gender equity in participation of women in decision-making processes and to establish processes and models aimed at gender equity in decision-making and greater participation of women.

Formulation and reflection of satellite accounts to capture the contribution of women to the economy by way of their activities in areas that go unreported like care economy, unpaid work in rearing domestic animals, etc.

Source: Ministry of Women and Child Development, 2007.

During the last decade, a number of international meetings have been convened that have the potential for transforming the reality of women's lives. At many of these meetings government, including Government of India, have committed to taking action to improve the situation of women. The following are among the international commitments to which Government of India is party:

- The Convention on the Elimination of All Forms of Discrimination against Women (CEDAW), which Government of India signed in 1980.
- The World Conference on Human Rights in Vienna (1993) asserted that women's rights are human rights.
- The International Conference on Population and Development (ICPD) in Cairo (1994) placed women's rights and health at the centre of population and development strategies.
- At the Fourth World Conference of Women in Beijing (1995), governments- declared their determination "to advance the goals of equality, development and peace for all women everywhere in the interest of all humanity".
- In the 1995 Commonwealth Plan of Action on Gender and Development governments declared their vision of a world "in which women and men have equal rights and opportunities in all stages of their lives".

CONCEPT OF GENDER BUDGETING

Gender Budgeting refers to a method of looking at the budget formulation process, budgetary policies and budget outlays from the gender lens. Gender Budget, with regard to the government at any level, does not refer to a separate budget for woman, rather it is an analytical tool which scrutinises the government budget to reveal its gender-differentiated impact and advocate for greater priorities for programme and schemes to address the gender-based disadvantages faced by women. In fact, gender budgeting, as an approach, is not confined to government budgets alone; it also includes analyzing various socio-economic policies from the gender perspective. As per Council of Europe's Group of Specialist on Gender Mainstreaming, gender budgeting is an application of gender main-streaming in the budgetary process. It means a gender based assessment of budgets, incorporating a gender perspective at all levels of budgetary process and restructuring revenues and expenditure in order to promote gender equality. The fundamental objective of gender budgeting is to refine budgets and relate policies with a view to promoting gender equality as an integral part of human rights. Thus, gender budgeting makes the gender specific effects of budgets visible and raises awareness about their frequently implicit dimensions of discrimination against women. Thus, it identifies the gender specific implications of public finance. Gender budgeting is crucial tool for monitoring gender mainstreaming activities, because public budgets involve all policy areas. Gender budgeting also increases the transparency of and participation in the budget process. It aims at democratising budgetary process as well as budget policy in general. Gender responsive budget initiatives can contribute to growing practice of public consultation and participation in the preparation of budgets and in monitoring their outcomes and impact. Gender budgeting also contributes to better targeting of policy measures and hence to the pursuit of effectiveness and efficiency. Gender budgeting may be regarded as an important strategy in the pursuit of equity in distribution of resources and helping to redress inequalities and to reduce poverty. Thus, gender responsive budgets are tool for strengthening economic and financial governance. A gender responsive budget is a budget that acknowledges the gender patterns in society and allocates money to implement policies and programmes that will change these patterns in a way that moves towards a more gender equal society. Gender budget initiatives are known by a range of different names such as gender sensitive budget, applied gender budget analysis, gender perspective budget analysis, etc. however, gender budgeting is the most popular term. Political will, accountability, allocation of specific human and financial resources, coordination of information and training and availability of gender disaggregated data can be regarded as preconditions of gender budgeting. Transparency, partnership and cooperation throughout the budgeting process are key principles of gender budgeting.

GENDER RESPONSIVE BUDGETING

The process of gender responsible budgeting eventually results in gender responsive budgets. The terms gender responsive budgets, gender-sensitive budgets, gender budgets and women's budgets are however often used inter-changeably:

- Refers to the process of conceiving, planning, approving, executing, monitoring, analyzing and auditing budgets in a gender-sensitive way.
- Involves analysis of actual expenditure and revenue (usually of the government) on women and girls as compared to on men and boys.

- It helps governments to decide how policies need to be made, adjusted and reprioritised.
- It is a tool for effective policy implementation where one can check if the allocations are in line with policy commitments and are having the desired impact.

Gender responsive budgeting is a tool or means to achieving gender equality and women's empowerment. Gender responsive budgeting helps in the following key functions:

- Monitoring of the achievement of the policy goals,
- Achieving gender equity/equality;
- Advancement towards the realisation of women's rights;
- Alleviating poverty more effectively;
- Enhancing economic efficiency;
- Achieving good governance;
- Enhancing accountability and transparency;
- Improving the allocation of resources to women;
- Supporting gender mainstreaming in macroeconomics;
- Strengthening civil society participation in economic policy making;
- Enhancing the linkages between economic and social policy outcomes;
- Tracking public expenditure against gender and development policy commitments;
- Contributing to the attainment of the millennium development goals (MDGs);
- The budget is the most important policy of government because, without money, government cannot implement any other policy successfully;
- A Gender Responsive Budget ensures that the needs and interests of individuals from different social groups are covered in the government budget. In particular, it ensures that the needs and interests of women, men, girls and boys are covered.
- Looking at budgets through a gender lens shows clearly where the collection and distribution of public money is unequal and inefficient. It also shows how discrimination affects national development.

- Budget analysis and advocacy by citizens brings together technical knowledge for effective and equitable policy-making with political and organising tools for engaging with powerful interests and institutions.
- Gender-responsive citizen budget initiatives complement anti-corruption strategies.

Gender is culturally and socially constructed roles, responsibilities, privileges, relations and expectations of women and men, boys and girls. In the Indian society, discrimination faced by girls and women through their life cycle as shown in Chart-5 demands for gender responsive budgets and gender budget.

Chart-5: Discrimination through the Life Cycle of Girls and Women

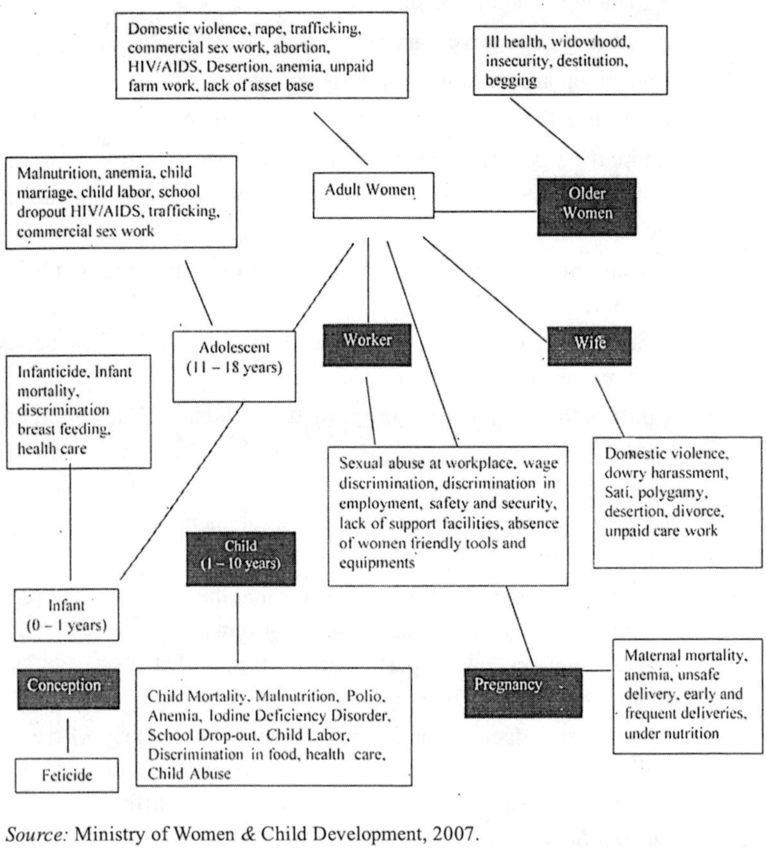

Source: Ministry of Women & Child Development, 2007.

Gender Budgeting serves varied purposes. These include, among others:

- Identifying the felt needs of women and re-prioritising and / or increasing expenditure to meet these needs;
- Supporting gender mainstreaming in macro-economics;
- Strengthening civil society participation in economic policymaking;
- Enhancing the linkages between economic and social policy outcomes;
- Tracking public expenditure against gender and development policy commitments; and Contributing to the attainment of the Millennium Development Goals (MDGs).
- Gender Budgeting does not propose separate budgets for women or for men;
- Focus on gender awareness and mainstreaming in all areas of budgeting at all levels;
- Promote the active participation of women stakeholders and other disadvantaged citizens who are excluded from public decision-making;
- Promote more effective use of resources to achieve gender equity and transparency;
- Look at the links between inefficient and inequitable use of resources based on gender and poor use of resources based on other axes of disadvantaged such as race, ethnicity, geographic location and age;
- Stress re-prioritising within and across sectors rather than only an increase in overall government expenditure.

BENEFITS OF GRB ANALYSIS FOR GOVERNMENTS

- It can improve efficiency and impact by ensuring that expenditure benefits those who need it most.
- It can be used to report on progress on the government's commitment to democracy, equitable economic development, and women's rights and equality.
- It can be used to improve transparency and accountability and to help implement policies effectively.
- It can be used to track budgets and so reduce corruption.

- It provides a space for government to work with civil society to enhance development impact, democratic governance and transparency.
- It can be used to report on government's progress on compliance with national and international gender-related commitments, recommendations and action plans (e.g. national gender policies and the Convention on the Elimination of All Forms of Discrimination against Women (CEDAW)).
- It strengthens advocacy and monitoring initiatives by citizens.
- It provides information to challenge discrimination, inefficiency and corruption and to propose feasible policy alternatives.
- It recognises the ways in which women contribute to the society and economy with their unpaid labour in bearing, rearing and caring for citizens.
- It provides a way of holding public representatives accountable for their performance.
- It recognises the needs of the poorest and the powerless.
- Around the world, Gender Budgeting trends to focus on women because:
- nearly two-thirds of the illiterate people in the world are women;
- in developing counties, maternal mortality continues to be a leading cause of death for women of reproductive age;
- women are under-represented in decision-making in both government and business sectors, especially at senior levels;
- Women's economic work continues to be very different in nature from men's. Women are engaged in less formal, lower status types of work and continues to receive less pay than men for the same work; and
- Women also continues to do most of the unpaid work of bearing, rearing and caring for children and other citizens.

STAGES OF GENDER RESPONSIVE BUDGETING

Gender responsive budgeting can be taken up at three stages of budget preparation and implementation:

- **Inputs:** (a) financial appropriations made in budgets vs. need, (b) appropriations vs. actual expenditure, (c) sector-wise shares of expenditure and (d) revenue side shifts between firms, individuals, households.

- **Activities:** supported by appropriations: public services, delivery costs, income transfers.
- **Outcomes:** expected from appropriations vs. actual outcomes including unintended ones: whether the money is being used in a manner that effectively achieves planned outcomes and what is the impact.

A government budget is a financial statement of the expected revenue and intended expenditure of the government over a given period. The government budget is not simply a technical instrument for compiling and reporting on government revenue and expenditure plans but it is also a

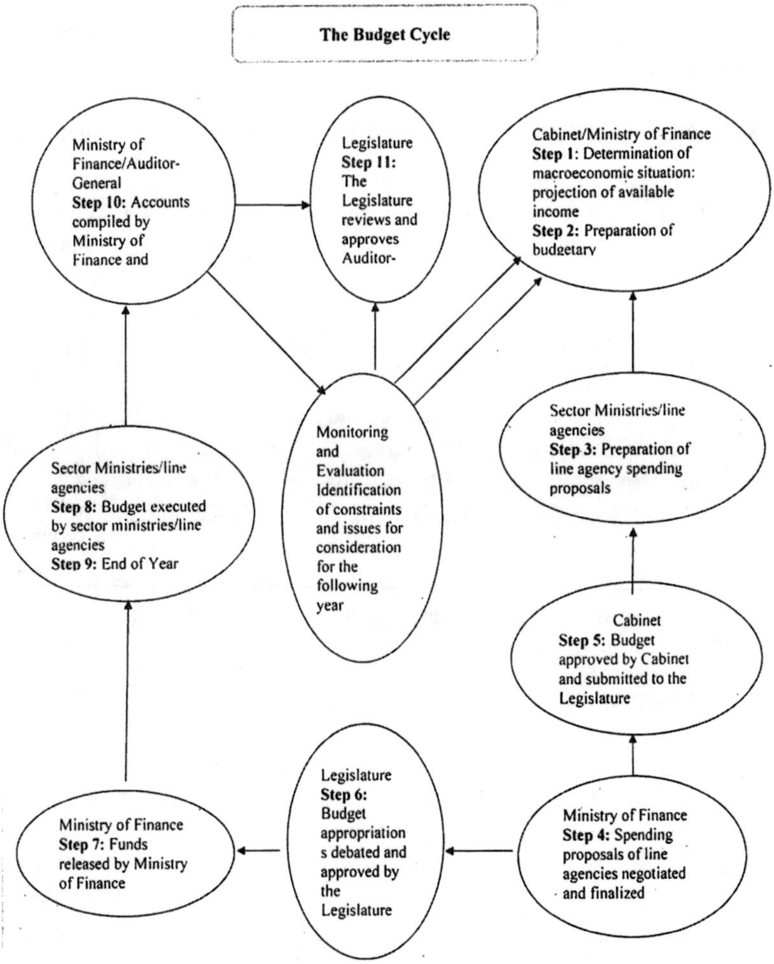

primary policy statement made by the government. The budget has three crucial economic functions viz. allocation of resources, distribution of income and wealth, and stabilisation of economy. Gender responsive budgets seek to uncover the impact of resource allocations on women, men, girls and boys. It is important to have gender disaggregated data in order to determine how different groups are affected.

A budget process consists of a cycle. The details differ from country to country, but in most countries the cycle includes the steps shown in Chart-6. The key steps of budget process in most countries are (1) determining the macro economic situation; (2) preparing budget guidelines and setting expenditure ceilings; (3) preparing sector ministry spending proposals; (4) securing legislative approval; and (5) monitoring, evaluation and accountability.

STAKEHOLDERS OF GENDER BUDGETING

A wide range of players may be involved in gender budgeting. Different stakeholders are involved in gender responsive budgeting. Government, Parliament, researchers and experts, international organisations, non-government organisations, trade unions and employer's organisations, etc. play key role in gender budgeting exercises. Governments may take up gender budgeting on their own initiatives or at the prompting of Parliament or civil society groups. However, awareness raising and training of officials at all levels is needed to provide necessary knowledge. Responsibility for management needs to be clearly assigned. Gender budget initiatives are most effective when the Ministry of Finance leads the initiatives, ideally with close involvement of Ministry for Women Development. While the top level budget decisions are made by Cabinet and other ministers, senior civil servants and advisors also play crucial roles. Gender budgeting represents an enormous challenge to the civil servants' whose job is to draft the details of budgets.

Parliament and State Assemblies have crucial role in adopting the gender budgeting. The politicians particularly the decision-makers in Parliament and State Assemblies are supposed to submit their demand for budgetary resources on women specific and pro-women programmes. Gender budgeting requires in-depth research and analysis. Academics can, therefore, make valuable contributions in particular with regard to providing know-how, implementing gender impact assessment, developing methodology and indicators, auditing budgetary outcomes and training government officials.

International organisations can also contribute to gender budgeting initiatives at national level by setting an example through the application of gender budgeting to their own activities and by organising joint projects and exchange of experiences, thus stimulating political interest in gender budgeting. Civil societies, trade unions and employer's organisations play an important role in organising and articulating collective will which contribute to process of gender budgeting. They have different roles and carry out different activities:

- The Ministry of Finance
- The Planning Department or Planning Commission
- The Ministry of Women's Development
- Sector ministries
- Researchers/Economist
- Statisticians
- Civil society organisations, especially women's groups
- Parliamentarians and other representatives of the people at state/ district and sub-district levels
- Media
- Development partners/Donors

Gender budgeting initiatives may be launched by players inside or.outside governments. However, potential for change in the budget process depends on government involvement. The involvement of Ministry of Finance is crucial for everlasting effect of gender budgeting. All policy areas are relevant to gender budgeting since they all affect gender relations. Gender budgeting initiatives should take all steps of budgeting process into account and promote gender budgeting throughout the process, including planning, preparation, implementation, audit and evaluation. The five major steps for gender budgeting are shown in Chart-7. These mainly include the prerequisite for gender budgeting, gender relevant data base, entry points for gender budgeting and availability of tools for budget analysis. The prerequisites for gender budgeting are mainly gender orientation and sensitisation, disaggregated data on budgetary allocations, participatory planning, spatial mapping, gender appraisal for all new programmes and schemes, preparing guidelines for review of public expenditure and policy, analysis of public expenditure and outcome assessments of budget.

Chart-7: The Five Step Framework for Gender Budgeting

Step 1:	An analysis of the situation lor women and men and girls and bovs (and the different sub-groups) in a given sector.
Step 2:	An assessment of the extent lo which the sector's policy addresses the gender issues and gaps described in the first step. This step should include an assessment o f the relevant legislation, policies, programs and schemes. It includes an analysis of both the written polios as well as the implicit policy reflected in government activities, Il should examine the extent lo which the above meet the socio-economic and other riuhts of women.
Slep 3:	An assessment of the adequacs of budget allocations lo implement the gender sensitive policies and programs identified in slep 2 above.
Step 4:	Monitoring whether the money was spent as planned, what was delivered and to whom. This involves checking both financial performance and the physical deliverables (disaggregated by sex)
Step 5:	An assessment of the impact of the polios / programs / scheme and the extent lo which the situation described m step ! has been changed, in the direction of greater gender equality.

Source: UNIFEM-UNFPA Gender Responsive Budgeting and Women's Reproductive Rights: Resource Pack.

TOOLS & METHODS FOR GENDER BUDGETING

There are a number of tools" that can be used for gender responsive budgeting. Some of these are mentioned below. Either one or a combination of two or more of these 'tools' can be used at a time (Chart-8).

Chart-8 Tools of Gender Budgeting Source: UNIEM

Sl.	Type -of Tools	Aim of the Tool	Questions the tool tries lo answer
1.	Gender-Aware Budget Statement	To review the budge using some of the other too s ant to summarise its implications lor pender euualilv with different	Does the budget statement of the government give an account of the progress in reducing gender-disparities?
2.	Sex-Disaggregaled Beneficiary Assess-ment of Public Service Delivery and Budget Priorities	To collect and analyze the opinions of men and women on how lar current forms of publie service delivery meet their needs and how far current patterns of public expenditure lit in with their	Are effects and outcomes of policies in line with the political intention? Are needs of women and men addressed equally?
3.	Sex-Disaggregated Public Expenditure Benefit Incidence	To analyse the extent to which men and women, girls and boys, benefit from expenditure on publicly provided	How are the benefits of public spending distributed among women and men. girls and boys?
4.	Sex-Disaggregated Revenue Incidence Analysis	To analyze the impact of the kind of revenues raised by the government on women and men.	What percentage of government's revenues is paid by men and women respectively? What kinds of tax/user fees reforms are more beneficial for the

(*Cond...*)

			poor/poor women? Which sources of revenues have a progressive and which a regressive nature? Does the tax system provide labour market incentives for
5.	Gender-Aware Medium-Term Economic model and To incorporate, gender variables into model on	To question gender-blind assumptions of Macro-economic models and to incorporate gender variables into models on which medium-term public expenditure planning are based.	Which realities do assumptions of macro economic models reflect? Are gender-specific constraints in behaviour of economic actors considered in the model? Are sex-disaggregated data included in the model? Are gender-aspects taken into consideration in the guidelines for
6.	Sex-Disaggregated Analysis of the Impact of the Budget or times Use	To analyse the impact of government resource allocation on the amount and the way time is spent in households.	How are national budgets and the way time is used in households interlinked? Who is most affected by changes in public spending? Are costs transferred from the public sphere to
7.	Gender-Aware Police/Programme Appraisal and Impact Analysis	To analyze policies and programmes funded by the budget from a gender perspective by asking in what ways policies and their associated resource allocations are planned and actually do reduce or increase gender inequalities.	Are policies and programmes likely to reduce or enhance gender inequalities and imbalances? Do budgetary allocations follow policy commitments oil gender equality?

Whereas public expenditures are directly linked to specific policy areas, public revenues form a policy area of their own. The tools and methods for gender budgeting reflect three basic steps of gender budgeting including expenditure and revenue related. These mainly include the analysis of gender relations in a specific area of related policies and budget allo-cations; development of gender sensitive policies and their translation into budgetary allocation; examination of impact of gender sensitive policy; analysis of impact of specific revenues on gender relations; development of a gender sensitive revenue policy and its implications; and examination of the impact of gender sensitive revenue policy.

BUDGET ANALYSIS

A review of Ninth Plan budget shows that about 43 percent of funds of gross budget support for Women Component Programmes from the 15 ministries and departments where ostensibly spent on women. Of these Family Welfare contributed 70 percent of gross budget support. Health, Education and Indian Systems of Homeopathy contributed 50 percent of gross budget support while the contribution of Rural Development and Labour 42 percent and 34 percent respectively. Others spent less than 30 percent of their gross budgetary support on women. During 1997-01 Rs 471.33 crores were spent on women's specific programmes. The larger amount was spent on Balika Smridhi Yojana, STEP and NORAD Schemes. Similarly, during Ninth Plan allocation, a larger amount was allocated for Balika Smridhi Yojana. Indira Mahila Yojana and Swashakti Projects. Rs 245419 was allocated for 2004-2005 and a large chunk of amount was allocated on ICDS Scheme and its related components.

The Eleventh Plan made the provision that gender budgeting and gender outcome assessment will be encouraged by all ministries/depart-ments and centre and state level. During the Eleventh Plan Period, Rs 48420.51 crores have been allocated as gross budgetary support under the Ministry of Women and Child Development for pro-women programs. Out of total budgetary support, a large chunk of amount has been earmarked for children. A few new schemes have been introduced in the plan for women empowerment (Table 2).

Table 2: Projected Budgetary Support for Women in Eleventh Plan (2007-12) (Rs In Crores)

	Schemes/Programmes	Plan Projection	
		2006-2007	**Current Price**
A.	**Central Sector Scheme**		
I.	Child Development	645.43	730.00
	(i) Rajeev Gandhi National Creche Scheme	486.28	550.00
	(ii) NCPCR	30.95	35.00
	(iii) NIPCCD	30.95	34.00
	(iv) Conditional Cash Transfer Scheme for Girl Child	70.95	80.00
	(v) Combating Trafficking of Women	26.52	30.00
II.	Women Empowerment	637.47	721.00
	(i) Hostel for Working Women	66.3 1	75.00
	(ii) STEP	88.42	100.00
	(iii) NCW	22.10	25.00
	(iv) RMK	95.49	108.00
	(v) Swadhar	95.49	108.00
	(vi) GIAloCSWB	229.88	260.00
	(vii) Scheme on Relief of Victims of Rape	22.10	25.00
	(viii) Gender Budgeting	17.68	20.00
B	**Centrally Sponsored Scheme**		
I.	Child Development	46494.92	52474.00
II.	Women Empowerment	543.75	615.00
	(i) Swavamsiddha	442.08	500.00
	(ii) Priyadarshini	83.99	95.00
	(iii) Scheme for Leadership	17.68	20.00
	Total (A + B)	**48420.51**	**54765.00**

Source: Eleventh Five Year Plan, Govt. of India, 2008.

Gender budgeting helps assess the gender differential impact of the budget and takes forward the translation of gender commitments to budgetary allocations. During the Plan, efforts will continue to create Gender Budgeting Cells in all ministry and departments. During 2005-06, gender outcome assessment of fund flows has been covered 10 departments and the total magnitude of gender budget was recorded at 4.8 percent of total union government expenditure. In 2006-07, 24 departments of union government were included in the magnitude of the gender budget was 3.8 percent of the total budget estimates. By May 2007, Gender Budget Cells were established in 51 departments and ministries of Central Govern-ment (Box 2). During the Plan period, the existing system of gender based planning is likely to extend to other ministries and departments. It is also likely to seek to make all national policies and programmes gender sensitive right from their inception and formulation stages.

Ministries and Departments with Gender Budget Cells

1. Department of Agriculture & Cooperation
2. Department of Biotechnology
3. Department of Chemicals & Petrochemicals
4. Department of Civil Aviation
5. Department of Coal
6. Department of Commerce
7. Ministry of Culture
8. Department of Consumer Affairs
9. Ministry of Defence
10. Department of Development of North-Eastern Region
11. Department of Drinking Water Supply
12. Ministry of External Affairs
13. Department of Elementary Education and Literature
14. Ministry of Environment and Forests
15. Department of Family Welfare
16. Department of Fertilisers
17. Department of Foods & Public Distribution
18. Department of Industrial Policy & Promotion
19. Ministry of Information and Broadcasting
20. Ministry of Information Technology
21. Department of Heavy Industry
22. Department of Health
23. Ministry of Home Affairs
24. Ministry of Labour & Employment
25. Department of Legal Affairs
26. Legislative Department
27. Department of Mines
28. Ministry of Non-Conventional Energy Sources
29. Department of Ocean Development
30. Ministry of Overseas Indian Affairs
31. Ministry of Panchayat Raj
32. Ministry of Petroleum & Natural Gas
33. Department of Posts
34. Ministry of Power
35. Ministry of Rural Development
36. Department of Science & Technology
37. Department of Secondary Education & Higher Education
38. Ministry of Small Scale Industries, Agro & Rural Industries
39. Ministry of Social Justice & Empowerment Education & Literacy
40. Department of Scientific & Industrial Research
41. Department of Shipping
42. Ministry of Statistics and Programme Implementation
43. Department of Telecommunications
44. Ministries of Textiles
45. Ministry of Tourism
46. Ministry of Tribal Affairs
47. Department of Urban Development
48. Ministry of Housing & Urban Poverty Allevia-tion
49. Ministries of Women and Child Development
50. Ministry of Water Resources
51. Ministry of Youth Affairs & Sports

Despite the plethora of women-specific programmes, it is surprisingly to note that a significant declining trend in the amount allocated to all these schemes as a proportional of total expenditure is noticed. The budget allocated to especially women-specific programmes was reported to be Rs 36.8 billion, constituting only 0.82 percent of the total public expenditure during 2002-2003. The shares were 1.02 percent in 1998-99, 0.94 percent in 1999-2000, 0.88 percent in 2000-2001 and 0.87 percent in 2001-2002. The direct allocation for women in the budgets as a proportion of GDP, after increasing from 0.10 percent of GDP in 1995-96 to 0.15 percent in 1998-99, decline to 0.13 percent in 2001-2002 and remained constant at 0.13 percent in 2002-2003. A significant deviation of revised estimates from budget estimates is noted for the women specific programmes. For instance, the plan allocation for especially targeted programmes for women constitute only 0.84 percent of total expenditure in 2001-2002 in revised estimates as compared to 0.87 percent of total expenditure in the year in budget estimates.

Notwithstanding significant pronouncements in the budgets for 2001-2002 and 2002-2003 on gender, and the commitment of the Ninth Plan to increase allocations of development resources to women, the share of women specific programmes under various ministries has not shown any major increase. The share of women specific programmes in certain ministries constituted around 1 percent of their total expenditure. The allocation for women related programmes in the Department of Family Welfare as high as around 30 percent of the total outlay until 2001-2002. This is mainly because of the fact that budget were provided for RCH programme which covered both mother and child care. However in the subsequent year, the budgetary allocation for women related programmes in the Ministry declined sharply. There is no significant deviation between the budget estimates and revised estimates for the pro-women allocations for most years under the various departments and ministries. The significantly high ratio of the Department of Agriculture and Cooperation in 2000-01 is mainly because of revised estimates of the National Watershed Development Project in Rain fed Areas exceeded its budget estimates. There is fluctuating trend in the deviation of selected public expenditure with pro-women allocations if we analyze the ratio between revised esti-mates and budget estimates of public expenditure. Selected public expenditure with pro-women allocations in different ministries, and departments is shown in Table 3.

Table 3: Selected Public Expenditure with Pro-Women Allocations

Ministry/Department Agri-culture and Co-operation	Public Expenditure With Pro-Women Allocation National Watershed Development Programme for Rainfed Area
Health and Family Welfare	Assistance towards expenditure on hospitalisation of poor Family Welfare Services Urban Family Welfare. Services Strengthening of Immunisation & Eradication of Polio. Transport
Education	Sarva Shiksha Abhiyan Operation Blackboard. District Primary Education Programme (DPEP). National Nutritional Support to Primary Education. No informal Education. Shisksha Karmi.
Youth Affairs and Sports	Sport Authority of India. Sports Scholarship Scheme. Miscellaneous Schemes. Nehru Yuva Kendra Sangathan. National
Labour	Employment and Training: (a) Women's Vocational Training Programmes (b) Establishment of Placement Cells at National Vocational Training Institute (NVTI)
Non-conventional Energx Sources	National Project on Biogas Development (NPBD) National Program on Improved Chulas (NPIC) Indian Renewable
Small-Scale Industries and Agro & Rural	Prime Minister's Rozgar Yojana (PMRY). Khadi and Village Industries Commission. Rural Employment Gene-ration Program
Rural Development	Swarnajayanti Gram Swarojgar Yojana (SGSY). National Social Assistance Program. Jawahar Gram Samridhi Yojana (JGSY). Indira Awas Yojana (IAY). Rural Sani-tation Program.
Housing & Urban Poverty Alleviation	Swarna Jayanti Shahari Rozgar Yojana
Social Justice and Empowerment and Tribal	Post-matric Scheme for Scheduled Castes Machinery for Implementation of Protection of Civil Rights Act. 1955 and Prevention of Atrocities Act. 1989. Pre-matric Scholarship for

Source: UNIFEM- NIPFP, Delhi, 2005.

During 1993-1994 to 2002-2003, total expenditure on women development has increased from Rs.1083.57 crores in 1993-94 to Rs 3719.16 crores in 2002-2003. The share of Central Government in expenditure on women has ranged between 40 to 50 percent. Expenditure on health is the largest component in expenditure on women for both states and Centre with contribution of Centre exceeding that of the state.

Expenditure on women in need is dominated by state contribution in the form of widow pension scheme etc.

According to budget estimates, Rs 31177.96 crores was expected to use exclusively for women during 2007-08. The total magnitude of the gender budget has gone up from Rs 22251.41 crores for 2006-07 (RE) to Rs 31177 crores in 2007-08 (BE), an increase of almost 40 percent. As a percentage of total union government expenditure, this constitutes a rise from 3.8 percent to 4.8 percent. As a percentage of GDP, this is an

Table-4: Composition of Gender Budget.

Sectors	2006-07	%age	2007-08	%age
Education	7513.7	38	8439.99	31
Health	3593.325	18	6483.03	24
Pood Security	4321.77	22	5906.4	22
Livelihood	2444.35	12	3582.87	8
Housing	1498.39	8	2067.55	8
Protection	195.473	1	306.733	1
Awareness Generating	153.41	1	177.43	1
Total	**19720.418**	**100**	**26964.003**	**100**

Source: Compiled from Gender Budgeting Statement.

appallingly low figure of 0.5 percent and 0.6 percent for the year 2006-07 and 2007-08, respectively. There has been an increase in the number of Ministries and Departments undertaking gender budgeting exercises that form the basis of gender budgeting statement of the government. The Ministry of Finance reported that it has also pointed out that 50 ministries/ departments have set up gender budgeting cells. The composition of the gender budget pool simply demonstrates that the largest share goes to women's education, health and food security and nutrition. The major chunk of allocation for women's education can be accorded to allocations in Sarva Shiksha Abhiyan.

According gender budget statement, almost 65 percent of total budget provisions under the Department of Health and Family Welfare are meant substantially for the benefit of women (See table alongside). All the budgetary allocation in the Department of Women & Child Development was devoted to the expenditure for the benefit of the women. Similarly, around 94 percent of the budget in the Ministry of Social Justice and Empowerment was made for the benefit of the women. Interestingly, more than one-fourth of the budget in the Ministry of Youth Affairs & Sports was meant for the benefits of women in the budget estimates for 2005-06.

According to the gender budgeting statement, out of entire allocations of the Union Government for Police (Ministry of Home Affairs) only 0.03 percent is women specific, which indicates that allocations of meagre resources for women specific programmes/schemes could be one of the major reasons for prevalence of high levels of crimes against women. While around 45 percent of allocations under the Department of Elementary Education and Literacy are earmarked for women specific, only 23 percent of allocations under the Department of Secondary and Higher Education have been accorded by the government as a woman specific. During 2006-07, less than 18 percent .of allocations under the Department of Rural Development have been earmarked for women specific, which includes the inclusion of 100 percent allocations for Indira Awas Yojana.

Gender budgeting has been internationally recognised as a key tool for empowering women by incorporating gender perspective and concerns at all levels and stages of development planning, policy, programmes and delivery mechanism. Government of India has adopted budgeting for gender equity as a mission statement, and is widely disseminating tools and strategies across ministries and departments. The importance of gender budgeting has been stressed time and again in different forums. In order to provide further impetus, the Finance Minister in his budget for 2004-05 mandated the setting up of gender budget cells in all ministries and departments and highlighted the need for budget data to be presented in a manner that brought out the gender sensitivity and budgetary allocation. During 2005-06, budgetary allocation under 10 demands for grants, estimated at total of Rs 14379 crores were shown in a separate gender budget statement. An estimated allocation of Rs 28737 crores for benefits of women under 24 demands for grants in 18 ministries and departments were given in the 2006-07 budget. This statement was extended in the budget of 2007-08 to include 33 demands for grants of 27 ministries / departments.

GENDER MAINSTREAMING IN URBAN SECTOR

The constitution of India has made provision of establishment of Local Self Governments in order to decentralise the planning process and governance. 73rd and 74lh constitutional amendments Acts were introduced which made provisions for three tire system of decentralised governance. The constitutional amendment Acts also ensured the provision of reservation of women in local governments. One-third seats were reserved in urban local bodies also. A few states such as Bihar, M.P., and Rajasthan have also made provision for 50 percent reservation for women in local governments.

Thus, the gender mainstreaming in decentralised governance has been initiated, however women's share in policy perspective and resources allocation in urban sector has been reported to be very low. With the launch of JNNURM and other infrastructure programmes and schemes, gender mainstreaming is getting momentum. JNNURM and reforms agenda seek to improve the effectiveness, accountability, efficiency, sustainability and service equity in cities. It also aims to reduce class and gender fragmentation by making socio-political-economic institutions, processes and resource allocations more equitable. Thus, gender based urban development is about promoting cities that respond, equally to men and women. Urban women experience cities differently and thus meeting their needs becomes critical for promoting sustainable and equitable urban development.

Women being underrepresented in planning process. JNNURM provides an opportunity to build gender fair and inclusive cities, it seeks to promote planned urban development and equitable cities. Though, urban space, infrastructure and services which contribute to cities economic development, however men and women perceive their utility differently. Infrastructure development is not gender neutral. Lack of basic services affects both men and women; however women in cities especially in low income communities and slums are more severely affected by inadequate and poor services. In absence of access to toilets, women are forced to defecate in open which is unsafe and undignified while it is also a serious health and environmental threat. Women have traditionally been excluded from land ownership and it has contributed more marginalisation of women as they are insecure and live in poverty. Women either do not work for wages or earn less than men. Because of their low earnings they cannot afford to buy a house or land for construction of house. Since, women often lack education and technical skills, they tend to be predominantly in informal economy. The informal sector is under regulated and social safety network is lacking. Among the poor, forced evictions from illegal spaces (slums) are a major cause of insecurity. The demolitions of slums, not only destruct homes, but also destroy the informal livelihoods. The women being the most vulnerable and disadvantaged group, are mostly affected by such evictions. Women living in slums and low income groups also face problem of domestic violence as the family income is very low to sustain the family. Women and children experience domestic violence through physical abuse, sexual assault and threats. Urban violence against women can be attributed due to lack of their power that comes from non-ownership of property and shelter. Urban women are also more dependent on public transport to move in the city however, men usually own personal transport. Women use transport differently from men based on the type of work they do. Urban women are bearing more burdens of diseases. Urban poor women are more anemic and modality, rate among them is higher.

Ministry of Urban Development and Ministry of Housing & Urban Poverty Alleviation need to set out a clear urban gender policy that will provide the framework for the gender integration. A general policy must have four key components:

1. Bring a gender perspective into all aspects of planning, policy and legislation and activities that are within the domain of the Ministries.
2. Create an enabling environment for women and thus to realise their full human rights in cities and particularly for women belonging to poor and marginalised groups.
3. Outline sustainable mechanism for the equal participation of all including poor women in city development.
4. Promote equitable access and control over the urban resources for women and men.

Gender mainstreaming is about promoting inclusive and participatory planning and development of the cities. Women empowerment is essential for inclusive development. Women empowerment through mobilising and organising in groups that promote micro-finance and ensure their participation in development planning and livelihoods is imperative. Public private partnership with civil society's involvement for gender equality is an effective instrument for improving basic services to urban poor including women.

Gender budgeting is a tool used for achieving gender equality. In the context of JNNURM and urban reforms encouraging inclusion of women in planning and decision making is imperative. The tools for gender inclusion in the budgeting and planning process include:

1. Spatial maps to assess women's access to physical, social-economic infrastructure to develop a mix of macro and micro level plans.
2. Gender profiling of public expenditure with impact assessment studies to understand gender based spending.
3. Gender based auditing and beneficiary assessment.

This is high time for the Ministry's to develop its gender policies for an integrated national urban policy. A review is required for all the urban policies and programmes from a gender perspective to make these gender equitable and pro-poor. Gender analysis involves an examination of gender issues across sectors using gender disaggregated data, looking at indicators separately for men and women, their differences, needs and priorities. Integrating gender concerns in urban development will be successful only when the administrators, municipal officers, people's representatives and other concerned persons are well convinced of the need for gender mainstreaming. Therefore capacity building of people's representative and concerned municipal officers and city managers is imperative to promote the concept of gender budgeting in ULBs.

Though, initiatives from government and outside of the government have been taken for gender budgeting, however, only a few departments and ministries have adopted the gender budgeting analysis. There is imperative need for crucial interaction between analysis and the structures of gender that currently exist in society as well as with the elements necessary for transforming gender relations. The serious efforts are required for opening a meaningful dialogue with policymakers and other key players to make the appropriate for adopting the gender budget analysis.

ISSUES

- Women and men contribute to city development and have a right to equal access to basic services and resources;
- Women and men access urban services in different ways;
- Infrastructure development is not gender neutral;
- JNNURM is an opportunity to integrate gender into urban policy, programme, planning and development;
- More men than women use the motorised road. More women use smaller roads. Similarly women are more dependent on public transport while men are usually own their personal vehicles for city transport;
- Women have less access to technology such as mobile phones and need to be able to move around safely in cities;
- Women are accompanied by children and aged and carry bags while using footpath and public transport and thus inadequacy of public transport facility severally affects them;
- Women are primarily responsible for water collection and storage. The public services based on user charges must be made gender friendly;

- Capacities of women must be enhanced to engage with local governments so that they can contribute meaningfully to planning for water supply and sanitation;
- Women in slum settlements need access to toilets as the absence of toilet facility to them creates problems of security, safety and environmental health hazards;
- Without access to toilets, women are forced to defecate in open which results in serious health problems and insecurity;
- A very few women own houses and eviction of slums adversely affects women both in terms of loss of livelihood and shelter;
- Women use home for productive activities besides performing their household activities thus housing conditions matter more for women than for men.
- A few women own properties hence property tax regime tends to be male oriented. Women headed households may find it difficult to pay property taxes unless there are gender friendly provisions;
- Women have low level of education and knowledge of computers therefore their access to e-Governance will be critical;
- Women councillors need more orientation and capacity building regarding different issues of urban development and governance in order to enhance their role in urban governance and management;
- Women's groups engaged in thrift & credit activities and self employment may be given opportunity to share the responsibility of urban sanitation and managing solid wastes;
- Self help group based micro financing is an effective instrument for empowering poor women living in slum and low income groups;
- Gender analysis of policies, programmes, schemes and projects in urban sector oriented towards women empowerment is imperative.

REFERENCES

Bannerjee, Nirmala & **Roy, P.** Gender in Fiscal Policies: A Case of West Bengal. Snap Shot of Gender Budget Initiatives in South Asia. UNIFEM, New Delhi. 2003.

Bannerjee, Nirmala, Roy, P., What Does the State Do for Indian Women. Economic & Political Weekly. October 30, 2004.

Bannerjee, References Nirmala & Krishnaraj, M. Sieving Budgets for Gender. Economic & Political Weekly. October 30, 2004.

Beall, J., Participation in the City: where do women lit. Gender and Development. Vol. 4(1). 1996.

Beneria, L. Towards a Greater Integration of Gender in Economies. World Development. Vol. 23, No. 11. November, 1995.

Bridge, Cutting Edge Pack on Gender & Budgets. Institute of Development Studies University of Sussex. Brighton, 2002.

Budlander, D. The Political Economy of Women in Budgets in the South. World Development, Vol. 28, No. 7, July, 2000.

Budlender, et.al., A Practitioner's Guide to Gender Budgeting: Understanding & Implementing Gender Responsive Budgets. Commonwealth Secretariat. London, 2003.

Chakravarty, Lekha, Macro Scan of Union Budget. 2003 in India: A Glimpse Through Gender Lens. UNIFEM, New Delhi, 2003.

Council of Europe, Gender Budgeting. Equality Division. Directorate General of Human Rights. Council of Europe, 2005.

Das, Subrat & Mishra Yamini, Gender Budgeting Statement: Misleading and Patriarchal Assumptions. Economic & Political Weekly. July, 29, 2006.

Elson Diana, Gender Responsive Btidgel Initiatives: Key Dimensions and Practical Examples. Heinrich-Boell Foundation. Berlin. February, 2002.

Elson, Diane, Integrating Gender Issues into National Budget Polices & Procedures: Some Policy-Options. Journal of International Development. Vol. 10, 1998.

Finat, G.A., Women and Transport Mobility is Gender Specific, The Uropean Commission, 2007.

IIPA, Seminar Proceedings of First Regional Workshop on Gender Budgeting. Organised by Indian Institute of Public Administration. November, 23-24, 2005.

Kapdi, N.Y., Gender Budgeting in Urban Local Bodies in Framing Module on Urban Poverty Alleviation. RCTUES. Mumbai, 2008.

Khosla, Renu, Women and Sanitation: The Urban Reality. Experiences of Government Programs. NGOs and CBOs. Social Change. CSD. Vol. 30, pp. 1&2, New Delhi-2000.

Lahari Ashok, et.al., Gender Diagnosis and Budgeting in India. NIPEP. December. 2001.

Lahari, Ashok, et.al., Gender Budgeting in India. NIPEP. July, 2002.

Lahari, Ashok, et.al., Gender Budgeting in India. UNICEF-NIPFP. Follow the Money Series. No. 3, 2003.

Mehta, A., et.al., The Budget: A Gender and Poverty Sensitive Perspective. National Commission for Women. New Delhi, 2004.

Mishra, Yamini & Bhumika Jhamb, What Does Budget 2007-08 Offer Women? Economic & Political Weekly. April 21, 2007.

NPC, State Gentler Development Report. National Productivity Council. New Delhi, 2005.

Patel, Vibhuti. Gender Budget: A Case Study of India. Working Paper. Department of Economics. University ofMumbai, 2003.

Planning Commission, 11th Five Year Plan. 2007-12. Oxford University Press. New Delhi, 2008.

Planning Commission, Approach Paper to the Eleventh. Five Year Plan. Planning Commission. New Delhi, 2006.

Prabhu, K. Sita & Kalyani, M.S., The Budget: A Quick Look Through a Gender Lens. Economic & Political Weekly. Vol. 36, No. 4, 2001.

Sarraf, E., (Sender Responsive Government Budgeting. IMF. Working Paper. Washington. 2003.

Sen, Gita. Gender Mainstreaming in Finance Ministries. World Development. Vol. 28, 2000.

Sen, Gita, Sender Mainstreaming in Finance: A Reference Manual for Governments and other Stakeholders. Gender Management System Series. Commonwealth Secretariat. 1999.

Sharp, R. & Broomhill, R., Women & Government Budgets. The Australian Journal of Social Issues. Vol. 25, No. I, 1998.

Sharp, R., Budgeting for Equity. (Gender Budget Initiatives Within a framework of Performance Oriented Budgeting. UNICEF. New York, 2003.

Sushan, H., Tools for Budget Impact Analysis: Taxes & Benefits. UNIFEM-OFCD. Brussels. October, 2001.

Taylor, V., A Quick Guide to (Sender Mainstreaming in Development Planning. Gender Management System Series. Commonwealth Secretariat. 1999.

Thorat, Minakshi, Gender Budgeting in Disaster Relief: Need for a New Methodology. Economy & Political Weekly. April, 26, 2008.

UNDP, Addressing Gender Concerns in India's Urban Renewal Mission. UNDP, Delhi, 2009.

UNDP, (Gender Sensitive Budgeting. October, 2002.

UNIFEM, Gender Budget Initiatives: Strategics. Concepts & Experiences. UNIFEM. New York, 2002.

UNIFEM, (Gender Budgeting in India: Follow the Money Series. Vol. 3. UNIFEM. New Delhi.

UNIFEM, (Gender Budgeting: Frequently Asked Questions. United Nations Development Fund for Women. New Delhi, 2007.

UNIFEM, Gender Responsive Budgeting and Women's Reproductive Rights: Resource Pack. New York, 2007.

UNIFEM, Gender Responsive Budgeting. United Nations Development Fund for Women. New Delhi, 2007.

WCD, A Report of the Sub-Group on Gender Budgeting for Eleventh Five Year Plan. Ministry of Women & Child Development. Govt. of India. 2006.

WCD, Annual Report. Department of Women & Child Development. Ministry of Human Resource Development. Govt. of India. New Delhi. 2004-05.

WCD, Gender Budgeting Handbook for Government of India. Ministries & Departments. Ministry of Women and Child Development. Govt. of India. 2007.

World Bank, Engendering Development: Through Gender equetily in Rights. Resources and Voice. World Bank Policy Research Report. Oxford University Press. Washington, 2001.

World Bank, Integrating Gender into the World Bank: A Strategy for Action. World Bank. Washington. 2002.

YAHSADA-UNDP, Special Issue on Gender Budgeting. National Resource Centre on Urban Poverty. YASHADA. AIILSG. Pune. March-2008.

Annexure

Gender Budgeting Frequently Asked Questions

What is Gender Budgeting?

The process of gender budgeting eventually results in gender responsive budgets. The terms gender responsive budgets, gender-sensitive budgets, gender budgets and women's budgets are however often used interchangeably. Gender budgeting:

- Refers to the process of conceiving, planning, approving, executing, monitoring, analyzing and auditing budgets in a gender-sensitive way.
- Involves analysis of actual expenditure and revenue (usually of the Government) on women and girls as compared to on men and boys.
- Helps Governments to decide how policies need to be made, adjusted and reprioritised.
- Is a tool for effective policy implementation where one can check if the allocations are in line with policy commitments and are having the desired impact.

What is not Gender Budgeting?

- Gender budgets are not separate budgets for men and women.
- Gender budgeting (GB) is not about dividing the budget - 50% for women and 50% for men.
- GB does not always imply an increase in the allocations for women - it is about prioritising as well.
- GB is not only for Government budgets. Budgets of public and private sector units, institutions, civil society organisations, NGOs etc can be made gender responsive as well.

Is gender budgeting an end in itself or a tool to achieve something?

Gender budgeting is not an end in itself. It is a tool or means for achieving gender equality and women's empowerment.

My ministry/department is committed to reducing gender discrimination, but how exactly can gender budgeting help in achieving this?

GB can be very effective in reducing gender discrimination and addressing socio-economic discrimination against women because:

- Many policy commitments can only be achieved if sufficient funds are allocated for their implementation.
- Women's and men's needs, concerns and priorities differ due to their different roles in society.
- The way a government raises and spends money can have a negative impact on women.

I don't have any spare time, why should I do gender budgeting?

Because gender budgeting helps in the following key functions which are generic and essential for any department to ensure efficiency, effectiveness, accountability, gender equality and value for money:

- **Monitoring of the achievement of policy goals**

  It provides a tool to monitor the achievement of the Millennium Development Goals/a country's plan goals and other policy goals in a gender-aware manner.
- **Achieving gender equity/equality**

  Achieving gender equity requires equality of outcomes for women and men. This implies the recognition of different needs, preferences and interests, which affect the way women and men benefit from policies and budgetary allocations.
- **Advancing the realisation of women's rights**

  Gender-responsive budgeting attempts to measure the gaps between policy commitments in respect to human and women's rights instruments (including CEDAW), the adequacy of resource allocations, and the outcomes of both.
- **Alleviating poverty more effectively**

  It is widely acknowledged, that social indicators for women are far worse than men belonging to the same social-economic strata, that women and men experience poverrty differently and face different constraints to overcome poverty. Women are also more affected by time poverty than men. If women's needs are not taken into account, poverty reduction policies risk failure.

- **Enhancing economic efficiency**

  Several studies have shown that there is a positive correlation between diminishing gender inequality and higher growth rates. Women's productivity increases disproportionately if their access to information, credit, extension services, inputs, and markets is enhanced and their time burden is reduced through, for example, the investment in labour-saving infrastructure.

- **Achieving good governance**

  The process of improving the delivery of goods and services to women, men, girls and boys in a fair, just, and responsible way has to be considered as an integral part of the definition of good governance. Good governance requires a participatory approach, so that the different perspectives of different groups of citizens, including women, are represented.

- **Enhancing accountability and transparency**

  GB is a powerful tool for highlighting gaps between international commitments (such as those established at the Fourth World Conference on Women in Beijing in 1995, CEDAW and in national policy documents) and the amount of public spending earmarked for the achievement of gender- specific benchmarks and targets. GB necessitates the availability of sex- disaggregated data and the accessibility to programmatic information. By tracking how allocated money is spent, GB increases both accountability and transparency.

Does gender budgeting have to be done for the whole budget?

Not necessarily. Gender budgeting can be done for:

- The whole budget, or
- Expenditure of selected departments or programmes and their impact, or
- Design and gender sensitivity of new programmes and projects, or
- Selected forms of revenue and changes in tax system, or
- New legislation.

Who are the different players/stakeholders in gender budgeting initiatives?

There are a number of different stakeholders who are involved in Gender Budgeting. They have different roles and carry out different activities. Some of them are:

- The Ministry of Women and Child Development (nodal ministry at the central level, in India
- The Ministry of Finance (at the Centre and in the States)
- The Planning Department or Planning Commission (at the Centre and in the States)
- Sectoral ministries-each and every department/ministry can do gender budgeting-albeit some more than others, (at the Centre and in the States)
- Researchers/Economists
- Statisticians
- Civil society organisations especially women's groups
- Parliamentarians, MLAs and other representatives of the people at state/district and sub-district levels.
- Media
- Development partners/Donors
- The women and men for whom the specific policy, programme or budget is intended.

Our budget for this year has already been prepared; does that mean it is too late to do gender budgeting?

It is never too late to start. Gender Budgeting can be taken up at various stages of the budget preparation, post-budget preparation, implementation and post-implementation, as described below:

- **At the budget preparation stage:**
  (a) Ensure financial appropriations made in budgets match the needs.
  (b) Analyze budget estimates (B.E.) for the current year vis-à-vis revised estimates (R.E.) or actual expenditure (A.E.) of the previous year and ensure corrective steps are taken for sufficient and proper and full utilisation of budgets of current year.

- **At the post-budget stage:**
  (a) Analyze sector-wise or ministry/department-wise shares of allocations and expenditure (indicates government's priorities).
  (b) Analyze the revenue side too - what are the sources of revenue, subsidies etc. and how will they impact men and women. Look at trends and shares - e.g. increases or decreases, percentage share etc.

  - **At the budget implementation stage:**

    Is the budget being spent in the way it was intended and to the full extent? What are delivery costs? Who is receiving subsidies? For whom is (what?) intended?

  - **At the post-implementation stage:**
    (a) What have been the outcomes and impact of the budget: analyze expected outcomes from appropriations vs. actual outcomes including unintended ones: whether the money is being used in a manner that effectively achieves planned outcomes and what is the impact.
    (b) Impact assessment of programmes, projects and schemes. Have they met their objectives and purposes?

How can one do gender budgeting? It seems complicated to me, where do I start?

It is really not that complicated. There are a number of Entry Point Tools that can be used to do Gender Budgeting. The most appropriate in the present Indian context are mentioned below. You can use either one or a combination of two or more of these tools, at any given time. Start with whatever you feel comfortable with and that seem most appropriate for your sector.

Participative Planning and Budgeting:

- Involvement of women in decision-making is seen as a key to success of all gender budgeting initiatives.
- It is not enough to say that women's needs and concerns have been taken into account.
- Women have to be treated as equal partners in decision-making and implementation rather than only as beneficiaries. For this there may be need for capacity building.

Spatial Mapping — Macro level planning for Micro level Needs

(Corresponds to Step 1 of the Five Step Framework for Gender Budgeting)

Women's empowerment is a holistic concept which entails adequate resource allocation in all areas including health, education, water sanitation and nutrition, sustained employment, access to credit and asset ownership, skills, research and design technology and political participation. Regional imbalances (rural-urban) have to be corrected. Spatial mapping of social infrastructure and access to employment opportunities for women would clearly highlight resources available, overall gaps, resource allocation required based M size of population and yardsticks for availability of facilities etc. These spatial maps can then form the basis for concomitant state plans.

Gender Based Profile of Public Expenditure

(Corresponds to Step 3 of the Five Step Framework for Gender Budgeting)

Preparation of the profile facilitates review of all schemes and public expenditure from a gender perspective and isolating the gender component by way of expenditure and physical targets. The profile would give a clear situational analysis of constraints like non-availability of sex disaggregated data; need to determine reasons for non-adherence to targeted expenditure on women etc. Trend of the gender component, allocation and expenditure, is indicative of extent to which budgeting is gender responsive.

The Government of India is using a two category format designed to assist government officials with the analysis of the budget and as the basis of presentation in the Gender Budget Statement in the Union Budget.

(i) Pro women allocations, where 100% of the allocation is meant for women.

(ii) Pro women allocations where between 30 to 90% of the allocation is meant for women.

Impact Analysis through Impact Assessments, Evaluations and Field Level Surveys

(Corresponds to Step 5 of the Five Step Framework for Gender Budgeting).

It is essential to evaluate the impact of programmes and schemes of the government and to see if they are meeting the objectives for which they were started. What has been the gender impact of these programmes and schemes? Results of impact assessment of programmes from a gender perspective help identify barriers in accessing public services/expenditure by women and help to identify challenges and identify solutions which may be very fundamental and structural or may just require minor changes of design and modalities of implementation.

Gender appraisal for all new programmes and schemes

(Corresponds to Step 2 of the Five Step Framework for Gender Budgeting)

All new programmes, projects and schemes (PPS) must be passed through a gender lens. This will ensure that gender sensitivity and women's participation is built into new all new PPSs from the start. It will also ensure that the implementation modality of the PPS is gender sensitive and that gender impact assessment is built into the design of the PPS.

Guidelines for gender sensitive review of public expenditure and policy:

(Corresponds to Step 2 of the Five Step Framework for Gender Budgeting)

Specific guidelines have been formulated by the Ministry of Women and Child-Development in the form of Checklists I and II. Checklist I is for programmes that are beneficiary oriented and consciously target women. Checklist II covers mainstream sectors. These guidelines help in reviewing public expenditure and policy from a gender perspective to enable identification of constraints in outreach of programmes and policies to cover women and to enable suitable corrective action.

Revenue incidence analysis

Show proportion of income paid in taxes and user charges by different categories of individuals / women / men or households. Who bears the burden of user charges?

Five Steps of Gender Budgeting

This is well known international took encompassing most of the above tools.

Step 1: An analysis of the situation for women and men and girls and boys (and the different sub-groups) in a given sector.

Step 2: An assessment of the extent to which the sector's policy addresses the gender issues and gaps described in the first step. This step should include an assessment of the relevant legislation, policies, programmes and schemes. It includes an analysis of both the written policy as well as the implicit policy reflected in government activities. It should examine the extent to which the above meet the socio-economic and other rights of women.

Step 3: An assessment of the adequacy of budget allocations to implement the gender sensitive policies and programmes identified in Step 2 above.

Step 4: Monitoring whether the money was spent as planned, what was delivered and to whom? This involves checking both financially and the physical deliverables (disaggregated by sex).

Step 5: An assessment of the impact of the policy / programme / scheme and the extent to which the situation described in Step 1 has been changed, in the direction of greater gender equality.

My department is as it is short of funds. How am I supposed to find more money for Gender Budgeting and Women's Schemes?

You do not necessarily need more money to do Gender Budgeting. You could just reprioritise and see where to put your existing money to get the maximum benefit. You could also examine the impact of previous schemes and programmes to make sure they meet the objectives they were planned for and if necessary make changes in the schemes and programmes or the way they are implemented. However you do have some additional funds they could be used to ensure your policies are matched with appropriate budgetary allocations or build on an existing scheme or develop a new scheme to meet the objectives of women's empowerment and gender equality.

What is the difference between Gender Budgeting and Gender Auditing?

Gender Auditing is part of the Gender Budgeting process. Gender auditing is the process that is conducted after the budget has been adopted and implemented. It is the process of reviewing financial outlays — looking at trends over time, percentage shares etc; analyzing and assessing systems actually put in place, processes adopted, outcomes and impacts of budgetary outlays vis-à-vis what was planned - all this through a gender lens. The figure below shows the various steps in the entire process of Gender Budgeting, of which there are 3 major components:

Policy Appraisal, Gender Budgeting and Gender Auditing.

Source: **UNIFEM.**

C. Technology and Decision Making

6

Geospatial Technology Applications in Disaster Management

Prof V Madhava Rao

Introduction

Disasters are sudden disruption to life, property, infrastructure, and bring human, material, and economic or environmental losses, broadly classified as natural, manmade and geological. The natural disasters are mostly floods, wild fires, drought, cyclone, etc, while the geological disasters are earthquake, landslide, Tsunami, volcanic eruptions etc. Among the manmade disasters the fire, explosion, accidents, epidemics, and the like.

Man always felt weak to tackle the disasters and got victimised by the onslaught of the disasters over centuries. However, technology, adaptability, mitigation measures, assessment, prediction, decision support and modern technologies have reduced the impact of disaster to a reasonable level.

Disaster

A serious disruption of the functioning of a community or a society causing widespread human, material, economic and environmental losses which exceed the ability of the affected community/society to cope using its own resources.

Disaster Risk Reduction

The systematic development and application of policies, strategies and practices to minimize vulnerability and disaster risks throughout a society, to avoid (prevention) or to limit (mitigation and preparedness) adverse impact of hazards, within the broad context of sustainable development.

Mitigation

Structural and non-structural measures undertaken to limit the adverse impact of natural hazards, environmental degradation and technological hazards.

Natural Hazard

Natural process of phenomena occurring in the biosphere that may constitute a damaging event.

Emergence Management

The organisation, management of resources and responsibilities for dealing with all aspects of emergencies, in particular, preparedness, reponse and rehabilitation. A disaster reduction strategy is a global challenge today and for the future. It is a strategy to find a way to live with these phenomena, rather than die from it, since natural disaster cannot be prevented and people are caught unaware when it happens.

Seismic Risk = f (Hazard, Exposure, Vulnerability, Location).

Hazard is characterised by the occurrence of an earthquake of sufficient Magnitude (hence, the Intensity at the epicentre) capable of causing damage to the man-made structures.

Exposure are objects and structures built by man which are exposed to the effects of the 'hazard', namely, buildings, bridges, dams, power plant, life-line structure, etc.

Vulnerability is the damageability of the 'exposure' under the action of the hazard, such as weaker ones being more vulnerable and 'risky' than the stronger ones.

Location

(i) Exposure site situation from the Hazard location the nearer ones being in greater danger than those far away.

(ii) Local site conditions which can modify the hazard and/or affect the stability of the exposure, such as topography, soil deposit, water table, etc.

The elements of Risk depends on hazards, it's vulnerability, exposure and location and externalities compound the effect of the hazards.

Elements of Risk

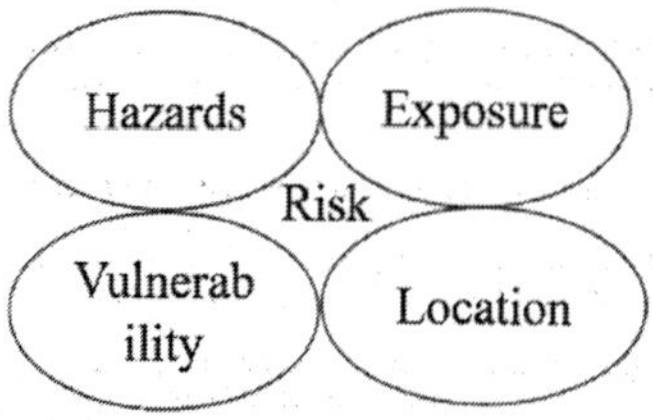

The Geospatial Technology like GIS, Remote Sensing and Navigation technologies help in the prediction of disastrous situations like impending drought, early warning of cyclones, floods, land-slides, and environmental degradation. Distance calculation, accessibility features and terrain conditions visualisation, help in rescue and relief measures, when any disaster strikes.

Early Warning System and responsiveness vital aspect of disaster mitigation strategies. Wireless Application Protocol (WAP), Satellite Dish Antennae (V-SAT), Cell Phones operating through Cell Towers, Fibre Optic based communication lines, including Wireless Communication and Ham Radio sets facilitate instantaneous communication linkages, comes handy tool for appropriate planning, coordination and monitoring of activities. Indicators like expected cyclone characteristics, rainfall pattern, water levels in rivers, environmental impact assessment, and vulnerability help model disaster consequences accurately and help evolve effective decision-making on logistic and infrastructure requirement and development in an area.

Satellite Remote Sensing, Geographic Information Systems (GIS) and Navigation System are handy tool for improved Real Time Decision Making, Rescue and Evacuation. India faces natural disasters every year which jeopardise the development pace and impair lives and property, through cyclones, floods, earthquake. The manmade environmental problems bring in urban sprawling, pressure on infrastructure, pollution, environmental degradation, global warming etc, while the developed World too has problems of environment, ecology, urban and climate change problems.

Policy learning from natural and man-made disasters evolve conscious and appropriate strategies to generate better preparedness among people and the make communities, officials, local bodies to tackle disastrous situations to reduce loss due to human and livestock deaths and property losses. Measures like vulnerability mapping, risk assessment, identify safer areas, affects on crops, assessment of damage, help for appropriate Action Plans for effective planning and reduction of effect of disasters in future.

The GIS based Watershed Plan implementation helped mitigate the impact of drought and better monitoring of watersheds and assess water balance and potential for use for various purposes. Geomorphological aspects help finding better recharge locations for rain water harvesting structures.

The lithosphere, hydrosphere, biosphere or atmosphere of the earth exert extreme impact on buildings, communication systems, agricultural land, forest, and natural environment, bringing insurmountable damage to the socio-economic system, rapid, as in the case of earthquakes, or slow as in the case of drought.

The difference between Hazard and Disaster is that a Hazard has potential damaging consequences and a Disaster is one that bring immense damage, loss or destruction. Disaster management consists of two phases that take place before a disaster occurs, disaster prevention and disaster preparedness, and three phases that happen after the occurrence of a disaster, disaster relief, rehabilitation and reconstruction (UNDRO, 1991).

The following table illustrate the origin of disasters and type of disasters:

Sl.No.	*Origin of Disaster*	*Type*
1	Geological Origin	Earthquake, Volcanic Eruption, Tsunami, Landslide Avalanche
2	Atmospheric – Oceanic – Hydrologic Origin	Cyclone, Storm Surge, Tornado, Flood and Drought
3	Anthropogenic Origin	Nuclear Accident, Chemical Spill, Forest Fire, Locust Invasion, Epidemic and Marine and Atmospheric Pollution by Toxic Agents

Disaster management is represented here as a cycle, since the occurrence of a disaster event will eventually influence the way society is preparing for the next one. The Disaster Management Cycle has the following phases, which completes the cycle:

1. Disaster Preparedness;
2. Disaster Event;
3. Rescue and Relief;
4. Rehabilitation;
5. Reconstruction;

6. Mitigation.

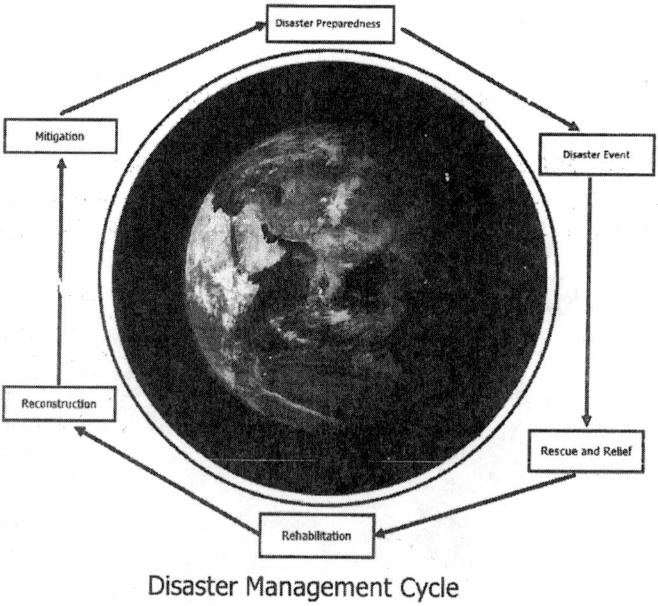

Fig. Disaster Management Cycle.

Remote Sensing, GNSS Geospatial Tools

The frequency, character, and magnitude of disasters has an important spatial component, in terms such as maps, aerial photography, satellite imagery, GPS data, other associated data etc, with different projection and co-ordinate system, to be brought to a common map-basis, to overlay and generate inferences.

Hazard, vulnerability, riskmapping, change detection, climate change, degradation, erosion, identification of adverse effect, variabilities of terrain properties, such as vegetation, water, and geology, both in space and time, help disaster signals, prediction, early mitigation measures, as precursors, identifying early stages of these events as anomalies in a time series and geospatial data availability at regular short time intervals, used for the prediction of both rapid and slow disasters.

Satellite remote sensing provide wide coverage, captures images from inaccessible areas, which help timely monitor the occurrence of the disaster, help planning of evacuation routes, identify safe regions for emergency operations, and provide disaster effects, reach, damage assessment, safety and rescue guidance.

Disaster Vulnerability-Cyclones

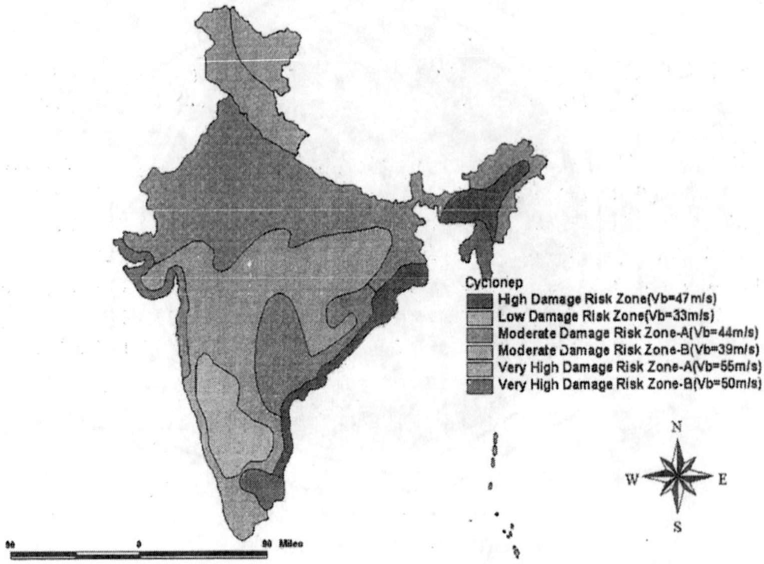

Disaster Vulnerability-Floods

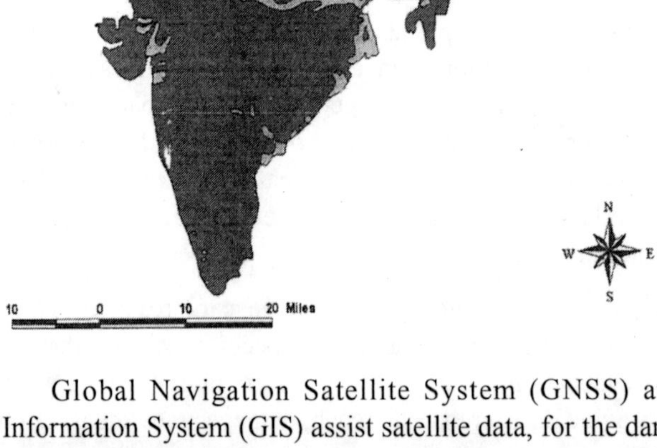

Global Navigation Satellite System (GNSS) and Geographic Information System (GIS) assist satellite data, for the damage assessment and aftermath monitoring, assist relief operations. Post-disaster phase, the rehabilitation, estimation of damage, reconstruction, and plan for preventive measures to minimise the impact of disasters in future, by better planning, regulation, disaster proof structures, early warning systems, awareness and exposure training and capacity building exercises to communities, field functionaries, and officials etc.

Disaster Vulnerability-Earthquake

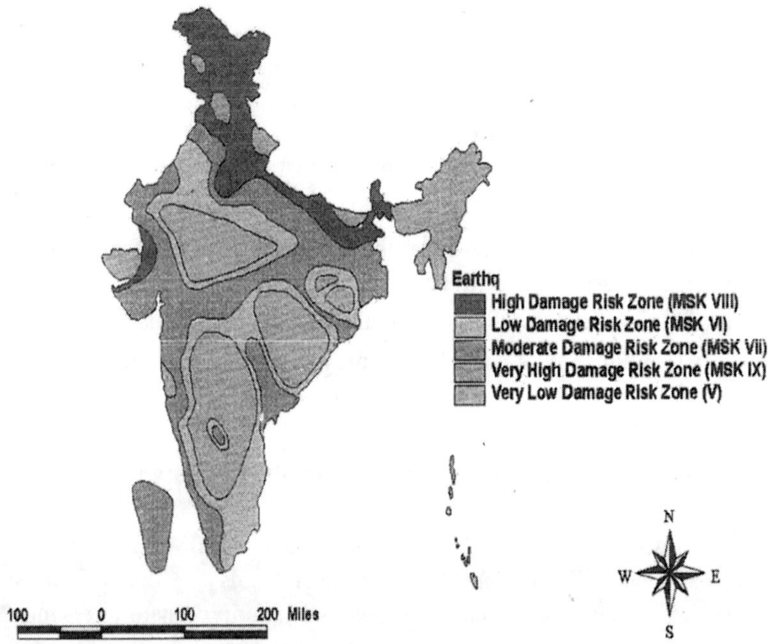

Disaster Management Information System (DMIS)

The State and Government of India have developed Geospatial based Disaster Management Information System for implementing structural and non-structural measures, on the basis of the past experience, knowledge and currently available information.

Information System for Disaster Management

Critical analysis and assessment of the implications of the occurrence of natural or man-made hazards need information comprising of both spatial and non-spatial related to factors influencing the hazards. If such information are available, it would be immensely useful in:

(a) Identification of the processes responsible for the hazards and the natural resources and socio-economic parameters associated with the process,

(b) Planning appropriate preventive measures/preparedness, and

(c) Assessing damage caused by hazards and to plan appropriate mitigation measures.

With the advent of Satellite Remote Sensing and GIS technology, the information generation related to earth surface has become easier in terms of database generation, storage, retrieval and data analysis. Further, creation of computerised database with Networking facilities has added a new dimension to the dissemination of Information, free flow of data and information exchange for speedy implementation of action plans and their monitoring.

Computerised database under the GIS environment has the following advantages with reference to hazards/calamities:

(i) Assessment of the situation through integrated analysis,

(ii) Implication of hazards in terms of risks and planning,

(iii) Spatial modelling, querying and map creation for efficient and effective implementation of Response Action System (RAS),

(iv) Simulation of models and visualisation of varying scenario of hazards.

Disaster Management Information System (DMIS) having a digital database under GIS environment is oriented towards providing information for decision-makers and encompasses information on natural resources. The integration of these data sets would aid in decision-making process for systematic planning and management of resources as well as disaster situations.

A wide variety of maps are required for the study of hazards. The maps with information on political boundaries, transport network, settlements, natural resources, LULC, etc, on which the spatial aspects of hazards are represented, with locational features, tectonic features, geological features, landforms, drainage, soils, etc. The information generated by these Thematic Maps are as follows:

(a) Geological maps help to identify the earth materials, geological hazards (e.g. seismic landslides, volcanic eruptions etc.) and river courses, etc.

(b) Geomorphology maps are helpful in creating an integrated picture of the natural land surfaces and its hazards (erosion, floods, landslides, subsidence and so on). Those maps form a part of a wider endeavour to understand the sensitiveness of geomorphologic processes to human interferences and the risks associated with development and settlements of hazardous sites.

(c) Soil maps depict the variation and changes in soil characteristics. Specialised pedological maps with collateral data enable area specific prediction such as landslides and mass washing, epidemic surveillance of soil borne diseases etc. They also help in providing information on drainage, water logging, erosion susceptibility, salinisation, etc.

(d) Land use / land cover maps depict the land use pattern such as animal, forest, scrub land, etc. These maps can be used for assessing the extent of damage as a consequence of hazards / disasters and valuation and also identifies the areas prone to hazards like floods, forest fires etc.

(e) In addition to the above, many other types of thematic maps that have direct or indirect bearing to hazards would also form a part of the RIS.

Non-spatial Database

The socio-economic and infrastructure data that reside in the database would be useful in the analysis of growth trends, demographic situations, the consequences of hazards depending on the demographic patterns, economic profiles, infrastructure status, communication networks and linkages and so on.

Geospatial Based Information Systems

The Geospatial data constitutes digital database, containing information about various resources such as land, water, vegetation and socio-economic situation, to generate Land Information System (LIS), Water Information System (WIS), Forest Information System (FIS), Disaster Management Information System (DMIS), etc, which find applications in various fields related to land, water, vegetation / forest, minerals, urban and rural development and specific area necessitating management of natural / anthropogenic hazards, development and management of facilities, transport, etc.

The DMIS is used for local, regional and State planning purpose, as well as a repository of information Hub on all disasters, namely, floods, epidemics, earthquake, accidents, industrial hazards, fire, cyclones, etc.

and an important requirement for the estimation of Vulnerability Analysis System (VAS) and in developing the Response / Action Plan System (RAS).

The Geospatial databases are sub meter and build on real time data, of great use in taking numerous decisions for managing, prevention and mitigation of impending disasters and protect life, property, environment and economy of the region, States and the nation. The DMIS Policy emphasizes on following aspect, for operational efficiency to meet the desired objectives:

- Community based Disaster Management, up to the last mile.
- Capacity Building and Training to all functionaries, at all levels.
- Consolidation of past initiatives and best practices.
- Networking with all stakeholder Agencies at national and international levels.
- A Multi-Disciplinary and Multi-Sectoral Approach.

Vulnerability

India with vast coastal area (about 7000 kms) in the West, South and East, causing Cyclones and Tsumani, Himalayan Mountain Range in the North prone to Seismic activities, Cloud Burst, Landslides, Perennial Rivers causing catastrophic floods, is vulnerable, to numerous disasters every year. It is estimated that more than half of India is prone to earthquakes of moderate to very high intensity; over 12 percent of its land is prone to floods and river erosion; coastline is prone to cyclones and tsunamis; more than half of cultivable area is vulnerable to droughts; and, hilly areas are at risk from landsides and avalanches. Further with industrialisation, India is also vulnerable to Chemical, Biological, Radiological and Nuclear (CBRN) emergencies and other manmade disasters, compounded by increasing vulnerabilities related to changing demographics and socio-economic conditions, unplanned urbanisation, development within high-risk zones, environmental degradation, climate change, geological hazards, epidemics and pandemics, necessitating a robust Disaster Management Policy and Programme.

Role of Geospatial Technology in Disaster Management

Earth Observation has improved tremendously, giving avenues to utilise it's potential for disaster early warning, mitigation and prevention measures. The Geospatial based decision support system involving integration of spatially referenced data in a problem solving environment, at various stages of natural disaster management (van Western, 2000) like:

- **Prevention Phase:** For analysing spatial database and to generate hazard zonation/risk/vulnerability maps.
- **Preparedness Phase:** For simulating natural disaster phenomena and to design evacuation plan and relief network.
- **Relief Phase:** To carry out search and rescue operation with the help of GPS.
- **Rehabilitation Phase:** To carry out damage assessment and evaluation of sites for reconstruction.

Further the Temporal monitoring of disasters identify the subtle causation factors and potential inhabiting measures to counter disasters, by the use of Geospatial technology applications.

Landslides

Landslides are triggered by heavy rainfall, earthquakes and volcanic eruptions or by human activities, such as quarrying and road construction. High relief areas of Himalayan terrain experience recurring landslides and slope failure phenomena due to geological reasons, climatic conditions and extensive human interference.

Landslide hazard assessment through two methods, namely, direct and indirect methods (Hansen, 1984). The direct method consists of a geomorphological mapping of past and present landslides identifying geomorphological indicators causing instability. The second category includes semi-quantitative and quantitative methods, namely the heuristic (knowledge driven), deterministic and statistical methods (Carrara *et al.*, 1995).

In the semi-quantitative method, landslide influencing geo-environmental indicators such as slope, rock type, landform, landuse etc. are ranked and weighted according to their assumed or expected importance in causing mass movements (Lakhera *et. al.*, 1992). This is based on a prior knowledge of the expert on causes of landslides in the area under investigation. The deterministic models, based on the physical process of landslide phenomena are site specific and used to predict slope instability for the design of control measures. Statistical models take into account spatial variability and are commonly used for prediction of slope failures on a regional scale (Carrara *et al.*, 1991; Yan, 1988 van Westen, 1993). These models are based on spatial distribution of landslides and quantitative analysis of geo-environmental indicators.

Spatial Modelling for Landslide Analysis in Himalayan Terrain

GIS based spatial statistical modelling techniques were applied to predict landslides in a structurally disturbed zone of western Himalaya (Lakhera *et.al,* 1996; Champati Ray, 1996). Various geo-environmental parameters, such as lithology, structure, slope, aspect, landuse, drainage, road excavations, vegetation cover and mass wasting areas were considered. Information on these parameters were derived from remotely sensed dataproducts by using digital image processing techniques, such as principal component analysis, image classification, vegetation coverage estimation (NDVI) and ortho-rectification. Terrain parameters such as slope and aspect were derived from DEM.

Statistical relationship between landslide occurrences and geo-environmental factors was established using information value (Yin and Yan, 1988) and weights of evidence. Finally, landslide hazard zonation maps were prepared using information value and weights of evidence modelling methods. It was observed that models predict around 60-65 percent of actual landslides in 17 percent of the predicted high hazardous area. Models were developed on limited number of known active landslides and were applied on a data set consisting of more number of slides to test the predictive power of the model. Two important conclusions could be made from this study – (1) information from remotely sensed data products can be integrated directly in a GIS based spatial predictive model; (2) the information value method and weights evidence modelling can predict reasonable number of landslides with the help of parameters derived from remotely sensed data products.

As a major initiative to explore the potential applicability of Remote Sensing and GIS in natural hazard assessment, Department of Space had taken up a National Landslide Hazard Zonation Project in 1999 along certain pilgrim/tourist routes in Himalayas of Uttaranchal and H.P. The project was taken up with prime objective to generate landslide hazad zonation maps on 1:25,000 scale using high resolution IRS LISS-III & PAN merged data, and to suggest management plans. The study was carried out under the umbrella of National Remote Sensing Agency in association with different centres of Dept. of Space and other central and state government departments, namely, Wadia Institute of Himalayan Geology (WIHG), Central Building Research Institute (CBRI), Defence Terrain Research Laboratory (DTRL), Indian Institute of Technology – Roorkee (IITR) and Remote Sensing Applications Centres of Uttar Pradesh and Himachal Pradesh.

In order to achieve the objective, 15 thematic layers (including three derivative layers) on terrain parameters were generated using satellite and ground data. These were integrated in a GIS environment using a specially developed knowledge-based decision support system to arrive at Landslide Hazard Zonation maps, showing six categories of Landslide Hazard Zonation from servere to low.

The final outcome is in the form of two Atlases on Landslide Hazard Zonation maps in Himalayas of Uttaranchal and H.P. (NRSC, 2001).

Earthquake Hazards

The Earthquake disaster is characterised by the neotectonic changes expressed in the form of diagnostic landform and relief changes, facture, fault zone, lineaments, etc which are captured by satellite sensors.

Geospatial based seismotectonic assessment in Lesser Himalayas and Kutch area, Gujarat

Lakhera *et.al* (1999) prepared a seismotectonic hazard zonation map of earthquake affected area around Chamoli and Rudraprayag districts of Garhwal in the Himalayas, where the satellite remote sensing data with ground checks were used to derive information on terrain conditions like rock type, slope morphometry (form and aspects), tectonic elements, soil cover and intensity of damage, and a Seismotectonic Hazard Map generated with five zones of very high, high, moderate, low and very low intensity.

The Bhuj earthquake of January 26, 2001 on terrain conditions using IRS LISS-III & PAN satellite data, helped prepare the Seismotectonic Hazard Map based upon terrain parameters like lithology, structure and soil condition etc. of the region and identified the damaged region in soil covered regions.

Cyclonic Hazards

Cyclonic hazards stands second most effected in term of number of occurrences specially in South-East Asian Region, most vulnerable to cyclonic disaster, and severity impact heavily due to lack of preparedness.

The Cyclonic hazards disaster management needs strong spatial and non-spatial databases and has the following processes:

A. Prediction, preparedness and planning :

    (1) Vulnerability map preparation

   (2) Protection of key installations
   (3) Selection of suitable areas for construction of Cyclone Shelters

B. During Cyclone Disaster Management:
   (1) Distance analysis
   (2) Safe Routes
   (3) Crowd Source Information
   (4) Broadcasting Guidelines
   (5) Movements/Air Dropping/Reaching Out with of Food, Water, Medicine etc.
   (6) Resource allocation
   (7) Coordination, Monitoring, Identification of areas for reaching out with help

C. Post disaster management:
   (1) Assessment of loss
   (2) Search and rescue
   (3) Rehabilitation and reconstruction
   (4) Insurance Settlements

D. Providing long term Policy and Programmes for Cyclone Disaster Management.

Flood Hazard

Floods have been causing untold misery and irreparable damages to mankind from time immemorial. Because of the rapid development in the flood prone areas and increased occupancy, thereby causing the overall susceptibility and increasing the damage potential, it has thus, become imperative for the flood administration come up with effective tools to combat the flood menace.

In order to combat such natural hazardous process, National Informatics Centre, Bhubaneswar, India has extensively worked in the area of flood management and developed a generalised GIS based model system which could be used by the district administration during critical flood situations for effectively monitoring the flood situation, estimating the likely damages and also efficiently administering rescue and relief operations (Rao, *et al*., 1997). The system is designed to work in a PC-ARC/INFO environment with an efficient communication network to get real time data from the lower levels such as blocks, tehsils, gram panchayats, villages etc.

In one of the case study taken along Dikrong river, tributary of Brahmaputra in Assam Duraga Rao *et.al* 1999 using RS & GIS techniques carried out study on flood forecasting, estimation of flood effected areas with varying magnitudes of floods and damage assessment due to flood.

Flood Monitoring

Satellite Imagery helps detection and monitoring of flood situations over large regions. Optical remote sensing from geostationary platform (INSAT-3D/3DR) provides rapid and valuable information on cloud patterns and meteorological parameters (rainfall). Microware remote sensing

Fig. Flood as Observed from SCATSAT-1.

techniques have advantage as these penetrate the clouds and senses the surface hydrological characteristics, hence the data from SCATSAT-1 (launched by PSLV-C35 on September 26, 2016) is used for the detection of the flood situations over India.

SCATSAT-1 is a continuity mission for Oceansat-2 Scatterometer for Ocean weather forecasting, cyclone detection and tracking. The satellite carries Ku-band Scatterometer and scans in a conical fashion HH and VV polarisations and allows developing high-resolution datasets due to high overlapping areas. SCATSAT-1 observations in Ku-band for backscattering and brightness temperatures have been analyzed for flood detection and monitoring over India.

Sentinel-1A, a C-band SAR imaging satellite high resolution data on July 24, 2017 helped to compare inundated regions over parts of Gujarat. Observations on flooding conditions are correlated in SCATSAT-1 and Sentinel-1A data.

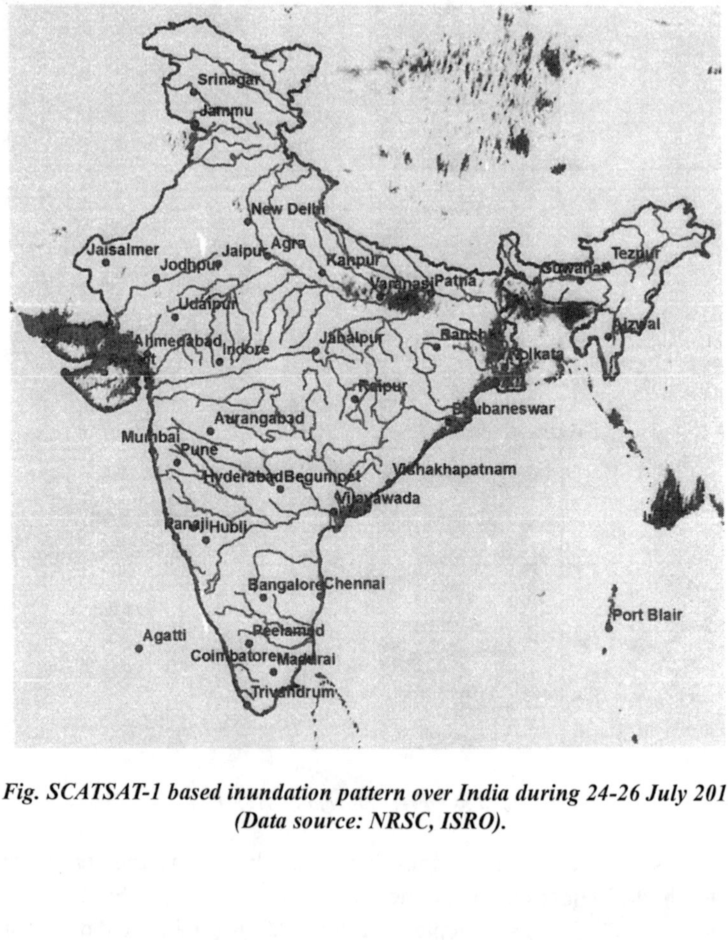

Fig. SCATSAT-1 based inundation pattern over India during 24-26 July 2017 (Data source: NRSC, ISRO).

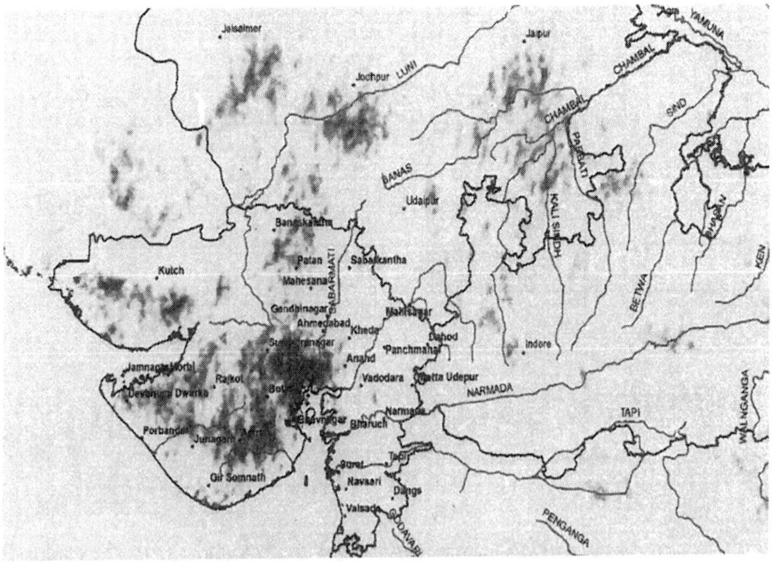

Fig. Flood inundation Change Analysis (6-10 July Vs 22-26 July 2017) over Gujarat and Neighbouring Regions using SCATSAT-1.

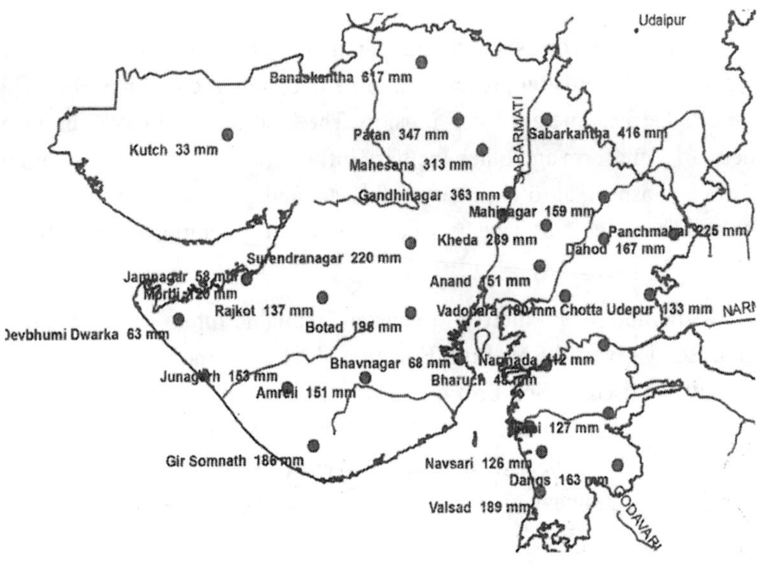

Fig. Observed Cumulative Rainfall (mm) in Different Districts of Gujarat during 21-26 July 2017.

(*Data source:* Gujarat State Disaster Management Authority)

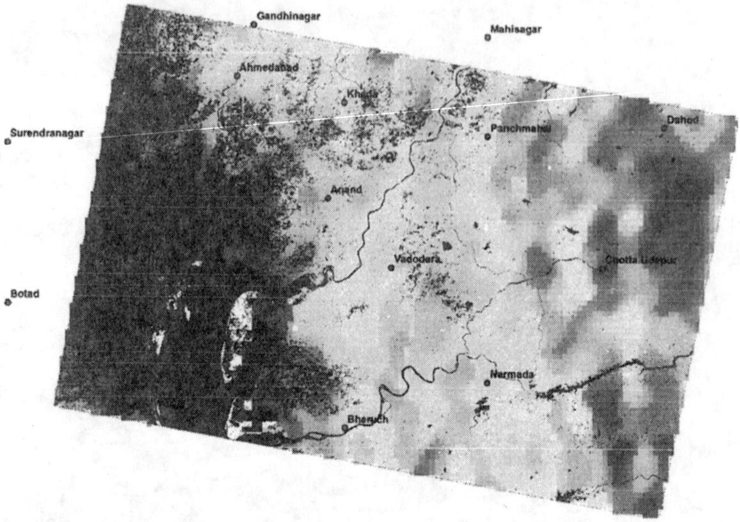

Fig. Merged Inundation Information from SCATSAT-1 (Ku-band, coarse resolution) and Sentinel-1A (C-band, high resolution) for July 24, 2017 in parts of Gujarat.

Soil Erosion Hazard

Soil erosion consists of terrain parameters and fluvial, aeolian, glacial etc impact the erosion process. Topographic, climatic and physiographic aspects help estimate the soil erosion. The land use/land cover, drainage network, landform and other ancillary information like slope morphology/ form and aspect, agro-climate, rainfall etc. and ground based information on soil characteristics have been considered, for generation of Soil Erosion Hazard Maps.

A number of Predictive Models are available for soil erosion hazard analysis. Universal Soil Loss Equation (USLE) is most common model widely practised for Soil Erosion Hazard mapping. The others like Sediment Yield Predictive Equation (SYPE) (Flaxman, 1971), Morgan, Morgan & Finney (1984), Model (MMF) and Sediment Yield Index (SYI) model (Bali & Karale, 1997) have also been used.

Land Degradation Mapping

Land degradation is temporary or permanent degeneration of productivity of land due to physical, chemical or biological factors. Regular updates and information on degraded land is essential for implementing necessary measures to tackle degradation processes and to plan for reclamation programmes.

National level land degradation mapping is prepared by the ISRO along with State Remote Sensing Centres and other Research Agencies, under Natural Resources Census (NRC) Mission of Department of Space, ISRO, in various scales, both multi-temporal and multi-spectral satellite data, with classification standards for generating reliable land degradation information.

DOS, ISRO has completed two cycles of land degradation mapping at 1:50,000 scale, for the timeframe 2005-06 and 2015-16, and generated spatial extent of the land degradation, changes between the 1st and the 2nd cycles, which are accessible in ISRO Bhuvan Geoportal.

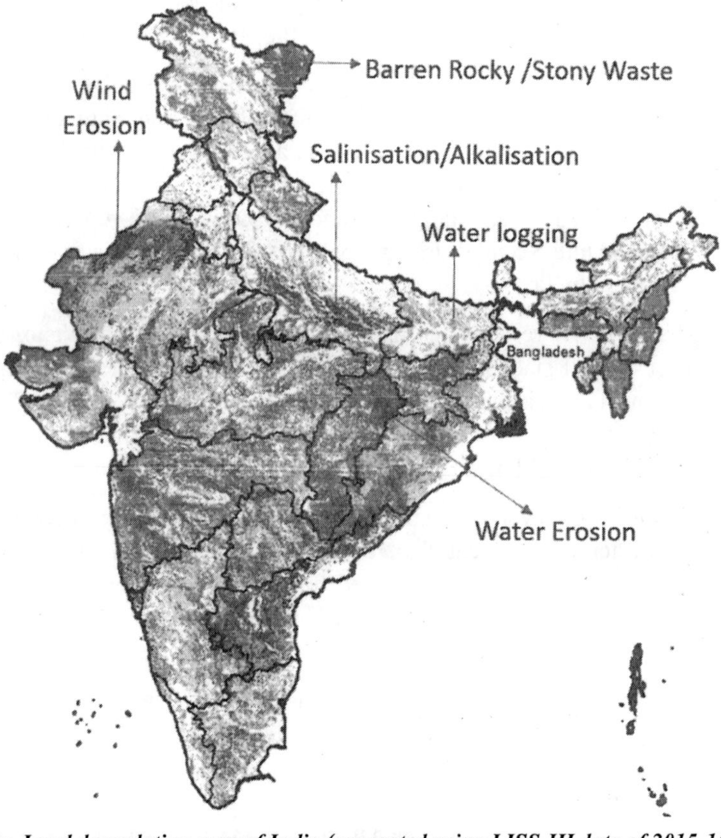

Fig. Land degradation map of India (generated using LISS-III data of 2015-16).
Source: NRSC, ISRO.

Geospatial Technology is proving as a decision support tool, for disaster management, with analysis of natural hazards on multi-dimensional and multi-disciplinary framework with a strong spatial component, which has strong data capture, co-registration, computational, using statistical and deterministic modelling techniques, with generation of 3D Mapping, real time mapping, analytical capability for effective monitoring of geo-environmental changes, which will facilitate scientific and management decision-making.

National Disaster Management Authority (NDMA)

The Apex Body for Disaster Management in India, is the National Disaster Management Authority (NDMA), headed by the Prime Minister of India, created for enabling environment for institutional mechanisms at Centre, State and District levels as mandated by the Disaster Management Act, 2005. NDMA lay down the policies, plans and guidelines for Disaster Management, for Prevention, Mitigation, Preparedness and Response.

The Indian government strives to promote a national resolve to mitigate the damage and destruction caused by natural and man-made disasters, through sustained and collective efforts of all government agencies, Non-Governmental Organisations and People's participation. This is planned to be accomplished by adopting a Technology-Driven, Pro-Active, Multi-Hazard and Multi-Sectoral strategy for building a Safer, Disaster Resilient and Dynamic India.

The NDMA reflects the aspirations of this National Vision, of empowering all stakeholders to improve the effectiveness of Disaster Management in India NDMA has five major divisions viz. Policy and Plans, Mitigation, Operations and Communications, Information and Technology, Administration and Finance.

At the State level, the State Disaster Management Plan, prepare the State Disaster Management Plan, to ensure that the issues of Disaster Risk Reduction (DRR) have been addressed, to prepare the risk and vulnerability assessments and preparation of annual vulnerability and risk reduction reports, laying down guidelines to integrate DRR into development process.

Geospatial technologies has been widely used in monitoring the occurrence of different types of natural disasters and in evaluating the losses and impact, timely early warning and by evacuation measures. The repetitively and synoptically captures data on land use, land cover, climate, atmosphere, and other natural phenomena within short span of time, within proven disaster mitigation measures.

The Geospatial inputs are critical in disaster management, including drought, flood, earthquake, cyclone, landslides, volcanoes, avalanches, forest fire, crop pest/diseases, etc. Its applications to drought, flood, cyclone and forest fire derived from satellite imageries on NDVI and vegetation conditions particularly moisture stress, for drought assessment, to provide early warning and monitoring the same for better resilience and preparedness.

Geoinformatics has proven its usefulness in disaster management by providing a data base from which the evidence left behind by disaster that have occurred before can be interpreted, and combine with the other information to arrive at hazard maps, indicating which area is potentially dangerous. Using remote sensing data, such as satellite imageries and Ariel photos, allows us to map the variabilities of terrain properties, such as vegetation, water, geology, both in space and time. Satellite images give a synoptic overview and provide a very useful environmental information, for a wide range of scales, from entire continents to detail of a few meters. Many types of disasters, such as floods, droughts, cyclones, volcanic eruptions, etc. will have certain precursors that satellite can detect. Remote sensing also allows monitoring the event during the time of occurrence while the forces are in full swing. The vantage position of satellite makes it ideal for us to think of, plan for and operationally monitor the event.

Thematic maps with tectonic features, geological features, landforms, drainage, land use/land cover, soils, etc form the basis for Hazard Maps depicting the following vital features:

1. Geological maps help to identify the earth materials, geological hazards (e.g. seismic landslides, volcanic eruptions etc.) and river courses, etc.
2. Geomorphology maps are helpful in creating an integrated picture of the natural land surfaces and its hazards (erosion, floods, landslides, subsidence and so on). Those maps form a part of a wider endeavour to understand the sensitiveness of geomorphologic processes to human interference and the risks associated with development and settlements of hazardous sites.
3. Soil maps depict the variation and changes in soil characteristics. Specialised pedological maps with collateral data enable area specific prediction such as landslides and mass washing, epidemic surveillance of soil borne diseases etc. They also help in providing information on drainage, water logging, erosion, susceptibility, salinisation, etc.
4. Land use/land cover maps depict the land use pattern such as animals, forest, scrub land, etc. These maps can be used for

assessing the extent of damage as a consequence of hazards/ disasters and valuation also identifies the areas prone to hazards like floods, forest fires etc.

About 5,700 km prone to Cyclones and Tsunamis out of 7,516 km long coastline.

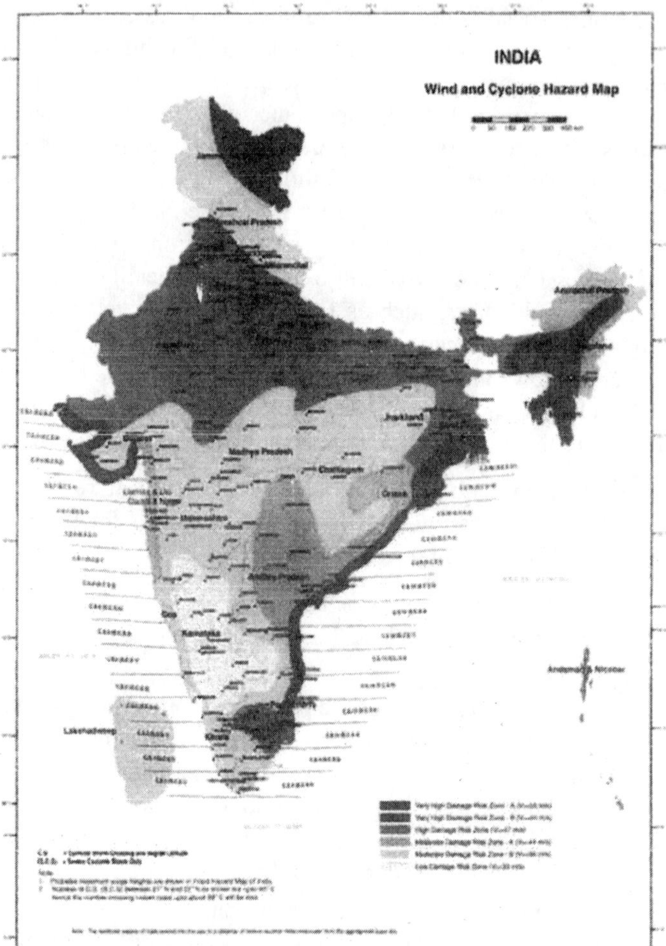

Fig. About 58.6 percent of the landmass is prone to Earthquakes of moderate to very high intensity.

Preparedness is paramount in a disaster situations and a quick rescue and relief mission is inevitable for minimising the impending damages on the onslaught of disaster where the role of the local community is vital in addition to the advanced forecasting systems, effective communications, institutional structure involving the government organisations, academic and research.

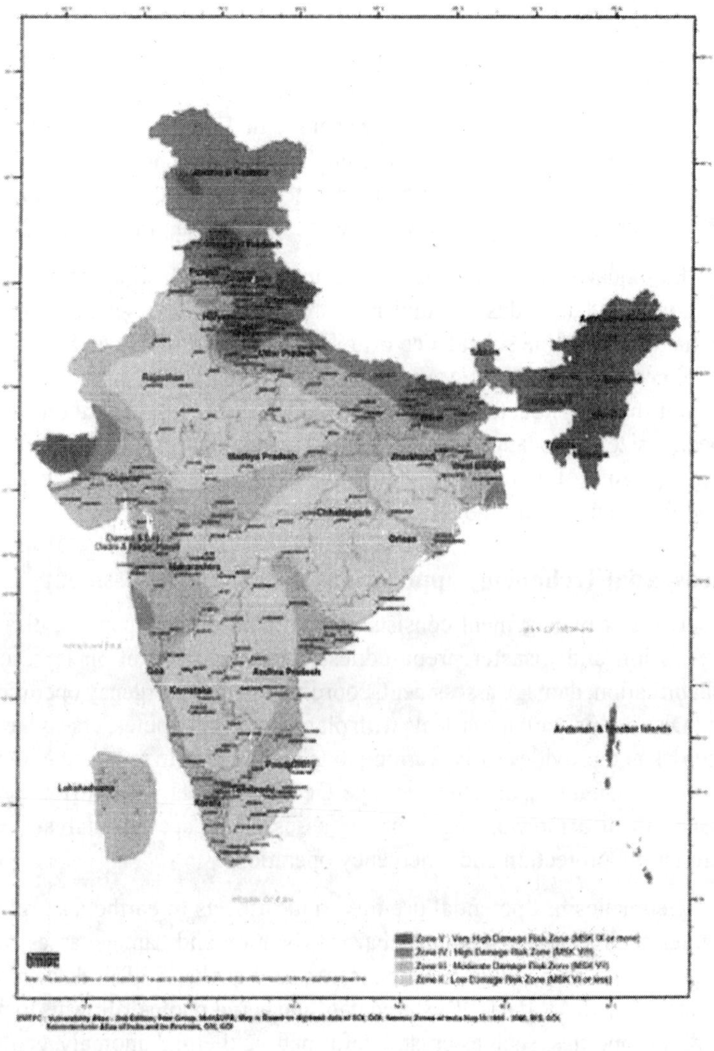

Role of Geospatial Technology in Earthquake Studies

Earthquake disaster emanates from Lineaments and faults, which are the sources of neotectonic activities, lead to an increase in seismic hazards of the region. Satellite imageries delineate lineament, fractures, faults which help in identifying the vulnerable areas, rick zones, mapping and promotion of earthquake proof infrastructures and regulation in these vulnerable areas.

The mapping of drainage pattern, surficial lithology and the geological structures reflect the morphotectonic processes, and identify the anomalies and tectonic movements (Ramasamy *et. al,* 2000). The Microwave Satellites provide the high-resolution imagery of earthquake prone areas, GNSS provides an ability to identify subtle changes on Earth's crust (Lunetta and Elvidge, 1999) and identification of nonhomogenous surface deformation (co-seismic deformation), which helped to monitor Latur earthquake, in 1993, where the surface deformation was 2.8 cms (Majumdar *et al.*, 2002).

Earthquake induced damage can occur due to liquefaction and or related phenomena, landslides, ground motion, tsunamis and seiches, ground rupture and tectonic subsidence or uplift. Seismic Zoning can be defined as delineation of geographic areas with varied potentials for surface faulting, ground shaking, liquefaction and landsliding during future earthquakes of specific size and location (Berlin, 1980). The geology, ground acceleration, legacy history of earthquake, spatial database, an associated database are used for the preparation of Hazard maps.

Geospatial Technology applications in Damage Assessment

Disaster management consists of two main phases, namely, disaster prevention and disaster preparedness. Disaster prevention is rescue, rehabilitation, damage assessment, coordinating the emergency operations, and Disaster preparedness deals with planning of safe routes, assess hazard and risk and provides early warning to take measures to reduce the impact of the onslaught of the disaster. The Geospatial data with attribute data assists in disaster warning, damage assessment, spatial analysis, loss estimation, protection and emergency operations.

Geomatics has potential use in various aspects of earthquake related studies such as active tectonics, hazard zonation and damage assessment and even act as possible precursors for earthquake. SRTM data, multi-spectral data, SAR data, IRS stereo data and aerial photos, allow us to map terrain properties, such as crustal deformation, thermal anomaly, geology etc, both temporally and spatially. SAR deformation, thermal anomaly, geology etc, both temporally and spatially. SAR interferometry and GNSS survey help in mapping of deformation, spatio-temporal analysis of earthquake data for hazard zonation and damage assessment.

Applications of Geospatial Technology in Disaster Management

Disaster	***Prevention***	***Preparedness (Warning)***	***Relief***
Earthquakes	Mapping geological lineaments land use	Geodynamic measurements of strain accumulation	Locate stricken areas, Mapdamage
Volcanic Eruptions	Topography and land use maps	Detection/measurement of gaseous emissions	Mapping lava flows, Ashfalls and lahars, map damage
Landslides	Topographic and land use maps	Rainfall, slope stability	Mapping slide area
Flash floods	Land use maps	Local rainfall measurement	Map flood damage
Major floods	Flood plain maps; Land use maps	Regional rainfall, Evapotranspiration	Map extent of floods
Storm surge	Land use and land cover maps	Sea state, ocean surface Wind velocities	Map extent of damage
Hurricanes		Synoptic weather forecasts	Map extent of damage
Tornadoes		Nowcasts; local weather Local weather observations	Map amount, extent of damage
Drought		Long ranged climate models	Monitoring vegetative biomass

Thematic Mapping	***Reflection***
Natural Resources	
Slope	Landslides, flood proneness, industrial hazards, drought.
Soils	Landslides, mass washing, floods, earthquakes, droughts, soil borne diseases, greenhouse effects.
Geology	Earthquakes, floods, droughts, fire.
Land use/Land cover	Floods, cyclones, droughts, damages. Assessment of industrial hazard, greenhouse effects
Drainage network	Floods, earthquakes.
Surface reservoirs	Floods, earthquakes, industrial hazards, fire.
Hydrogeomorphology	Industrial Hazards, earthquakes, drought, hazard preparedness and monitoring

Climate	***Reflection***
Rainfall pattern	Floods, cyclones, droughts, damages, Assessment of industrial hazard, greenhouse
Temperature	Cyclones, droughts, epidemics
Wind	Cyclones, droughts, epidemics, fire
Humidity	Epidemics, industries.

The Geospatial Technology have been used for many disasters including drought, flood, earthquake, cyclone, landslides, volcanoes, avalanches, forest fire, crop pest /diseases, etc. There is a direct relationship between vegetation (through NDVI and Vegetation conditions) and moisture stress, with occurrence of drought assessment has been successfully carried out with qualitative assessment of the drought conditions, which can be captured by the satellite data.

The Disaster Policy and Strategies to be adopted for reducing the impact of the Disasters, through the application of the Geospatial Technology, are as under :

(i) Reduction of disaster risks by Early Warning Systems,
(ii) Design and develop Disaster resilient Plan,
(iii) Robust Communication and Health Delivery System, through Mobile, broadcasting, television etc.
(iv) Rescue and Rehabilitation during and post-disaster reduction.

A robust Disaster management necessitate Disaster Prevention Planning, Better Preparedness Measures, Real time Monitoring, Relief, Assistance and Rehabilitation. The prediction and early warning, damage assessment and relief management constitute the core of the Disaster Management.

Geospatial technology application are used for flood monitoring, cyclone, forest fires and Hazard Mapping. The Thematic maps with tectonic, geological, landforms, drainage, land use/land cover, soils, and other features form the basis for Hazard Maps depicting the critical features as under :

1. Geological Mapping with land forms, geology, lithology, drainage, volcanic eruptions, river course etc.
2. Geomorphological Mapping with land surfaces, erosion, floods, landslides, subsidence and risks associated with hazardous sites.
3. Soil maps with soil characteristics, soil types, classes, drainage, water logging, erosion, susceptibility, salinisation, etc.
4. Land Use/Land Cover (LULC) mapping, with various impact and pressures on land use and natural coverage of the land, provides useful information on floods, forest fires, land slide, etc.

The UNOOSA/UN-SPICER (United Nations Office for Outer Space Affairs/UN Platform for Space-based Information for Disaster Management and Emergency Response), facilitates the use of space-based technologies for disaster management and emergency response.

The devastating impacts of natural disasters cause loss of lives and property around the world. To avoid sustainable development being undermined by natural hazards, disaster risk management based on effective early warning systems, improved understanding of risk and better information about the onset of disasters is crucial. Space technology such as earth observation, satellite telecommunications and navigation satellites can contribute to more effective disaster risk management and emergency response.

Acknowledging the benefits of space-based information for disaster risk management, the United Nations General Assembly established UN-SPIDER as a programme of UNOOSA with the mandate to provide universal access for all countries and all relevant international and regional organisations to all types of spaced-based information and services relevant to disaster management to support the full disaster management and cycle.

Through its activities, UN-SPIDER contributes to reducing loss of lives and damage to property and supports the implementation of the 2030 Agenda for Sustainable Development.

Hazard Areas

The board hazard areas can be summarised as under :

1. Avalanches, Landslides, Flash floods and Mudflows
2. Climate change and sea level changes
3. Coastal management, marine systems (including mangroves and coral reefs) and coastal erosion
4. Crop pests and plagues
5. Cyclones, Tsunamis and Storm Surges
6. Deforestation
7. Desertification
8. Drought
9. Earthquakes
10. Epidemiological and entomological risks
11. Extreme weather conditions (temperatures, thunderstorms, snowstorms, windstorms, and lightning)
12. Fires – Forest and grassland
13. Floods
14. Food security
15. Glaciers

16. Haze and Fog
17. Land degradation and soil erosion
18. Land mines
19. Oil spills
20. Refugee flows
21. Sand and Dust storms
22. Subsidence
23. Technological, industrial and nuclear risks
24. Transportation accidents
25. Volcanoes
26. Water pollution
27. Capacity Building
28. Development of IT and Space Technology Systems and Solutions

Lessons from Disaster

Tsunami Disaster 2004

The natural disaster such as a Tsunami hazard of 2004 was not known in India in the past. However, the devastation had led India to devise Geospatial based rescue management. The mapping of the disaster and vulnerability assessment for the affected coastal area, with Tsunami Disaster Mapping were overlayed with thematic map layers of villages, rivers, canals, national and state highway etc, to obtain the Tsunami affected features. The vulnerability was mapped using the buffering technique, with rivers buffered to 1 km radius, to identify the villages within the 1 km from the coast and villages worst affected due to tsunami on Dec 2004, used for further analysis and rescue and rehabilitation maps.

Flood Mitigation Modelling

Flood risk management strategies can be structured into pre-flood strategies and post-flood strategies, this is one of many possible categorisations of the different strategies:

1. Pre-Flood Strategies

The following strategies are adopted during Pre-Flood Phase:

(1) **Mitigation**

- Structural measures the levees, dikes, dams, and reservoirs.

- Non-structural measures are change location: relocate properties to less vulnerable.
- Change land use: coding, zoning, programming, and re-naturalisation.
- Adaptation
- Loss Sharing
- Flood insurance: Public, Private, and mixed (public/private)
- Response (Preparedness (Early Warning) and Awareness and Training)

2. Post-Flood Strategies (Recovery)

- Rehabilitation
- Community Support and Networking
- Governmental Support System and financial assistances
- Insurance Claims
- Public Support and Funding (Material and Non-Material)
- Reconstruction
- Disaster Proof Measures

Mitigation: Structural Measures

The most ambitious flood control measures are levees, dikes, and flood-walls. Apart from assisting in flood control these structures also provide for irrigation, drinking water and hydroelectric power. Levees are embankments along the course of a river. Many rivers produce levees naturally during floods when the overflowing river deposits debris along the bank.

Gradually this builds up and contains the stream into the channel. Artificial levees are constructed in much the same manner. They may be temporary, as when sandbags are used during flooding, or permanent when the banks are raised to keep the river in its channel during times of increased water flow.

Levees protect the surrounding country side from floods by holding more water in the channel. They also aid in navigation by deepening the channel. A flood-wall is very much the same as a levee, but built out of concrete or masonry instead of sand.

Dikes are similar to flood-walls in all respects except that they usually refer to holding back large standing bodies of water, such as an ocean. A system of dikes prevents the sea from flooding the inlands in coastal areas.

Mitigation: Non-Structural Measures

The most typical feature of the measures belonging to the group of non-structural measures, is that they do not alter the physical characteristics of the river. These measures instead aim at changing the consequences of floods.

For the last fifteen years, there has been a change in focus away from structural mitigation to non-structural mitigation measures. One possible non-structural solution is re-location. Families and settlements are moved out of the flood plain. This method is not commonly used, as there are many problems related to moving people. Even if such a policy would be economically rational, it is not often liked by the people living in the flood plain.

In a land area with a given risk of inundation, regulations prescribe what can be done. It might for instance be forbidden to build certain types of infrastructures in areas with a high risk of inundation. Because of the cost and environmental impacts of flood-protection structures, many parts of the United States rely on land-used regulations to prevent flood damages.

Response and Recovery

Different concepts such as flood forecast, flood warning, and evacuation programmes are grouped under this lable. Awareness programmes are tailored to the specific village or community at risk. The community engagement is very important for preventing a natural disaster or reducing the effects of a natural disaster. In very short time the event can occur, why external help may not reach its location in time.

The organisation and education of local volunteers is more and more recognised as an important flood risk management strategy.

Approaches to Flood Risk Management

1. **Hierarchical approach:** This approach promotes governmental responsibility, with no private responsibility. Large-scale structural measures are built and maintained by the government. If a levee fails, or if an unprotected area is flooded, the government compensates the victims.
2. **Individualistic approach:** The responsibility lies on the individual, private responsibility is extensive. People should be relocated if they live in a high-risk area, but they should receive compensation for this. A system of private insurance is an

ingredient, with a margin for private incentives; in order to get a reduced premium of the ground has to be waterproofed, for instance.

3. **Naturalistic Approach:** This approach considers floods as natural, it would be better to take down the levees and let the hydrological balance take over. The government should actively support sustainable development. Recently there is a change in focus away from large-scale structural measures to non-structural mitigation measures. There is a growing recognition that the problem of flooding cannot be successfully managed by structural mitigation solutions as these deal with the symptoms of the problem, and not the problem itself.

The increasing concentration of people and property in flood-prone areas raises questions of responsibility and vulnerability. By building flood-walls and dams the frequency of floods in an area is reduced, allowing for changes in land use. The flood risk is not eliminated, however. The structures only give protection up to a certain flood level, and there is also a risk of failure of the structures. Large expensive structural measures initiated and supported by the government, seems to be very much in the policy agenda for flood disaster management.

A new holistic view recognises the importance of working in harmony with nature and of approaching the problem of flooding in terms of responsible management and restoration of the natural function of rivers. Instead of spending public funds on flood mitigation structures, concrete channels are removed and the original meandering streams are restored which is an ecological approach.

Flood Insurance Policy

The cost for protection and loss reduction is peaking and thus it appears prudent to consider a flood management programme with insurance plans for vulnerable areas and people. One reason for such a programme is that it is a fairer way of sharing the losses from flooding. People who live in flood-prone areas carry a larger risk and financial burden which upsets their livelihood practices very often.

Spatial Data Analysis

Spatial data is at the core of a GIS and therefore, at the core of its application to flood emergency management. The primary source of spatial data has been Land Records and Reveue Data, Census and Local Panchayat Raj Institutions.

In the management of flood scenarios, the quality of decisions made with assistance from a GIS will depend completely on the timeliness, relevance, accuracy and currency of the data available. The data themes most relevant to flood management include demographic data, LEP zones, cadastral parcels, transport layers (roads and railway lines), address data, elevation data (contour, Digital Terrain Models (DTM) and Digital Elevation Models (DEM)), aerial photos and flood boundaries. This list is not exhaustive, as other data sets may be available from councils and other producers of local spatial data.

Many of the core data sets listed above are available however, to provide some essential data in the format that is required, such as road centre lines with street address attributes, and therefore, the need arises to look at alternate sources for this required data. An obvious source of current and well maintained spatial data are local councils whose own requirements for detailed spatial information provides one of the most important repositories of spatial data available. Council spend time and effort checking, correcting and maintaining spatial data for their respective areas, so it seems logical to extend the well-established relationship between gram panchayats and settlements to the supply of this digital spatial data.

Further to the supply of local digital spatial data, the local level applications would benefit greatly from the willingness of gram panchayats to extend the specification of flood studies carried out in their areas. The inclusion of such items as the output of one metre increment flood boundaries, identification of heights of possible evacuation routes and the range of rates of rise up to when evacuation routes are cut would greatly benefit the flood planning process.

Flood Emergency Management

The emergency management of floods begins with the data gathering or flood intelligence phase, continues through the planning phase and the conduct of community education about the problem and its management and, when necessary, culminates in the combat or operational phase. These phases should not be viewed as separate entities, as each informs and complements the others in a continuous process. Information about the effects of a flood event is added to the flood intelligence database and then used to update the Local Flood Plan and so on. While the role of GIS in each of the phases is described separately below, the phases themselves should be thought of as part of an ongoing process.

Using Geospatial Technology in Flood Planning

Using the GIS to display a combination of aerial photography, road centre lines, rivers, creeks, contours, cadastral and administrative boundaries has been particularly useful in the initial stages of planning. This combination provides a discussion focus and helps to illustrate local knowledge. Being able to create, enlarge and print a map has been a boon in familiarising emergency managers with an area prone to flooding.

Floods are not a true representation of real flood behaviour but they have proven to be an aid during the planning process when used in conjunction with other flood intelligence. Using the tools available in GIS, flood extents at two metre intervals were overlayed on a three dimensional Digital Terrain Model (DTM) of the Lowlands area of study area, and used to create an animation of potential inundation. Being able to present a growing flood enables researchers to better visualise and contextualise their local flood knowledge.

Projecting a map, with a rich set of underlying data, onto a wall screen and having the ability to manipulate aspects of the map during flood planning meetings has greatly improved communication between emergency managing officials and has led to a more detailed understanding of the problems to be addressed. During flood planning sessions for Venkat Durga Puram area in Machillipatnam Mandal of Krishna District, a need was identified for accurate height data at specific locations in the floodplain. The lowlands become isolated in the early stages of a flood, and many refuse to leave their homes until it is too late for safe evacuation to be undertaken.

To fully understand the implications for evacuation in this area a surveying technique called a Real-time Kinematic Global Positioning System (RTK GPS) can be tried out to capture very accurate Height Datum levels and locations and other characteristics of residences, road low points and intersections. This data can be incorporated into the planning process and flood simulations. This method of data collection shows great promise for use in all parts of the state confirming, or in many cases identifying, the height of levees, roads and other points of interest during the flood planning stage.

The researchers used existing spatial data as well as generate new spatial data. Further to this, the researchers used GIS to display the cadastral boundaries and overlaying incremental flood extents with the road network, priorities for flood proofing effort were easily identified.

GIS has also contributed to the Flood Plan as well, by providing customised sector and evacuation route maps of the area being planned for. These maps are exported in various image formats and inserted into the plan. These and other documents have been enhanced by the flexible output of maps from GIS.

Using Geospatial Technology for Community Education

Maps and imagery created in the GIS have been used at community information meetings to help describe the complexity of issues surrounding the study area. Three-dimensional models showing progressive inundation can be generated to demonstrate and explain the possible effects of flooding.

Factors such as population increase, population turnover and the time which has passed since the last major flood have meant that there are segments of the community with little or no knowledge or experience of flooding and its effects in the area. Hence, there is a need to be able to translate information on river heights into area flooded and the effects. Simply providing the general public with information on river gauge heights is not enough. This information needs to be supported by a description of the known and possible consequences, and by what actions should be taken.

Issues such as which major tributaries feed the River system, when evacuation routes are cut and how islands are created by rising flood waters are more easily explained using GIS illustrations and graphics.

These analytic presentations shows demonstrative effect on the possible behaviour and extent of a major flood over the terrain. In showing the 'where' of a flood, community members are also able to gain an appreciation of the 'why' of various aspects of the planning process such as locations of road evacuation routes and why it is necessary to evacuate early. These animations and 3D displays make the concept of a flood come alive and quickly break down barriers to acceptance of the idea that floods 'can happen here' and of a greater magnitude than can easily be believed.

Community Based Approach

PRA for Community Response

1. **Information Base** (Forecasting and Warning)
   (a) Source of information
   (b) Medium of information
   (c) Perception on early warning
2. **Adaptation/Coping practices** (of the People/Communities)
   (a) Types of measures considered/perceived

(b) Any collective actions considered by the community
(c) Any community-based facilitation to individual's/family's coping

3. **Assistance offered** (by any Quarter)
   (a) Sources of Assistance
   (b) Process of getting Assistance
   (c) Type of Assistance

4. **Assessment of Risk**
   (a) Type of Risk
   (b) Perception of risk (location-specific response)
   (c) Response to Risk

5. **Potential**
   (a) Potential internal/external facilitation
   (b) Perceived potential solution

Sl. No.	*Vulnerability Factors in Disaster Management*			
	Physical	***Social***	***Economics***	***Environmental***
1	Land-Use Planning	Literacy and Education	Poverty Ratio	Extent of natural resource depletion
2	Engineering and Architecture Density Levels	Peace and Security	National Economic Reserves	State of resource degradation
3	Design and Materials Used for Critical Infrastructure and For Housing	Access to Basic Human Rights	Socio economic Infrastructure	Loss of resilience of ecological system
4	Remoteness of a Settlement	Systems of Good Governance	Communication Network	Loss of biodiversity
5		Social Equity	Utilities, Supplies	Exposure to toxic and hazardous pollutants
6		Positive Traditional Values	Transportation, Water, Sewage and Healthcare etc.	
7		Knowledge Structures		
8		Customs and Ideological Beliefs and Overall Collective Organisational		

Earthquake Safety in Buildings

The Earthquake safety measures in the construction in buildings as per the Buildings constructed using the Indian Standard Codes and Guidelines are as under:

Masonry Building

Seismic Zone III 2-3%

Seismic Zone IV 3-4%

Most severe seismic Zone V 4-6%

Reinforced concrete buildings of 4 – 8 storeys

Seismic Zone III 2.6-3.2%

Seismic Zone IV 3.2-4%

Seismic Zone V 5-6%

(in each case, including about 0.7 percent only for ductile detailing)

Retrofitting of buildings, not initially designed for earthquake will cost:

2 to 3 times as much as the above mentioned costs.

Source: Prof A S Arya, National Seismic Advisor, MHA

Preventing Natural Disasters

The recommended disaster management preventive measures are enumerated in the Tables below:

Disaster	***Prevention***
Flood	Dams, Flood Shelters.
Drought	Afforestation, Rain-Water Harvesting
Cyclone	Advanced Warning, Cyclone, Resistant Housing
Earthquake	Earthquake Resistant Structures
Landslide	Slope Stabilisation, Plantation
Tsunami	Advanced Warning System, Plantation Along Coasts.
Avalanches	Anti-Avalanche Mesh
Epidemic	Adequate Health Care, System, Immunisation

Multi Hazards Zones in India

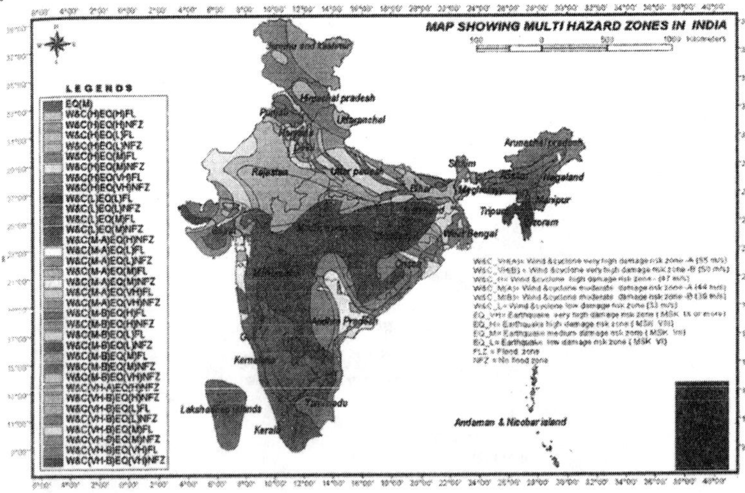

The Geospatial Technology application in Disaster Management has both Pre-Disaster and Post Disaster measures. The Pre Disaster management through the application of Geospatial technology has Vulnerability Analysis and Response Planning under the Preparedness, Disaster-wise prediction with forecasting models and vigilance system. In the Post Disaster phase the immediate response, Relief, Recovery, Rehabilitation and Impact Study are the measures recommended for disaster mitigation.

Geospatial Technology in Disaster Management

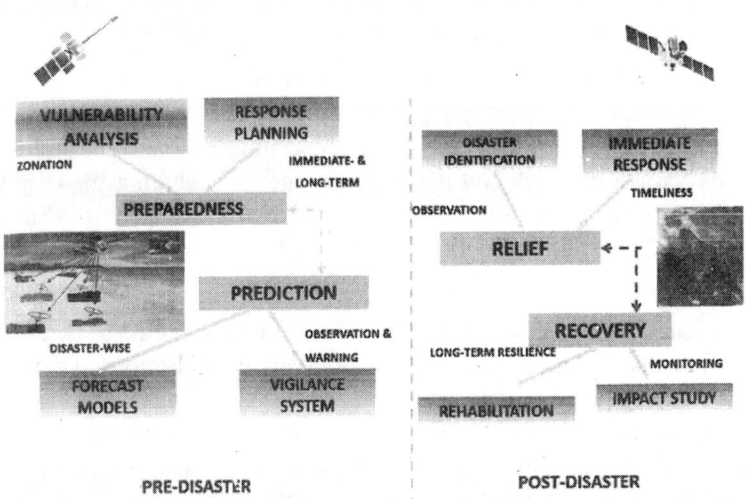

Case Studies

Flood Mitigation Model

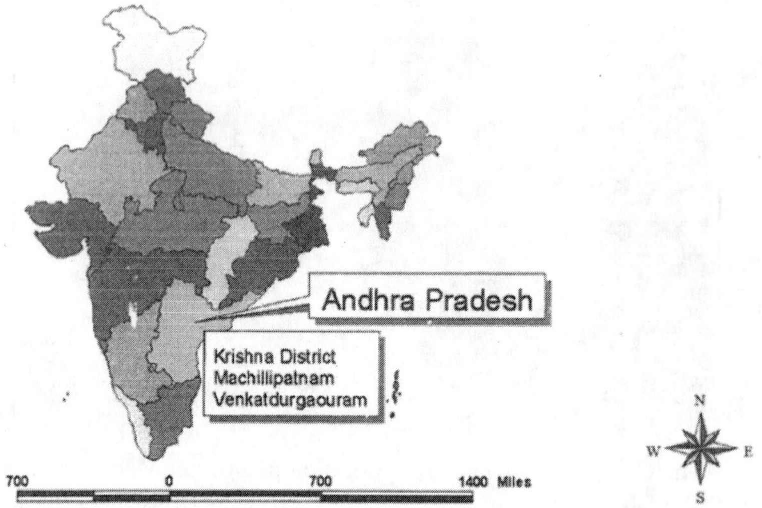

The Venkat Durga Puramin Gram Panchyat in Machillipatnam Mandal in Krishna district is perennially prone to storm surge and flooding, making agriculture and community life difficult to sustain.

The Cadastral Maps, Socio Economic Data, Rainfall Data, Cropping Pattern, Historical background of Flood and Cyclones, Housing structures and Infrastructure, Drainage Patterns, Land Use and Land Cover, attitude and perception of people towards preparedness, present Disaster Management set up for early warning, preparedness and response system etc.

There were also extensive interactions with Officials, NGOs operating in the area, Gram Panchayat functionaries, women group, youth groups, National and International Organisations operating in the area and discussed with various research and development agencies working for Disaster Mitigation measures. Survey of India Topo Sheets collected from Survey of India for the region and were digitized for generating vector layers based on which all other data are integrated for analysis.

The basic premise on which the Model Plan is aimed at is reliable database at Gram Panchayat level both spatial and attribute features including the local social and economic aspects of the area. The database comprise all the parameters like rainfall, rainwater runoff, drainage, slope, soil types, cropping pattern, vegetation, land use and land cover, settlement patterns, spatial spread of infrastructure, contours, topography and terrain, sedimentation, precipitation demographic profile and vulnerability. Data pertaining these aspects are collected and linked to various administrative units like district, mandal, gram panchayat, ward, streets up to household and land parcel and analysis on the same are generated.

Temporal data over time wherever available help understand the flood proneness and people's preparedness, response and coping mechanism to the cyclones and floods. Simulation and forecasting models are generated in a GIS platform for decision support system at the local level incorporating all aspects of disaster management practices. Rehabilitation in terms of identification of safe places, places suitable for storage of medicines, drinking water, food grains etc, appropriate drainage patterns and vegetative measures can be generated as an Action Plan for the Gram Panchayat micro level planning, monitoring, implementation and development process.

The following analytical treatment for the preparation of the Model GIS based Community Based Disaster Preparedness Plan is as follows:

(a) People's perception and attitude towards disaster preparedness
(b) Status of preparedness
(c) Peoples Involvement/participation
(d) Institutional Network engaged in disaster preparedness
(e) Socio Economic aspects
(f) Spatial Spread of Infrastructure
(g) Government policies and programmes
(h) Land Use and Land Cover Practices
(i) Agriculture and Cropping Practices
(j) Drainage, slope, soil and geomorphological aspects

The layers to be generated are as under:

(a) Base Maps for physical and social parameters
(b) Generation of micro zonation of vulnerability and risk analysis
(c) Community based Disaster Preparedness Plan for Emergency Response
(d) Long Term Disaster Mitigation and Reduction Plan

Based on the characteristics of hazard faced, type, location, magnitude, frequency, a combination of interrelated aspects of hazard mitigation need attention, which necessitate the following measures:

1. Land-Use Planning
2. Hazard Mapping and Risk Assessment

3. Early Warning and Management of Hazards
4. Protection against Hazards
5. Health aspects of Natural Disaster Reduction
6. Strengthening Institutional Frameworks for Disaster Mitigation

The Geospatial Technology has the potential applications in the following areas:

1. To map vulnerable areas.
2. To prepare maps of potential hazard areas for use in Physical Planning (Hazard Zoning Maps).
3. To forecast early warning of cyclones, flood, landslides, etc.
4. To identify safer zones, routes, etc during a disaster.
5. To assess the damage and help in rescue and rehabilitation during a disaster.

GIS/RS, then, has exhibited two principal advantages for natural hazard mitigation and research. First, the technology allows long-terms time-series studies and storage of the information which may prove invaluable in future situations. Secondly, GIS/RS improves information accessibility. Remote sensing platforms can provide large amounts of data quickly and inexpensively, relative to other means of collection, and GIS can bring together vast amounts of information from a wide variety of sources and make the information quickly visible and applicable in emergency situations.

Conceptual Framework and Planning Guidelines for Integrated Coastal Areas and River Basin Management:

The coastal areas, apart from being environmentally sensitive and highly productive, are extremely attractive for human population and, therefore, for economic development. Sixty percent of the world's population lives within 60 km of the coastlines, and this figure is forecasted to rise to 75 percent within the next three decades. River basins have been a unit for management of freshwater resources, which are indispensable for human life, economic development and maintenance of ecosystems.

Both the coastal and river basin systems support a variety of socio-economic functions as they provide space, produce resources and absorb unwanted products. With the expansion and increase in scale of human activities, functional linkages between coastal and riverine areas are ever more apparent. Economic activities in downstream areas benefit from upland resources, such as water, nutrients and pollutants and woods.

On the other hand, coastal areas provide space for settlement and industrial or tourist developments that have a positive benefit for the wider basin area.

These two areas are linked through a number of natural and socio-economic processes:

- The cycle of water which affects water quality and quantity and ultimately sea water quality affecting coastal ecosystems and human activities on the coastal zone (fishing/aquaculture and tourism/recreation opportunities);
- Sediment transport which affects soil and coastal dynamics ultimately having an impact on coastal ecosystems and human activities on the coastal zone (fishing/aquaculture, urban development, tourism, etc.); and
- Human activities in the river basin might affect also coastal ecosystems and human activities in the coastal zone in a positive way providing food, water and energy or in a negative way through water retention for irrigation and other uses, waste effluents dumped in the river, etc.

Under the Integrated Coastal Area Management, coastal managers, start recognizing that freshwater input to the coastal areas has strong impacts on the coastal environment and welfare of human being living in the coastal areas. River basin managers also initiated to manage freshwater systems, taking into consideration their influence over the coastal environment. As the logical consequences, a concept of managing coastal areas and river basins together in an integrated manner has been formulated. The priority issues in that respect are: capacity building, coastal land-use planning, river basin development and resource management, legislation, enforcement, coastal and river banks protection and conservation, etc.

In order to demonstrate the usefulness and applicability of the guidelines, the present paper aims at presenting proposed demonstration project, composed of a set of activities. Depending on nature of a target river basin-coastal area, priorities set and activities that were already carried out, some of the presented activities can be selectively implemented.

Approach

The overall goal of the demonstration project is to demonstrate the usefulness and applicability of the information in the guidelines, more specifically, approaches and tools that are introduced as the whole or part of the integrated Coastal Areas and River Basin Management that supports environmental conservation and management, which is of equal importance to economic efficiency and social equity. The relevant tools include Database, Geographic Information Systems (GIS), Decision Support Systems (DSS), Environmental Impact Assessment (EIA), Strategic Environmental Assessment (SEA), economic evaluation of costs and benefits, environment-development scenarios, Carrying Capacity Analysis (CCA), regulation and control or financial mechanisms, awareness, Capacity Building and Education, conflict resolution, etc.

The basic principles in the demonstration Geospatial based Flood Management Model requires the following aspects:

- Respect the integrity of the river basin or coastal ecosystem accepting limits on the use of resources;
- Ensure the strategic importance of renewable resources for socio-economic development;
- Allow for the multiples use of resources integrating complementary activities and regulating/separating conflicting ones;
- Ensure multi-sectoral and multi-level integration decision-making linking broad scale management to local level interventions; and
- Allow for participation of all actors particularly local population in the planning process to assure effective management.

The Model requires a high level of co-operation within and between institutional structures. A high level of horizontal co-operation is required particularly among sectoral institutions at the planning stage and a high level of vertical co-operation is necessary within institutions at the implementation stage. Therefore, the project demonstration also aims at demonstrating ideal structure for carrying out activities under the concept of flood, cyclone and river basin management.

Different scale requires varying attention, and roughly these levels are classified as: regional, national and local, suggestive modifications depending on the scale and different actors involved.

The coastline may not be influenced by river inputs, but as longer section of coastline are considered, the impact of rivers inevitably becomes greater. In the same manner, small river basins are unlikely to affect the coastal zone significantly, except in a few cases. However, as the size of a basin increases, the likelihood of outputs from the basin having some effect on the coastal zone increases. However, in many cases, large and complex river basin systems require specific attention to river basin issues, and impacts on or relation with the coastal areas may be given lower priorities. For large and highly urbanised coastal areas, issues relevant to river input or land based activities in the connecting river basins may often be given secondary attention.

Therefore, at the stage of demonstration of the logical framework and technical procedure of the guidelines, the following criterion can be applied to choose target areas for any demonstration project:

1. Medium sized river basins and associated coastal areas, not more than three countries are involved;
2. Involving medium sized cities or urban development, including both agricultural and industrial development;
3. Requiring an approach integrating various sectors; and
4. Where river basin activities have environmental and socio-economic impacts on the coastal areas, and vice versa.

Model Outcome

The demonstration Model is envisaged to generate the following outcome:

1. Demonstration of the usefulness, efficiency and economic and environmental benefits,
2. Demonstration of usefulness of individual tools that can be used under the overall framework,
3. Demonstration of efficiency and economic benefits of a policy coordination and institutional mechanism,
4. Demonstration of key linkages between river basins, coastal areas, flood and cyclones.

The overall Flood Model is composed of specific activities that aim to demonstrate usefulness of a specific tool that is introduced in the guidelines in support of the flood modelling project. These steps are:

1. Assessment and data/information management;
2. Mapping and Spatial Data preparation;
3. Integration of local information, DEM, River basin, etc;
4. Vulnerability Analysis and identification of various mitigation parameters;
5. Monitoring and evaluation of results.

Assessment and Data/Information Management

The overall results of the Assessment and Data/Information Management are to gather and collate information and data that can lead to formulation of goals and objectives and furthermore in the definition of management strategies for sustainable development in the river basin and the coastal area.

Development of an Environmental and Socio-Economic Profile

The environmental and socio-economic profile are designed to present in a simple manner key issues for the target river basins and associated coastal areas.

1. *Surveys on selected key-issues.* The survey for new data and gap identification.
2. *Analysis of the natural systems in both coastal areas and river basin.*

   Consists of the Following

   - Current rate of resource use according to existing socio-economic patterns;
   - Assessment of the impacts of resource use practices on the state and stock of natural resources;
   - Estimation/contribution of waste generated and of that which is being discharged into natural systems, calculation of the waste that is being generated in other regions but still discharged in the natural systems of the region under study;
   - Assessment of possible effects of climate changes (mainly related with the study of the coastal area); and
   - Impacts of socio-economic activities on natural resources/ecosystems.

   Information requirement for this phase is as under:

   - Basic environmental data, biology, topography, hydrology, geology;
   - Natural resources including water, agricultural land, forest, fishery and aquatic resources, natural heritage, minerals;
   - Environmental hazards including floods, slope and soil related hazards, cyclones, volcanic activities, etc.;
   - Spatial (terrestrial and sea) uses including all economic sectors, urban development, infrastructure; and

- Networks including water supply and drainage, waste disposal and transport;
- Data should also indicate seasonal changes, cyclical and other fluctuations.

3. *Analysis of the socio-economic context along with their spatial implications:* Within this context information around the following issues needs to be generated. Demography, economy, social structure, spatial patterns, institutional issues. A link to risk issues, such as sea level rise for the coastal areas, need to be made as well.
4. *Forecasting future developments:* This can be based on projections of existing trends and forecasts of the activities not currently affecting but expected to effect the natural systems of the river basin or of the coastal area, or of both in the future. This can be done with the help of cross-sectoral scenarios.
5. *Identification of key environmental and socio-economic issues:* Key environmental and socio-economic issues identified taking into consideration causal relationship of causes and issues and driving forces.
6. *Modelling and Decision Support System:* The results distributed to all stakeholders for their participation, feedback, interactions, roles and responsibilities.

As a support tool for data acquisition and management, data from satellite imagery, GNSS and GIS system, ICT and associated modern techniques are used and tested, with data presented in a GIS system so that the data/information can be presented for a easy understanding of a wide range of data users.

Environmental Carrying Capacity Analysis

Development pressure in an area is vital particularly if it is to modify the existing environmental conditions in the area. This calls for an assessment of relative capacity or threshold of the local system to cope with pressures. Carrying capacity can be best defined as the maximum load of activity (or maximum number of users) which can be sustained by a natural or man-made resource or system without endangering the character of that resource. Therefore, it is recommended that the carrying capacity for a certain activity be estimated prior to establishment of the framework for development and management of the areas under consideration.

Environmental Impact Assessment

Environmental impact assessment is a method of identifying: (i) The impacts of human and natural environments, and (ii) Options to reduce or mitigate negative impacts. The key activities proposed in the Strategic Action Plan will be reviewed in terms of their impacts on the environment.

The Geospatial Flood Modelling involve community, primary state holders, integrating all aspects of the local wisdom and the modern techniques to familiarise the local people with various technological tools and techniques available for disaster preparedness, early warning and mitigation, replicable in coastal areas, vulnerable to cyclone and flood.

The alleviation and mitigation of natural hazards is one of the critical real time application of Geospatial Technology, used for floods, cyclones, volcanic, earthquake, fire, landslide and other disasters, advanced at an unprecedented rate, and created new possibilities in hazard mitigation and disaster management approaches, in assessment of hazards and emergency management, including real time monitoring potentially hazardous situations and providing advanced warning and in improving management of emergency situations following a disaster, with decision alternatives for judicious decision making in emergency situations on real time basis.

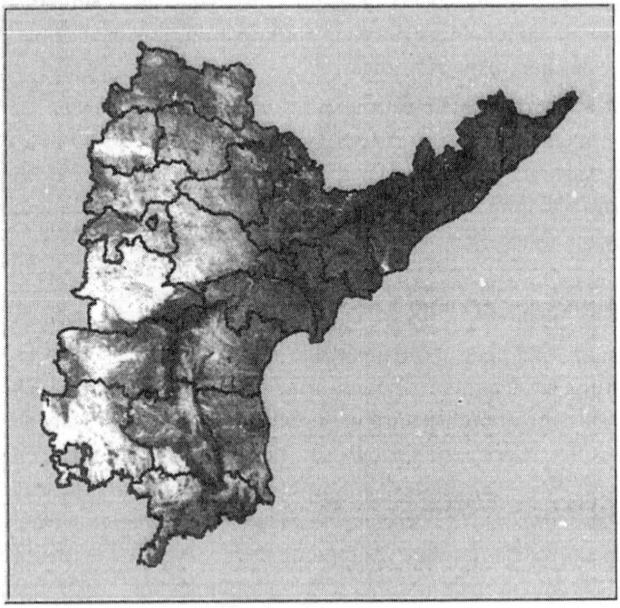

Fig. Erstwhile AP State.

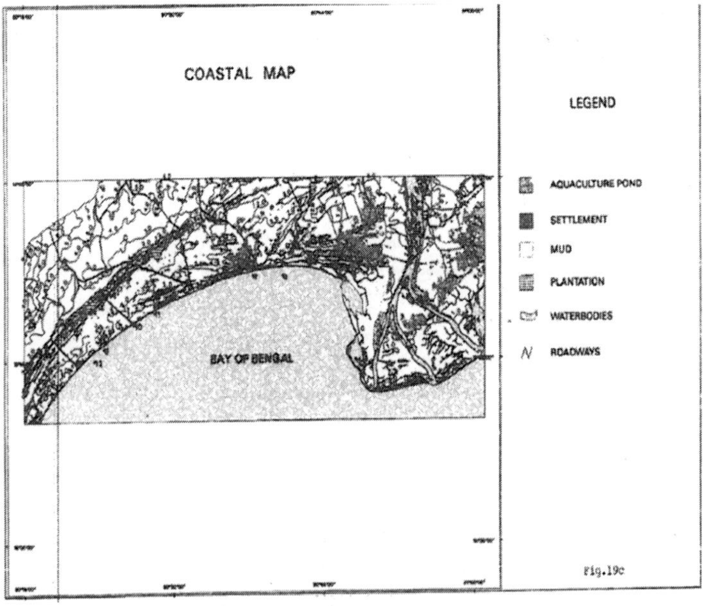

Fig. Coastal Topography Map.

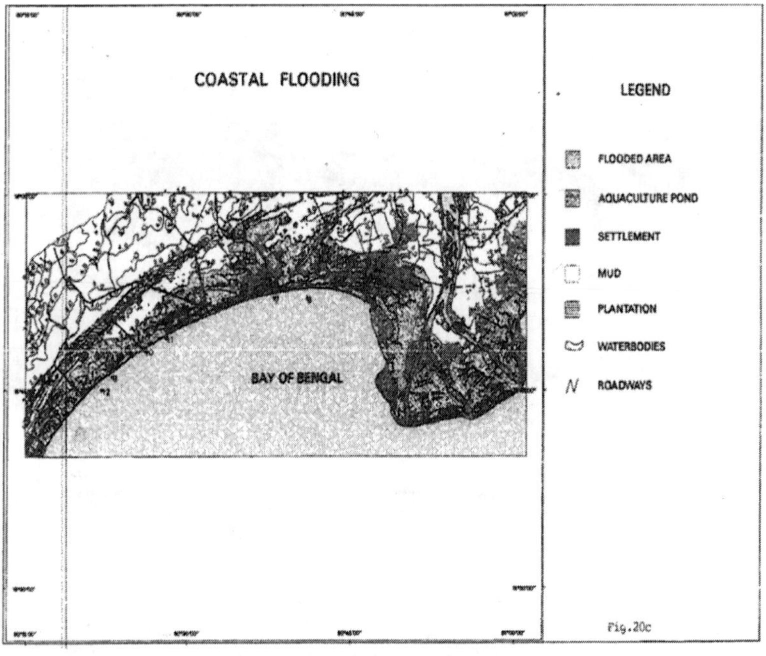

Fig. Coastal Flooding.

Fig. Krishna District with Mandals.

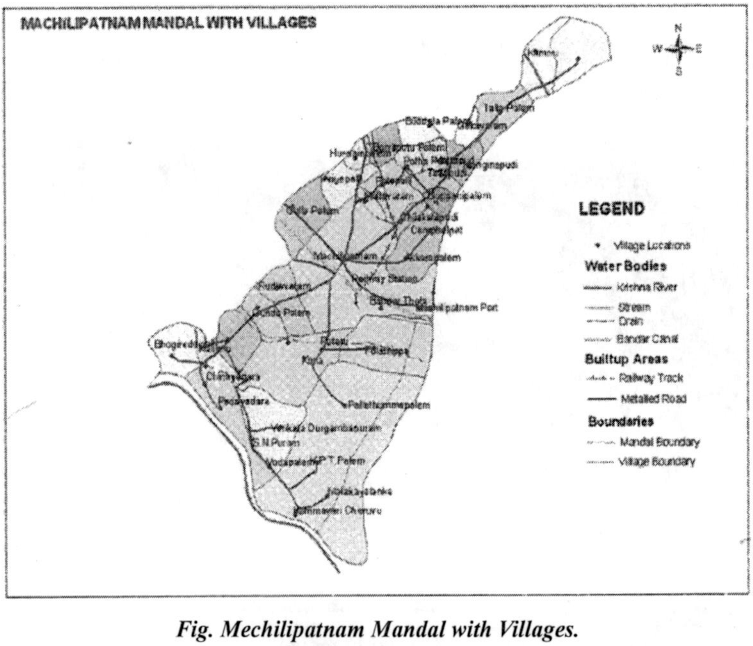

Fig. Mechilipatnam Mandal with Villages.

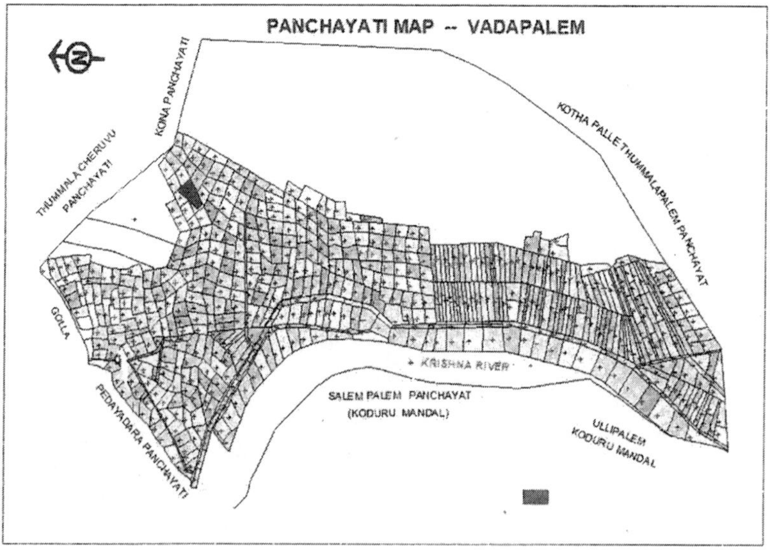

Fig. Panchayati Map– Vadapalem.

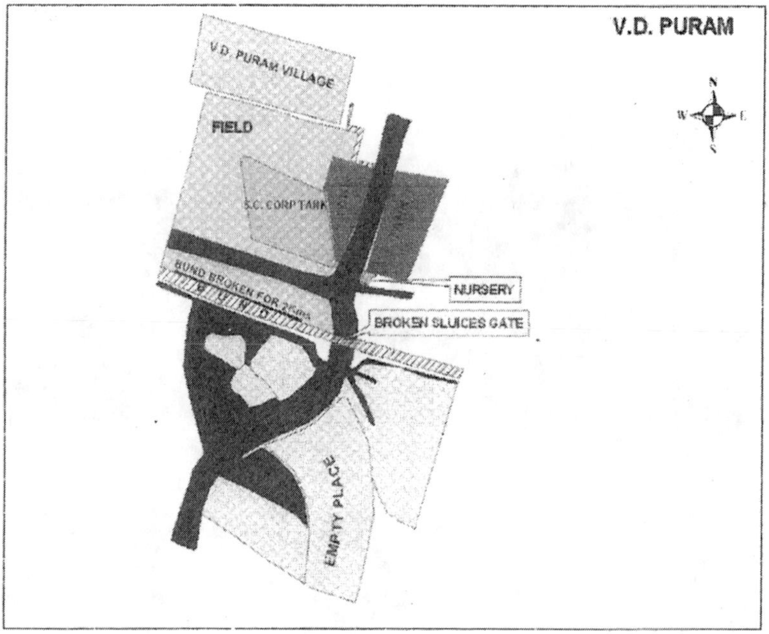

Fig. V.D. Puram.

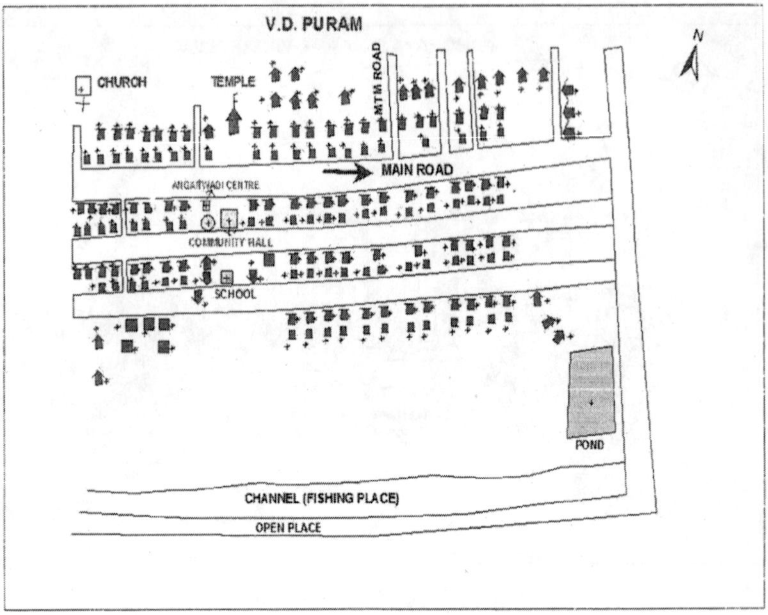

Fig. V.D. Puram PRA by Community.

Fig. Cyclonic Flood in V. D. Puram.

Fig. Cyclone Shelter.

Fig. Electronic Display Board on Cyclone by INCOIS.

Fig. Mangrove Degradation due to Aqua Culture along Kakinada Coast.

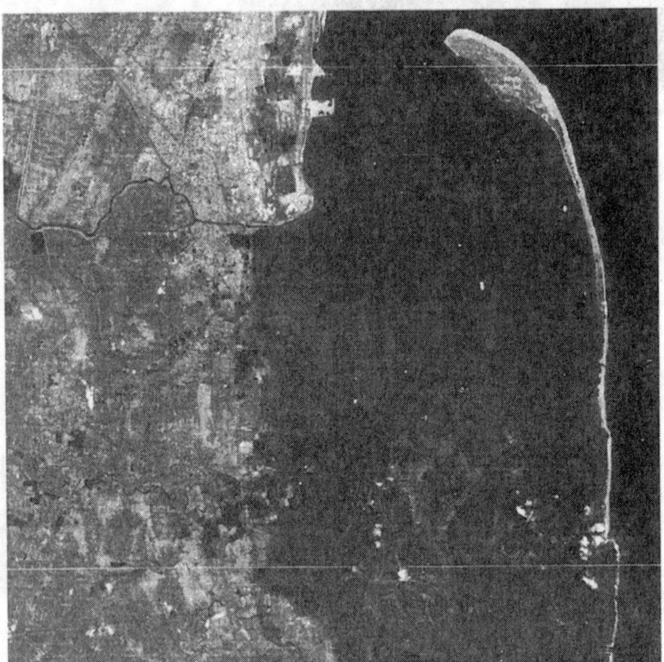

Fig. Damaged Aqua Culture in Kakinada and Surroundings.

Flood Disaster Impact Minimisation (FDIM)

Flood Forecasting system (FFS) Spatial Flood Warning System (SFWS)

Integration of RS/GIS with SCS-TR20 & MIKE-II Models	*Integration of RS/GIS & DEM*
• To generate Peak Flood Hydrograph	• Spatial Extent of Flooding
• Flood Routing for Decision Support	• Contingency Plan/Evacuation Model
• To improve accuracy of Forecast	• Flood Damage Assessment
• Lead/Warning Time of Forecast	• Converting Flood Forecasting water level into Spatial Flood Hazard Information

Pre Flood Scenario

BACKWATER WITH MANGROVES IN THE BACKGROUND

Area of Flood Scenario

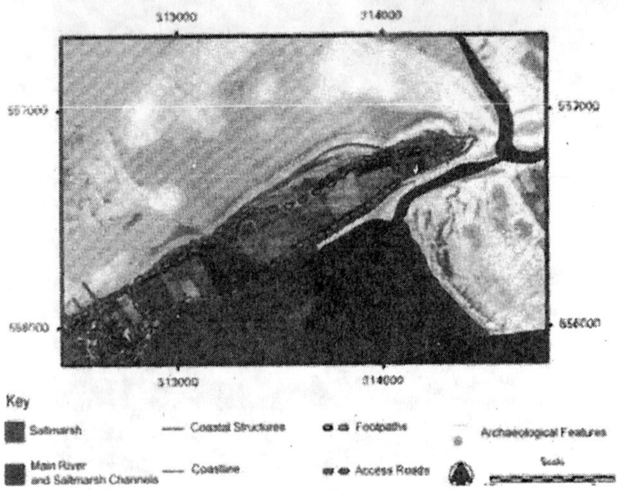

Fig. During Flood Scenario.

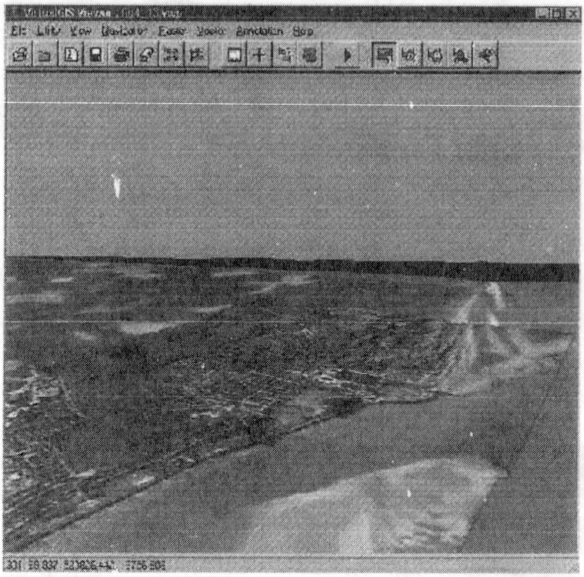

Fig. 3D Modelling.

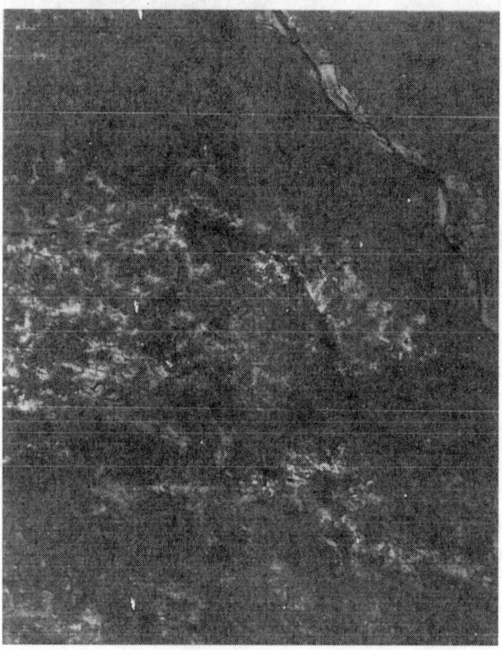

Fig. Brahmaputra River in Spate.

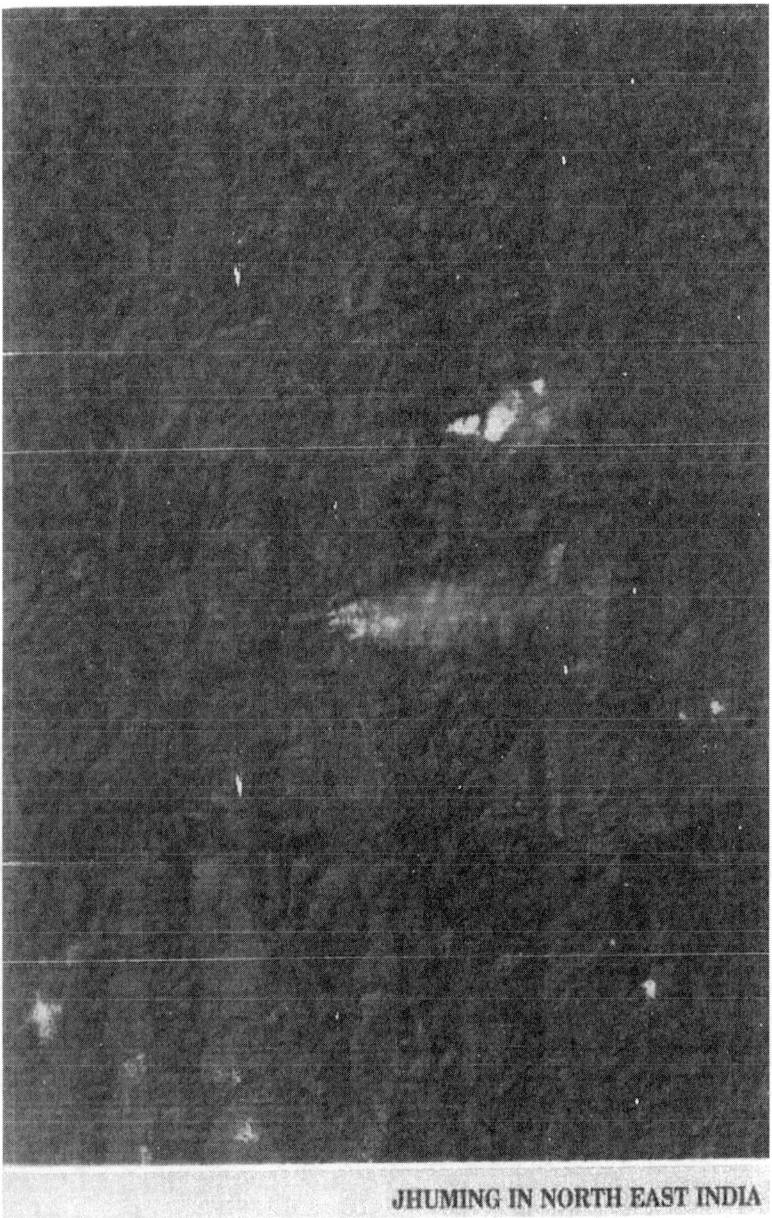

Fig. Shifting Cultivation in the North Eastern Region.

Forest Fire Monitoring

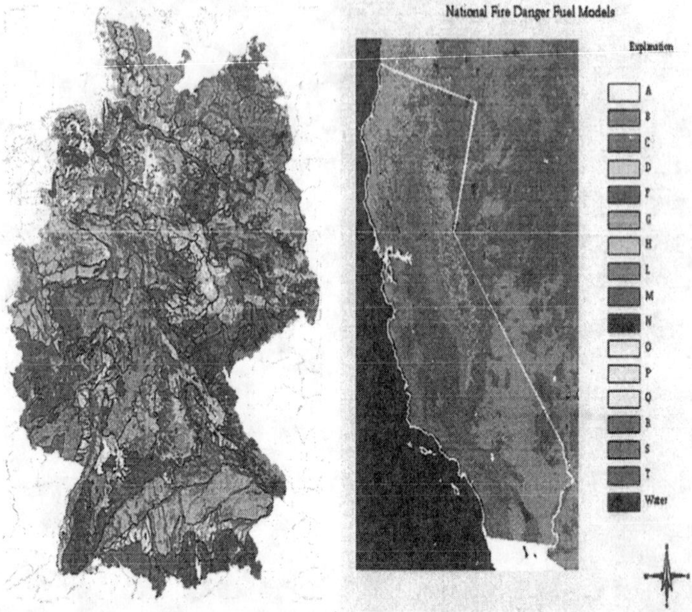

Pre and Post Volcanic Eruption

Land Slide Hazard

PRE-EARTHQUAKE (26.03.99) POST-EARTHQUAKE (30.03.99)

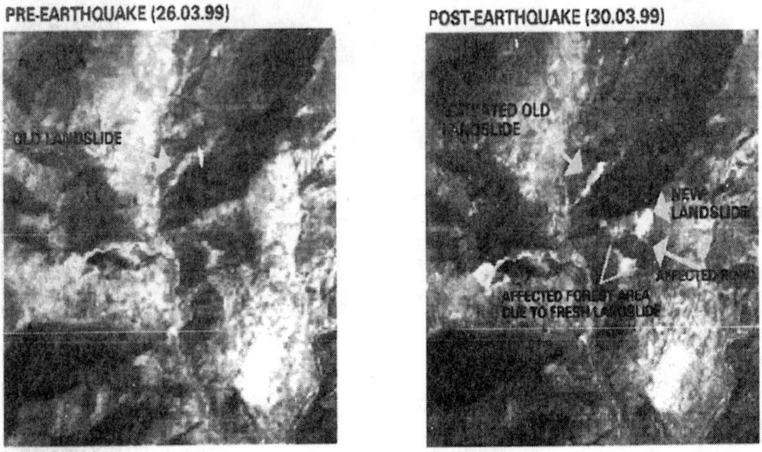

LOCATION - NEAR GOPESHWAR

DATA USED :
1. PRE-EARTHQUAKE IRS-1C LISS III
2. POST-EARTHQUAKE IRS-1D LISS III

Chamoli Earthquake - 29.03.99 Date of Analysis - 02.04.99 Geosciences Group / NRSA

Pre and Post Earthquake Scenes

Flood due to cyclone (29th October 1999) off Orissa coast

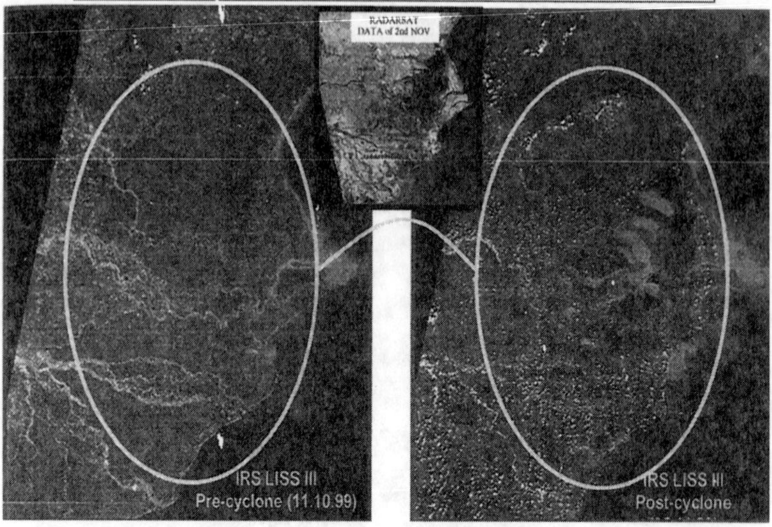

Change Detection

1. DENSE FOREST
2. DEGRADED FOREST
3. AGRIL. PLANTATION
4. LAND WITHOUT SCRUB
   ROCKS
5. WATER
6. OPEN FOREST
7. AGRIL. CROPS
8. LAND WITH SCRUB
9. [illegible]

Change Matrix

Name of the Class	*2001-area in Sqkm.*	*2005-area in Sqkm.*	*Change*
Agricultural crops	84.69	70.34	-14.35
Agricultural plantation	40.63	20.14	-20.49
Dense forest	190	234.84	+44.84
Open forest	105	156.77	+51.77
Degraded forest	127.87	51.27	-76.60
Land with scrub	61.24	135.33	+74.09
Land without scrub	124.23	73.37	-50.86
Water bodies	4	4.6	0.60
Barren rocky area	52	43	-9.00
Total	**789.66**	**789.66**	

Drought measures through Micro Watershed – 1997

Drought measures through Micro Wastershed Boundaries –2006

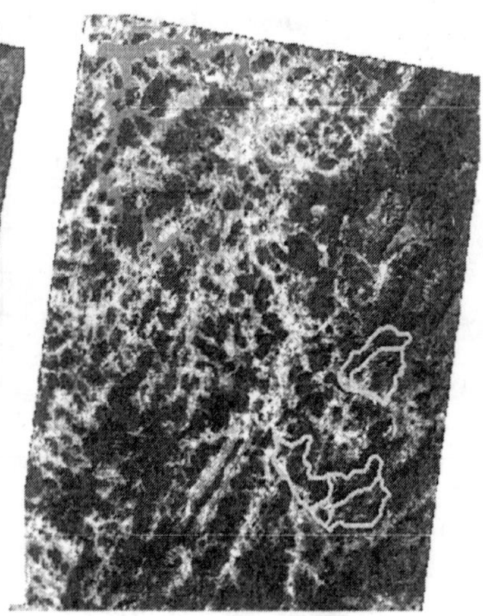

Change Detection by Satellite Imagery

1997 2006

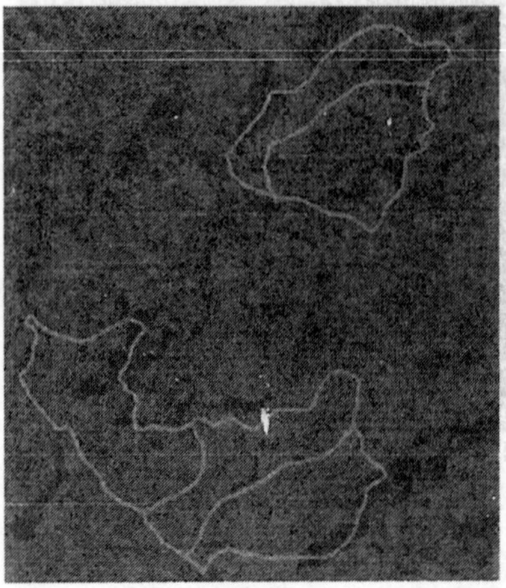

Drought Impact through Watershed Measures

Land Use Pattern	*Area in Sq.m 1997*	*Area in Sq.m 2006*	*Change in Sq.m*
BARREN	90260	125629	35369
CROP	533834	349903	-183931
DENCE FOREST	76462	2985883	2909421
FALLOW	1473503	3341043	1867540
OPEN FOREST	3222136	587515	-2634621
SCRUB	1243718	501200	-742518
SALT EFFECTED	1403705	152445	-1251260
Total	8043618	8043618	

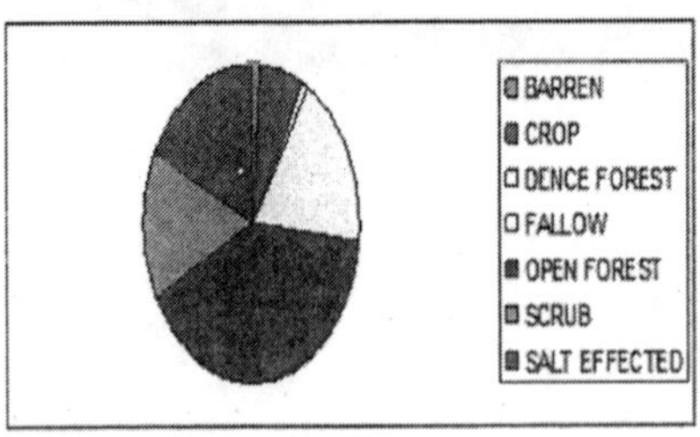

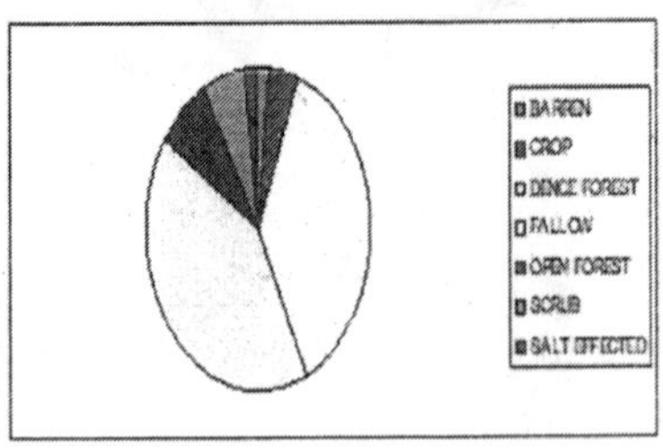

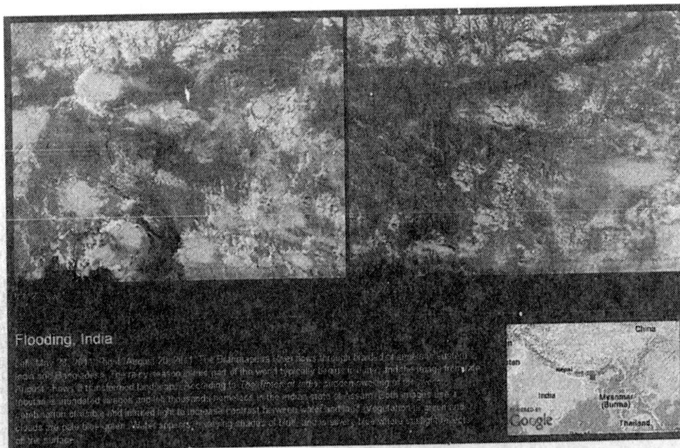

Bhuj and its Environs as Viewed by Indian Remote Sensing Satellite (IRS)

PRE-EARTHQUAKE IMAGE OF 4 JAN, 2001

POST-EARTHQUAKE IMAGE OF 29 JAN, 2001

PARTS OF BHUJ TOWNSHIP BEFORE AND AFTER EARTHQUAKE AS VIEWED BY INDIAN REMOTE SENSING SATELLITE

PRE-EARTHQUAKE PAN IMAGE OF 4 JAN, 2001

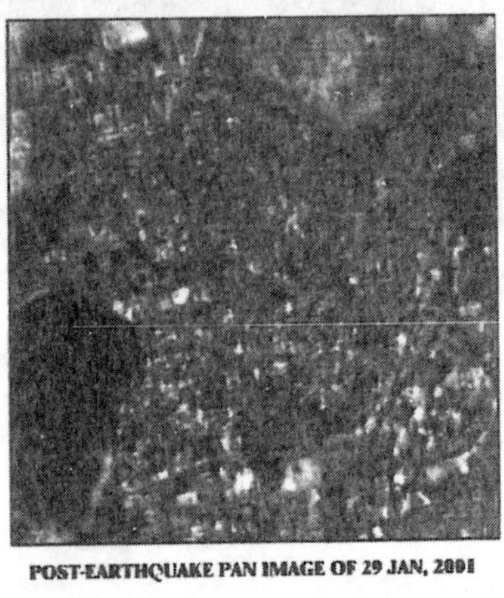

POST-EARTHQUAKE PAN IMAGE OF 29 JAN, 2001

VOLCANIC ERUPTION
IN BARREN ISLAND,
ANDAMAN AND
NICOBAR ISLANDS

CYCLONES
OVER ORISSA
COAST
INSAT IMAGES
SHOWING THE
CYCLONE MOVEMENT
DURING 28 OCT TO
30 OCT, 1999
......AND THE AFTERMATH
• NEARLY 3.75 LAKH Ha. INUNDATED
• ROAD, POWER AND COMMUNICATION
NETWORKS SEVERELY AFFECTED IN 10
COASTAL DISTRICTS

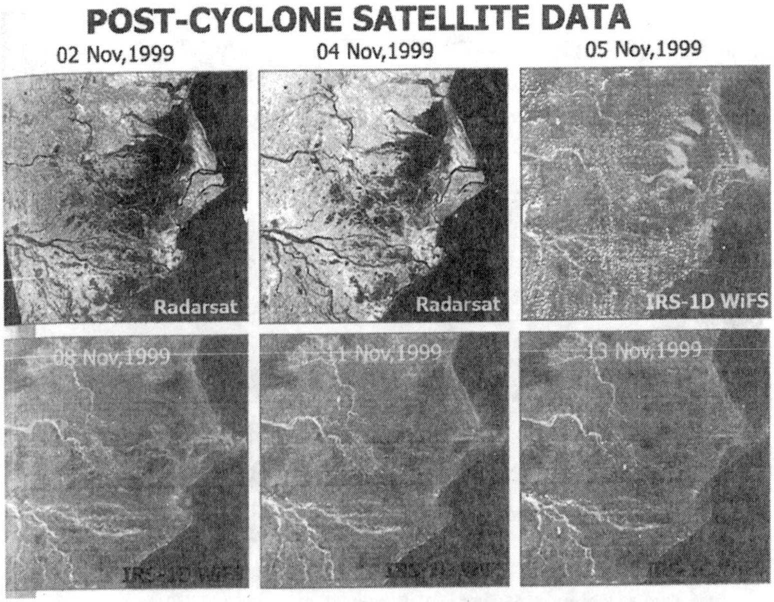
POST-CYCLONE SATELLITE DATA
02 Nov,1999
04 Nov,1999
05 Nov,1999
Radarsat
Radarsat
IRS-1D WiFS
08 Nov,1999
11 Nov,1999
13 Nov,1999

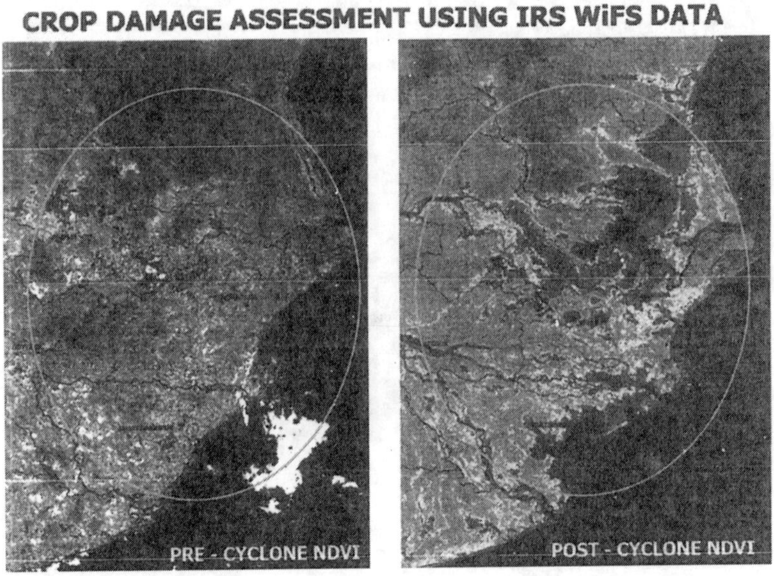
CROP DAMAGE ASSESSMENT USING IRS WiFS DATA
PRE - CYCLONE NDVI
POST - CYCLONE NDVI

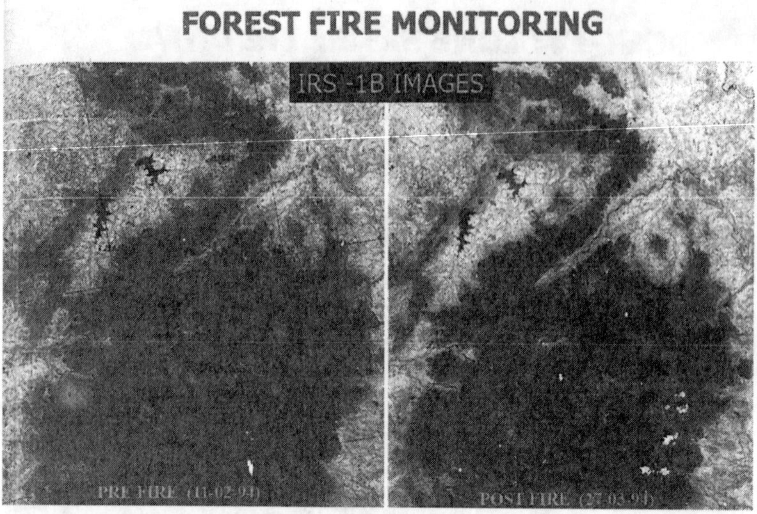

Fig. Kutch Earthquake Disaster Impact.

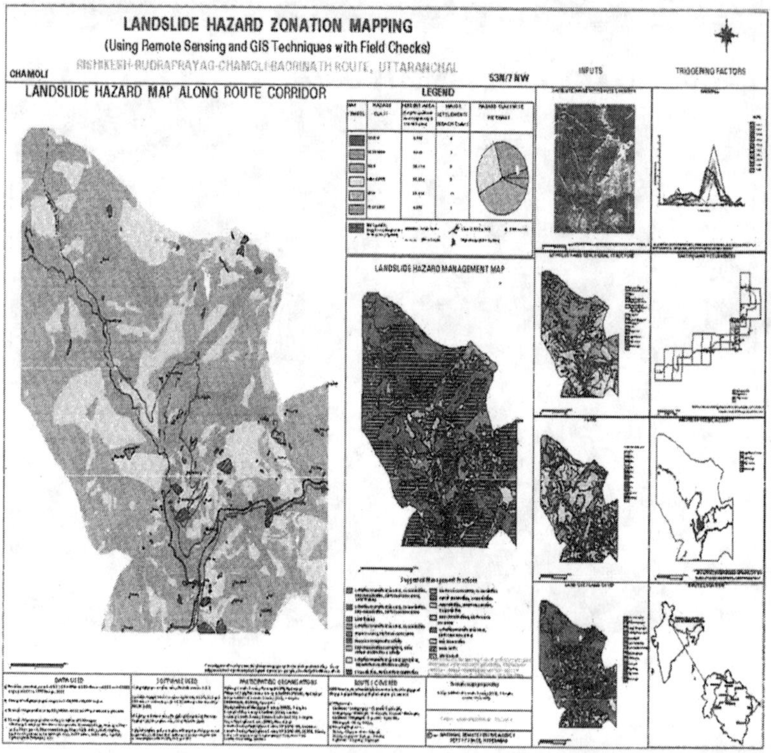

Geomorphological Changes in Greater Rann & Banni Plian Gulf of Kutch. Gujarat

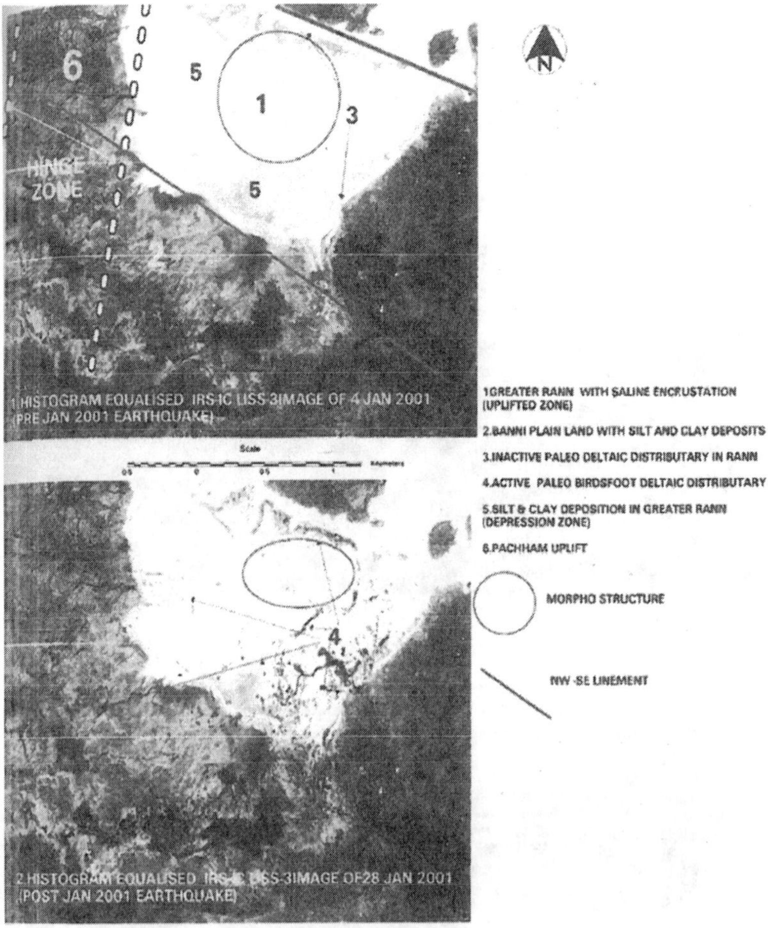

The Geospatial Technology has advantages for natural hazard mitigation and generating decision alternatives for judicious decision making in emergency situations on real time basis. First, the technology allows long-term time-series studies and storage of the information which may prove invaluable in future situations. Secondly, GIS and RS improves information accessibility. Remote sensing platforms can provide large amounts of data quickly and inexpensively, relative to other means of collection, and GIS can bring together vast amounts of information from a wide variety of sources and make the information quickly visible and applicable in emergency.

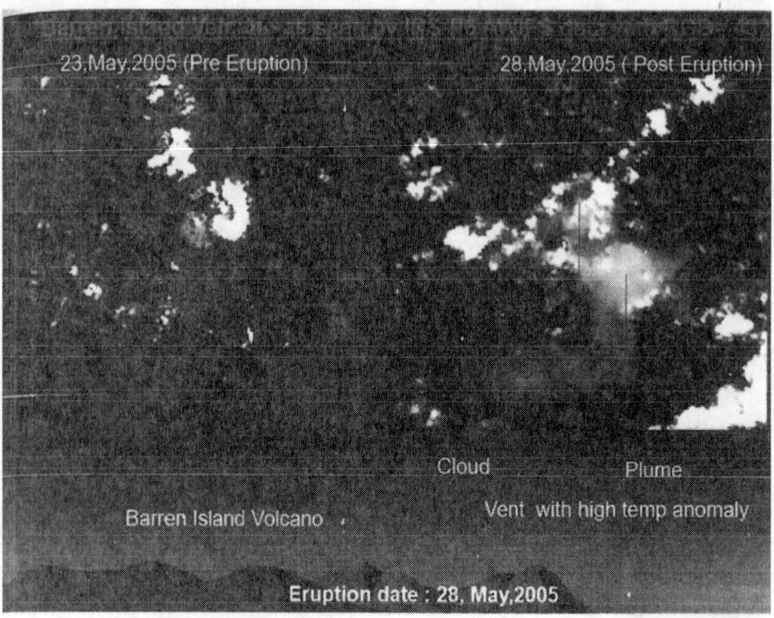

Sharing important knowledge during emergencies

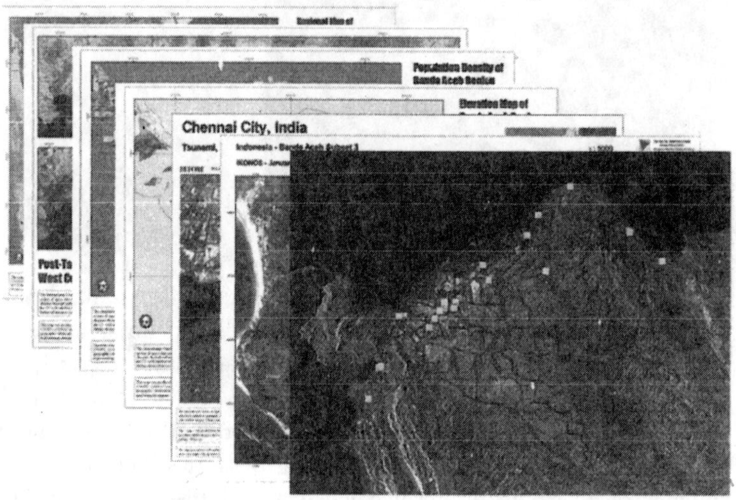

7

Role of Blockchain Technology in Asia - A Relook at China and India in Banking Sector

Dr. CH. Kishor Kumar

Beijing's expected launch of a digital yuan next year is part of a bigger plan to take a global lead in the future of the internet. There is no stage bigger than the Olympics for the athletes and the host country/Modern China announced its arrival 13 years ago when 2008 synchronised drummers wowed the world at the Beijing Summer Olympics opening ceremonies. In February, China is expected to use the Beijing Winter Olympics to unveil a creation of intense international interest; the digital yuan, the first major central bank digital currency, or CBDC.

Consumers are unlikely to notice much difference shopping with e-CNY as the currency is officially KNOWN. It will be worth the same as cash and will activate with a tap, swipe or QR code. But the questions this form of money raises are profound. As governments around the world move to phase out physical cash, what will become of financial privacy? How will state sponsored digital money affect China's economy, its trading relationships and most weighty of all the future of the global financial system now dominated by the United States and the dollar?

The question is "not whether China's CBDC will upend the current, rules of global trade and commerce" said Pauline Loong, director of Hong Kong based research consultancy Asia analytics. The only question is "how far reaching the ramification will be across issues related to who controls access to capital and its movements."

But for all of the digital yuan's consequences, it is a toe peeking out from a giant red curtain. Behind is an ambitious and largely invisible infrastructure programme to rewire the country and its economy with a distributed ledger technology known as blockchain. China has moved deliberately to secure first mover advantage in what it believes is the future of the internet. If the digital yuan is Beijing's tender for the digital frontier, its block chain initiative is its bid to build the railroads.

A New Money

The story of how China came to settle the technological frontier begins with the 2008 financial crisis. Just one month after the Summer Olympics an under regulated US financial sector tripped the world into recession. It was a vulnerability that China decided it was no longer willing to accept. As the crisis was unfolding then President Hu Jintao called upon like minded nations at the G20 summit to Steadily promote the diversification of the international monetary systems. Receiving a muted response, China forged ahead in creating parallel institutions to those dominated by the US In 2010 when Washington's sanctions effectively locked Iran out of the international financial system. China's focus on cross-border currency flows intensified.

By then domestic concerns were spurring creative thinking around monetary policy. One was how to get 400 million "Underbanked" Chinese out of poverty, e-Commerce giant Alibaba introduced a mobile payment system in 2008, taking advantage of the country's high rates of smartphone adoption: By 2015, 800 million Chinese would be using smartphones, according to the Pew Research Center. But such private payment systems left the Bank of China on the sidelines and did little for rising Communist Party leader Xi Jinping's anti-corruption strategy which required closer state monitoring of money.

Then around 2012, regulators began to observe strange patterns in power grids across the country. From Xinjiang to Inner Mongolia, huge amounts of electricity were surging into warehouses packed with powerful computers and colossal servers. The processors were crunching numbers to produce—or— "mine" —a new kind of money called Bi te bi in Mandarin. At their peak in the late 2010's Chinese miners are thought to have produced 95 percent of the world's Bite bi or Bitcoin.

This money had no connection to a bank, or any centralised authority at all. It was entirely digital and uniquely secure. Every transaction was broadcast to every computer within a network for confirmation and recorded permanently in a long series of distributed ledger entries or blocks. Chinese officials grasped the implications of this unregulated activity immediately.

In 2014, its People's Bank of China (PBOC) began studying the possibility of a government version of Bitcoin. With each passing year, the disappearance of paper yuan from the economy made the idea more plausible. By 2019, PwC reported 96 percent of Chinese regularly shopped online.

"Before many governments even knew the basics of Bitcoin. Chinese authorities started to take leadership in the security of the network on the mining side," said Ian Wittkopp, vice president at Beijing based Sino Global Capital. This led to the development of a strong blockchain and crypto eco-system.

By October 2020, the digital yuan was ready for pilot testing to China's masses. All told, 750,000 people chosen by lottery were given 150 million e-CNY ($23 million in US Dollars) to spend at roughly 70,000 brick and mortar businesses plus a slew of online retailers. Six months later, new trials allowed open participation. This marked the first release of the digital yuan into the wild. By June, nursing homes in Chengdu were teaching elderly residents how to use the new money.

Such care and expense are necessary to ensure the Olympics debut is as well rehearsed as those 2008 drummers, according to Peter Cai, who studies China's economy and trade policy at the Lowy Institute in Sydney. "The cost of getting something wrong on this is tremendous" he said. Chinese officials are right to talk about the digital currency as if it's a new frontier. What are the full implications for financial, banking and payment systems. Or the conduct of a monetary policy? I don't think anybody has a firm grip on that. And that includes China".

The Next Internet

During two decades of historic economic growth, China has had a mixed record on high technologies. It has struggled to attain self-sufficiency, never mind dominance in the production of semiconductors and chips. It was ahead of the curve on 5G broadband, but lags behind the West in field of arguably greater strategic value such as artificial intelligence.

When it comes to blockchain, China appears to have taken a lead in a technology of consequence. After President Xi in 2019 promised blockchain would lead the next wave of the digital transformation of China, thousands of companies reportedly initiated blockchain projects related to everything from retail banking to global shipping and supply chains. This profusion of activity continues apace. Said Wittkopp. "It's a field of one. No other country is even close".

These projects are transforming a digital ecosystem that was already among the world's most sophisticated according to a recent McKinsey study China has 850 million internet users and more than a quarter of the world's most successful start-ups. One of them is Hangzhou based Ant Group. The financial services giant has over 50 blockchains based decentralised apps or dApps, in areas such as shipping, insurance claim processing and charitable donations. Internet search firm Baidu, the Google of China has 20 dApps, including one that has handled 35 million pieces of electronic evidence for China's "Internet Court". It's not just tech companies staking territory on the blockchain frontier. A division of the Industrial and Commercial Bank of China has developed dApps for retail and corporate use. Insurance giant Ping An uses them to finance public works projects. A dApp used by the China Construction Bank has helped local banks facilitate $134 billion in loans.

"Blockchain will make tech and our society work better", said Yifan He, blockchain evangelist and CEO of engineering firm Red Date Technology. "It can make all the IT systems in the world communicate like they are in one room". He predicts in 10 years all transactions that require more than two parties will be blockchain based.

The state of blockchain today is like the internet of 1993. He said Back then, most companies couldn't afford the entry costs of the nascent internet (which began as a public infrastructure project overseen by the Pentagon).

In April 2020, China formalised its bet on blockchain by creating the Blockchain based Service Network or BSN, managed by Red Date. It is an infrastructure platform that allows private entities, especially small and medium sized businesses to overcome the two biggest barriers to entry — interoperability and prohibitive costs.

"We built everything for you already: you just connect to it and work on your smart contract said He, who says the development cost of a simple dApp within the BSN could be as little as 1 percent of commercial blockchain.

By its first anniversary in April 2021 the BSN had attracted 20,000 users and more than 2,500 projects across 120 "nodes" throughout China plus Johannesburg, Northern California, Pairs, Sao Paulo, Singapore, Sydney and Tokyo. S- Labs A Beijing startup has used it to develop applications that have helped over 5,000 SME's find more than 500 million yuan loans during the pandemic. S labs CRO Li Ming said the BSN is easy to use because it meets Chinese government standards and helps them find customers. "The biggest convenience of BSN is its brand effect."

If He has his way, today's youth will be the first blockchain native generation. This fluency is already being developed in high schools where the BSN is exploring how to teach students including by holding programming contests with cash prizes. Blockchain should be a basic skill said He. The idea is to help more people become comfortable using the technology. In June, Red Date closed on $ 30 million in Series A funding that was notable for its global reach. Major investors from Saudi Arabia, Switzerland and Thailand participated.

BENEFITS OF BLOCK CHAIN

India could take a leaf out of Europe's book instead a calling for a blanket ban on crypto currencies:

> The Banning of Crypto currency and Regulation of Official Digital Currency Bill, 2009 has proposed stringent penalties, including 10 years of imprisonment, for holding, selling or dealing in crypto currencies such as Bitcoin. Given the high chances of crypto currencies being misused in money laundering, various government bodies such as IT, CBDT, and the customs departments have endorsed this endeavour.

While it is important to put mechanisms in place to deter bad actors, a blanket ban on all forms of cryptocurrency transactions will result in India missing out on what may become one of the biggest technology revolutions since the Internet.

CONCLUSION

From the present paper, the following conclusion is drawn:

> While an oversimplification, blockchain can be described as a way for people to share extra space and computational power in their computers to create a global supercomputer that is accessible for everyone. Every network helps validate and record transactions. People who connect their computers to a network are known as validators and receive transaction fees in the form of tokens.

Many technologists believe that the blockchain industry is poised for an explosion similar to what happened to the smartphone industry. None of us could have imagined services such as Google Maps or Uber which came to fruition due to the new mobile platform. Startups have already built thousands of apps on blockchain platforms like Ethereum. However, these apps aren't easily available to non-tech savvy consumers through an app store, and hence their usage remains low. They also face technical problems including suitability and slowing down of the network when many people use these apps simultaneously. New companies such as Algorand and Casper Labs are investing millions in research and development and are close to solving these issues.

Blockchain technology has the potential to create new industries and transform existing ones in ways we cannot imagine. For instance, it has the capacity to facilitate nano-payments proportionate to an individual's contribution and value creation in the Internet, making it an ideal wealth redistribution tool for our digital age.

Even big technology companies have started to take blockchain applications seriously. Facebook for instance, recently announced its own cryptocurrency to facilitate payments globally with minimal fees and no dependency on a central bank. Venture capitalists invested $2.4 billion in blockchain and cryptocurrency start-ups in 2018. So far, 2019 is poised to exceed this benchmark.

None of the above is possible without the underlying tokens that facilitate transactions in a blockchain network. A law to ban holding or transacting in cryptocurrency would not only prevent Indians from reaping economic benefits by participating in blockchain networks as validators and earning transaction fees, but also stifle any innovation related to this disruptive emerging technology.

SUGGESTIONS

The following suggestions are offered to strengthen the Blockchain applications in Pharma and Biotech Start ups:

I. Blockchain technology is not just for techies

(a) Blockchain technology has gone far beyond its association with crypto currency and is finding relevance in a variety of fields including banking, healthcare and logistics.

(b) Blockchain is particularly useful when cross organisationsal data is involved. The technology makes it near impossible to modify the data, and that enables trust within the network of organisations involved.

(c) In India, over 14 states including Karnataka, Andhra Pradesh and Telangana, are running blockchain pilots and projects, and various organisations that have traditionally been competitors are coalescing into industry consortiums to leverage the technology.

(d) Blockchain in India is still in its initial stages, says Manish Jain, partner digitasl and fintech-KPMG India. "We could see hiring happening more at the senior architect level. Mass hiring is still some time away". He says.

(e) Digital lending company Cred Righf's co-founder Neeraj Bansal says "the startup has been looking for Ethereum (blockchain based platform) developers who can work with other blockchain based third party products. The demand for blockchain developers and project managers is very high, but availability of talent that can guide starts ups is very limited" he says.

II. Who should upskill

(a) Blockchain technology is relevant for coders who could look to build blockchain products. It is also relevant for tech managers/ project managers/tech architects looking at product development and architecting solutions.

(b) It is relevant for banking and finance, legal and other professionals who are evaluating use cases for blockchain application.

(c) Blockchain coders need to have coding experience, preferably in Java and a good sense of mathematics. It's also essential to have knowledge of both the foundational development aspects of Ethereum, Hyper ledger Fabric and Composer and functional aspects (hands on projects and case studies).

(d) Mayank Kumar, co-founder of edtech platforms up Grad, says while the majority of the learners who enrol for the blockchain programme is from tech backgrounds, 30% are finance professionals and 10% are healthcare professionals "We have seen over 120% quarterly rise in enrolments for our programme launched in September 2018," he says.

III. Job roles

(a) Development enthusiasts : Professionals with 2-5 years of experience who aim to understand, develop and deploy the network from scratch. They are well versed in development platforms like Hyper ledger and Ethereum.

(b) Tech architects: Professionals with 7-10 years of experience in the IT industry, with a strong affinity towards development and implementation of technology.

(c) Blockchain managers: Professionals who have spent over 10 years in the IT industry and who can understand the business applications of the technology and are domain experts.

IV. The future of Cloud computing in India

(a) Over 1 million cloud jobs will be created in India by 2022.

(b) Cloud hiring based on experience doesn't help, changes are too rapid".

(c) The second edition of Times Techies on Wednesday spoke about how working professionals and students can go about becoming cloud computing experts, an acute demand-supply gap in cloud skills.

Companies of all hues and sizes are moving their data and also building their services on the cloud for the speed, flexibility and scalability it provides. Research by edtech platform Great Learning says more than 1.7 million cloud jobs worldwide are vacant. Their research also says that over a million cloud computing jobs will be created in India by 2022.

Sridhar Pinnapureddy, founder and CEO of Cloud4C opines that a progider of managed services on the cloud, said India's cloud spent is about 1.6% of the country's GDP for 2018 while the global average stands at around 3% "It is estimated that we may require around a million and a half cloud certified professionals by 2025".

Unlike IT skill shortages in the past, solving this skills gap is challenging as cloud computing brings a new set of skills which weren't needed in the past. Which is why ed-tech platforms are seeing a boom in the numbers enrolling in their courses. "We are witnessing significant growth in our Microsoft Azure and Amazon Web Services (cloud) programmes' said Anand Narayanan, chief product officer at edtech platform Simplifiers.

Sunil Jose, country leader India for Salesforce, one of the companies that prioneered delivery of software via the cloud, said cloud application services (or software as a service-SaaS) is on pace to be the fastest growing market segment in India in 2019, and the growth of SaaS spending on customer relationship management (CRM).

Chaitanya Peddi, co-founder of Darwinbox, a cloud based human capital management (HCM) platform, said the cloud computing space is constantly evolving and hiring decisions driven by past experience do not have global merit any more.

Mr. Chaitanya Peddi opines that: "Even a senior resource who has worked on PHP or Java in the past might have to start afresh with angular or node on their next assignment. The challenge in hiring is to assess the learnability of individuals."

Peddi also feels that another major techy hiring challenge in the SaaS space is to find talent that is oriented towards building products. "We have talent aplenty which is oriented towards problems solving for services that are tailored to one particular client's use case as opposed to building a solution architecture that suits the requirements of 1,000 companies. They should also be able to build it with the flexibility to handle future possibilities. He said:

Deepak Visweswaraiah, MD at NET App India, feels that the hybrid cloud (combination of public and private clouds) is the future of data. "And with data becoming the lifeblood of organisations, cloud computing is a highly lucrative skillset to acquire. This field requires young engineers to focus on building their tech muscle in domains such as Agile Development. Dev Ops and Containers.

References

1. Banking Frontiers—Vol. 18/No.7, November, 2019, p. 44.
2. Outlook Business-September 13, 2019, p. 60.
3. Forbes India-August 17, 2018.
4. Banking Frontiers—Vol. 16/No. 10, February 18, p. 48.
5. Chartered Secretary—Vol. 47/No.16/p. 1-140, June, 2017.
6. Chartered Secretary—Vol. 49/No.02/p. 1-132, February, 2019-12-06.
7. The Management Accountant—Vol. 51/No. 9 p. 124, September, 2016.
8. The Management Accountant—Vol. 51/No. 10/p. 124, October, 2016.
9. The Hindu Publications, Hyderabad.
10. The Times of India Publications, 2018 and 2019.

8

Role of Board of Directors in Policy Formulation and Decision Making

Ms. M. Sangeetha

A board of directors (B of D) is an elected group of individuals that represent shareholders. The board is a governing body that typically meets at regular intervals to set policies for corporate management and oversight. Every public company must have a board of directors. Some private and nonprofit organisations also have a board of directors.

By specific statute in most states, board approval is required for the following actions: (i) Amendments to the corporation's bylaws, (ii) Issuance of shares by the corporation, (iii) Declaration of dividends or repurchase of the corporation's shares, (iv) Recommendations to the shareholders of plans to amend the articles of incorporation, dissolve the corporation or merge, consolidate or sell substantially all the assets of the corporation.

Further duties include: (i) Ensuring legal and ethical conduct, (ii) Selecting, evaluating, compensating and where necessary replacing the CEO and other senior executives, (iii) Approving corporate strategy, (iv) Providing general oversight of the business, (v) Evaluating board processes and performance, including selecting and compensating directors, (vi) CEO succession planning, (vii) Evaluating major investments. (viii) Advising management on significant issues facing the corporation, (ix) Statutory v/s Advisory Boards, (x) Statutory: Working for the company, (xi) Fiduciary responsibility, (xii) Responsibility for management succession, (xiii) Evaluate performance of CEO's and key executives, (xiv) Hire and fire CEO, (xv) Review and approve major corporate objectives, policies, budgets and strategies.

Advisory: (i) Working for the Owners/CEO, (ii) Good way for wary CEO's to test drive a board, (iii) Don't get ensnared in minutes of audits, compliance and regulatory matters and (iv) Minimal liability.

THE STRATEGIC BOARD CONTINUUM

So, here is a board benchmark, the Strategic Board Continuum to help you determine your board's value. No list is magic. Scoring a 10 on the Strategic Board Continuum is not synonymous with good governance.

Of course, what drives the value of any board is the quality of the directors and their willingness and ability to assume the tremendous obligations inherent in board membership. No set of systems and no checklist can ever ensure good governance. Only good people can. The magic comes when outstanding directors combine with best practice. Here is a list of the ten most critical mistakes:

1. Failure to recruit strategically.
2. Too many insiders.
3. Too many paid consultants.
4. Too much family.
5. Too many cronies.
6. Getting the money wrong.
7. Fear of diversity.
8. Information block.
9. Passive directors.
10. Failed leadership.

These ten mistakes are the symptoms of a toxic captive board. If your board exhibits these weaknesses, look to see where else there is weakness in your company. How was the board recruited? How is the board used? What is the attitude of management toward corporate governance? Why are they indifferent to one of the most powerful tools available to management today? These ten mistakes are the indicators of a failed board and perhaps a failing company.

WHO NEEDS A BOARD?

Small and private companies are best positioned to leverage a strategic board, because they lack the resources, the resilience, and the scope of the Fortune 500s and because of their fragility. Strategic small company boards tend to be more helpful and action oriented, more hands on, more mentoring, more informal and more likely to help build strategic relationships than the more formal Fortune 500 boards.

ADVANTAGES OF A STRATEGIC BOARD

1. Allows a company to gain valuable expertise available in no other way.
2. Enables strategic relationships and provides access.
3. Facilitates financing.
4. Serves as a think tank for big issues and strategic thinking.
5. Establishes accountability.
6. Supports and bolsters management.
7. Relieves isolation.
8. Attracts the best employees.
9. Facilitates cross-fertilisation and exposure to new ideas.
10. Balances stockholder interests.
11. Helps to avoid mistakes.
12. Proactively manages change.
13. Provides extraordinary value for minimal expense.

WHAT IS STOPPING CEO's?

If boards are a strategic force in a company's success, why doesn't every company take advantage of this tool? Here are the key reasons:

1. Perceived threat to independence. 2. Focus on tactics. 3. Makes extra work 4. Resistance to change. 5. Ego. 6. Insecurity.

WHAT CHANGES THE CEO's MIND?

What triggers the decision to move to a strategic board? Change. Competitive pressure. Internet time that compresses one year into ninety days or less/ The speed of change where you compete against yourself instead of your peers. Globalism. And often crises Business plan projections are unmet. A new round of funding is needed. A key member of management is leaving. The management team is failing. Or a new high financed competitor surfaces. The company is going public. Or is on the block. At some point, you realise you can learn faster and easier through others. If you are smart, you learn this early.

When a company is healthy, management and directors are inclined to think they have all kinds of time to make decisions. As a company slips, the next stages accelerate towards the crisis stage where only 13 percent of companies emerge whole. By this time, Its almost always too late for a board to save the company. Yet, it is often at this time. It is usually a turnaround situation, with a totally separate set of imperative.

Business is blocking and tackling observes Micheal Burke, people get up early to produce at the lowest possible price. I don't know anybody selling products for more money than either years ago and most are selling their products for substantially less. Adds Burke who sits on nine boards in the Cincinnati area. 'Its tough stuff. If someone is not keeping an eye on the horizon, it's dangerous. You need the guy with instant replay who can see your play in conjunction with others. You need someone to say. I've tried to play on third down before. And it doesn't work.

Lots of entrepreneurs who are potential board members are frustrated coaches. That's why they are so valuable. Bob Hartman, CEO of Universal Technical Institute, decided to form a board after the founder retired and left a void of critical thinking. We were stagnating, treading water at a time when about 40 percent of his industry had gone out of business/The board brings critical thinking, different perspectives on options, perspective, development of the management staff and the opportunity to see how we ought to be thinking and what we should be thinking about. We think more globally. It's brought great growth to our organisation.

The dramatic untold stories are the hundreds of companies public and private that have avoided crises, because of the advice and counsel of strategic boards of directors. As Ken Derr", CEO of Chevron, says there's nothing more important to a company's fortunes than a strong board. Ultimately if we don't, govern ourselves, the government will do it for us. So, who needs a board anyway? You do.

NINE STEPS TO STRATEGIC RECRUITING

Recruiting can be the responsibility of the full board, the board governance committee, or, if it is a new board, a collaboration of management with perhaps an objective outsider. In all cases, the process should include management's thinking. There are nine steps involved in strategic recruiting.

1. Create a board charter.
2. Create a board matrix.
3. Define the board structure.
4. Develop a measurable profile for each director slot.
5. Know and specify why directors will want to serve.

6. Recruit proactively to each profile.
7. Interview and reference potential directors in the context of your board.
8. Provide comprehensive orientation.
9. Recruit in a continuum.

The following intangibles determine just how effective is your board will be :

- **Integrity:** Strength of character. Will the new director make decisions for the right reasons? Or will he be co-opted by false allegations or potential gain?
- **Business sense:** Does the potential board member bring enough business acumen to approach problems from a broad knowledge and experiential base.
- **Thinking strategically:** How does she approach problem solving? Does she leap to judgment and then retract or modify her option? Does she wait to see what everyone else says? Is there any original thinking? Does she substantiate her opinions? And is she indeed willing to change her opinion?
- **Good nature:** is the director easy when she is on the offside of a debate. Instead of taking it personally? Do others seek her company?
- **Focus:** Does he get quickly to the essence of an issue, instead of straying off on tangents?
- **Sound judgment:** Common sense. Is he realistic and logical?
- **Scope:** Does he contribute in the context of the whole. Rather than the parts? And, does she have the breadth of perspective and experience to add value at that level.
- **Curiosity:** Does she have the courage to question, to speak up, to advocate for the shareholders when it is easier not to do so. As Steve McConnell, Principal of Solano Ventures, says, "you need people with a spine. A lot of people want to be polite and diplomatic on board. Today collegiality is not enough. You have to say what you feel when someone crosses the line".
- **Life perspective:** Humility. Sense of self. In today's strategic boardroom, there is no time for egotistical displays and consuming self-aggrandizement.
- **Ability to evaluate people:** When you realise that the single most important responsibility of a director is to ensure that the best

people are managing in the interests of the shareholders, the urgency of this criterion becomes obvious. Yet this aptitude is often underrated and diminished. So instead of focusing on this all important ability, CEO's tend to focus on skill sets and recruit directors because of their ability to do things.

- **Commitment to the CEO and the company:** Does the director just want to be on a board? Or does she want to make a contribution to the company and the shareholders? Does she understand the way to do that is to ensure that the CEO has all the support and resources possible?
- **Being not too hungry:** Whether it is hunger to state the ego, to fill the time, or to earn the money.

INTERVIEW AND REFERENCE POTENTIAL BOARD MEMBERS

Even seasoned directors should be interviewed in the context of your board. They need to understand your charter and what is expected of them. How will directors be measured? What do you hope to gain from their membership? Is yours a captive board beholden to the CEO or a strategic board in partnership with management- or somewhere in between? Where is your board on the strategic board continuum? Who else will they serve on the board with and how will they complement the mix and the culture?

Visit the candidates on their home turf- at their business and their home as well. Meet their families. It's a unique opportunity to see their culture and their leadership skills in action, to see whom they surround themselves with and where their priorities lie. Questions to ask prospective board members:

- Why do you want to serve?
- What is your opinion of our company?
- How will you contribute? Examples
- What are your specific areas of expertise? How will those add value to the board?
- How many other boards do you sit on? For profit and not for profit. What role do you play on those boards?
- What is your view of the role of a board and corporate governance?
- Do boards add value? How?
- What are the downsides?
- How do you use your board?

- What is your most rewarding experience on a board?
- How specifically have you added value? Examples
- What is your most difficult experience as a director.
- Are you willing to commit to the level of participation and support that we need?
- What committees would you like to sit on? Why?
- Do you prefer to be compensated in stock or cash?
- Are your goals and values compatible with those of our organisation? Describe.
- What are your concerns?

Discuss the criteria in the profile and ask directors to describe their strengths and weaknesses in that context. Ask experiential questions based on challenges and issues before your board. What conclusions do they draw from your financial statements? How would they approach some of your key issues? You will learn a lot about the potential director and a lot about your company. Invite prospective directors to your facility. Are they truly interested in your company? In your business? What kind of questions do they ask? How insightful are they ? Have they done their homework?

Referencing: Often, referencing reveals important nuances of personality. If you bring on a bureaucrat who isn't used to the decision making process. Whoever tends to drone on, it can quickly destroy the process. So can a monopolize or a chronic naysayer or the director who feels he has to say something about every subject that comes before the board. Or the director who micromanages and eats up the board's time, by going on about the layout of the brochure, the colour of the packaging, the price of the software, or his ski vacation. One director we interviewed boasted about batting 500 in removing CEO's from the management team of the boards he sat on not a quality that endeared him to the CEO recruiting him.

On the other hand referencing can confirm strengths and address seeming weaknesses. A quiet person may be seen to have tremendous depth. An understated prospect may prove to have invaluable access. It is a time saver. A face saver. And a courtesy to your existing board to do initial referencing before meeting a board prospect face to face. If an issue is raised, you can then address. It in your personal conversation. If the references are negative you can simply forgo any further discussion. Remember that every director you recruit is a reason for others to stay or to stay away.

USING OBJECTIVE RECRUITERS

Consider using an objective outsider to recruit for you. As David Me Laughlin observes, there is definitely a shift from cronyism and clubishness to a search process for selection. More thought is now being given to background and balance. Harvey MacKay says, you should always go to two or three shops. When looking for advice you should always have more than one opinion.

The advantages of outside recruiting are that it:

- Allows you to proactively recruit to your strategic plan to your critical issues.
- Gives you access to the broadest spectrum of targeted best candidates.
- Allows you to move beyond your own circle of influence.
- Gives you access to a higher level of individuality than through informal networks.

Provides a choice among highly qualified candidates, who become multipliers for you, whether or not they come on board.

- Validates the board to potential directors.
- Validates the board to your constituencies.
- Provides objective referencing and interviewing.
- Provides confidentiality and discretion.
- Does not waste the time of the CEO and directors on less qualified candidates.
- Maintains the goodwill of candidates and constituencies.

THE DIRECTOR'S CHECKLIST

The decision to join a board is as critical for the director as for the board making the offer. Perhaps more so. At stake are your resources and your reputation. You are going to pledge your commitment, your loyalty, access to your network, your time and your energy. What are the questions to ask?

- Where is the board on the strategic continuum? If it is more captive than strategic, do you care? Will it change?
- Why were you asked? How are you expected to contribute?
- Where do you fit on their needs matrix? Are you being pursued for your rolodex or your expertise?
- Is it a company whose business interest you? About which you know something? Can you learn to understand it well enough to accept the liability that goes with serving on the boards?

- Is it a valued board with appropriate independent authority?
- Is there a majority of independent directors?
- Is there a board charter? Are there committee charters?
- Do the independent directors ever meet alone?
- Who determines board procedures?
- Is the board actively involved in key management succession? Is the company clear in its mission? There must be that passion to serve its constituencies and a clarity of purpose. Why are they in business? How will the company move forward?
- Where will the company be in ten years? What is the exit strategy?
- What are the toughest issues facing the board now? Are there any unresolved lawsuits/Any major events or transactions?
- Ask yourself why you want to serve? Is it for the prestige? The camaraderie? The networking ? The money? The opportunity to make a difference? Does this meet with the board's expectations?
- Who else is on the board? Why are the directors there? As Betsy Sanders says "It is rewarding when they are there for their own personal integrity. They have reasons beyond prestige and pay/ They are actively involved and they lay their gifts on the table".
- What is the board selection process? Is the process healthy?
- Does anyone other than the CEO/founder have meaningful input? What does the process tell you about the board? Does the CEO quietly invite you onto the board? Does that. In itself, testifies to the respect the CEO has for the board.
- What kind of time commitment is involved?
- What kind of D & O insurance and indemnification is provided?
- How are directors compensated? If it's at least half stock that's a good sign.

The money is not enough to compensate you for the responsibility you assume or for that one idea or introduction that catapults the company to success.

INDEPENDENCE

- Do you own, or are you an officer, director or employee of any enterprise that competes with this company? Information sharing is the issue.
- Have you or your immediate family had any interest in a transaction or proposed transaction with this company?
- Is the company indebted to you for any advance of money?

- Have you or your immediate family been indebted to the company?
- Do officers or directors of this company serve on the board of any other companies you own, that employ you or of which you are an officer or director? In other words, would there be any interlocking directorships?
- What percentage of your gross income will consist of the fees that you receive as director for this company?
- Are you related to any member of the board of directors or to any officer of the company?
- In which charities are you involved? Are you employed by an organisation that receives benefits from the company?
- Do you have any other relationship with the company that could be construed to influence your ability to exercise your independent judgment as a director?

Decision making by BOARD

The most noteworthy in our interviews is the overall trust of the directors' thoughts on what makes for effective boards. In their view, effectiveness has little to do with regulators, laws, recent shareholders initiatives to change board elections, and so on, and everything to do with what transpires within individual boards. The determinants that shape boards' behaviour, in the eyes of our interviewees, are illustrated below. What really matters, they told us in a variety of ways, is for each board to achieve clarity about its role - that is, about the extent and nature of its involvement strategy, management succession, risk oversight, and compliance.

This conception of board activities has several important implications. If, as our interviewees insisted, EA boards effectiveness is directly attri-butable to its activities, it follows that boats have responsibility to define their own role with precision and to decide how to perform it in the light of nature of the firm, its management, its industry, and its particular challenges. To gain this understanding, boards will have to invest extended time in hard-headed discussions of both, leading to concrete and actionable conclusions.

The three interrelated issues:

I. **Board role:** 1. Level of involvement 2. Time commitment Activities: (i) Strategy, (ii) management, (iii) development or succession, (iv) risk management and (v) compliance.

II. **Boards and standing of the company:** (i) From management (ii) from outside sources and (iii) from prior experience.

III. Board management relationship: (i) Balance between challenge and support and (ii) Open and candid two way communication.

A Framework for strategic engagement

Directors are confronted with these numerous barriers. We often join a company's board because they would like to contribute to the strategic direction of the company. What is the best way to go about doing this? An easy recommendation would be to urge directors to spend more time on board work. However, given that most board members have already significantly increased their time commitment, this is not practical, unless we make board membership a near - full - time job.

Another seemingly obvious alternative is to recommend that all board members should have a DIP background and experience in the industry. This too is impractical for several obvious reasons. First, current independence requirements make it very difficult to identify potential board members within the industry who do not run a foul of potential conflicts. Second, even if one could create a board full of industry experts, it is not clear that this is necessarily a good idea. Today, boundaries are blurring across the industries, and globalisation and new technologies are giving rise to dramatically new business models. It consists of some industry experts but also some industry outsiders with horizontal thinking capabilities are more likely to spot and respond effectively to potential disruptive changes on the horizon. Third, increased compliance requirements on audit and compensation committees are making it necessary to recruit technical specialists with relevant expertise, whether or not they have relevant industry experience. So, realistically, altering board composition, while potentially helpful, is unlikely to be a panacea for increased strategic engagement.

A practical and sustainable approach to enhanced strategic management will focus on increasing the written on time already spent by board members, rather than asking them to spend more time on their board work. It also should facilitate engagement by board members who do not necessarily have a background in the company's industry, not just those with industry expertise. Finally, the approach should integrate strategic engagement with the general board work. Based on this criteria the following is the framework.

Step 1. Understanding strategy: 4 questions but every board should I ask

One of the most important reasons many board members feel that it is challenging to fully understand their company's strategy is because strategy presentations to boards consist of endless powerpoint presentations with the lot of jargon and unnecessary complexity. Simple prescription to address this is asking the management to provide short answers in a plain language to the following for three questions. 1 dancer is known to these questions at an intuitive level, as a board member we can be confident that we understand the essence of our company's strategy.

1. **What does the customer that we are targeting and what is our proposed solution?**

   The customer, not the company, is the right starting point for strategic thinking. Without satisfying significant customer needs, no company can hope to be in business for a long time. What should have a clear sense of unmet customer needs that their company is seeking to target and satisfy. The more clearly articulated the customer segment and its need is, the easier it is to understand and assess the nature of business opportunity the company is pursuing, the potential for growth and profitability, the capability is the company must have to address the customer need, and the nature of the competition it is likely to face in the marketplace. Strategic failures of an acca when companies try to be all things to all customers and, in the process, fail to solve any particular customer segment's need optimally. Silence also often occurs when a company's target customer needs that they assume exist, our solutions that there's your address the customer needs, but customers either do not feel the need of the company's offer does not address their real need.

2. **Vah rava competitions and how do we win against them?**

   In a free market economy, any meaningful customer need is unlikely to be targeted by just one company. Customers often have several offerings from which to choose, sweet is important for both to have a clear sense of the competitive landscape in which the company operates. Who are the relevant competitors? How are the competitors solving the customer's problems? What is the fundamental basis on which we expect to differentiate our offering from competitors' offerings -features, service, our brand image? 2 customers we value our differentiation? If customers cannot differentiate between our offering and those of competitors, our if customers do not value our difference, then the only basis on which we can compete and win in the market will be based on price—another word, we become a commodity, and everyone knows how challenging it is to make money in the commodity world.

3. **What do we need to do to make our strategy profitable?**

   Sound customer value proposition is necessary. But not sufficient, to make a strategy profitable. There are many examples of companies that create a lot of value for their customers but struggle to make money. A company's profitability is simply a function of the price it can charge and the cost it has to Inka to deliver value to its customers, price is a function of how unique and valuable the product or service is to the customer. Costs are influenced by necessary expenditures a company needs to Inka to create the capabilities and processes to deliver its unique value proposition. Whereas price is influenced by competition and customer's willingness to pay, costs are influenced by the nature of the company's relationship with its suppliers and how complex its value chain has to be to deliver its value proposition. Another factor that often influences a company's value to the customers, and hence its profitability, is its relationship with any companies in its ecosystem that might provide products and services to its customers that complement its value proposition.

   Whether or not a strategy leads to profitability, at least in the theory, is therefore a function of several factors. Some of these factors are determined by our company's business ecosystem—its relationship with its customers, competitors, key suppliers, and complementers—and some of these factors are determined by the key organisational and technical capabilities a company needs to invest in to achieve its differentiation. Board members need to have a clear sense of these key strategic factors to assume themselves that their company's strategy is likely to be a profitable strategy.

4. **What is the game plan for sustaining our competitive advantage for strategic renewal?**

   If our company has a winning strategy today, this does not guarantee that this strategy will be a winner tomorrow. One of the greatest business risks facing a company is that, as the world changes around it, it does not remain vigilant and renew itself to retain its competitive edge. Threats to a company's competitive position emerged from many different sources. Customer tastes and needs change over time. Competitors will figure out a way to imitate what you do uniquely and to reduce or eliminate your differentiation, new business models using innovative new technologies provide compelling alternative solutions to our customers. Globalisation brings in a host of new competitors that provide good enough solutions to your customers at a significantly lower price. Many great companies of yesterday are no longer around today as a result of their inability to foresee or to respond to these types of changes. Therefore, boards must have a continual discussion about potential strategic threats and how the company's strategy will adjust to changes in the marketplace.

Boards interested in being strategic alien gauged should ask their CEO and top management to provide simple and short answers to these questions. It is the boards job to ask these questions, the company's CEO and management team have the responsibility for proposing the answers.

Step 2. Monitoring strategy execution

Boards do plenty of performance monitoring, so how exactly is it different from monitoring strategy? To understand the difference consider the following figure. Per strategy to lead to decide financial outcomes, a company needs to continuously monitor whether or not it is continuing to invest in and nurture the key capabilities and processes; whether or not these capabilities and processes are being applied to deliver the proposition that was promised to the customers; and whether or not the next financial consequences of both these activities result in sufficient profitability over the long-term to meet or exceed investor expectations.

From strategy to profits——strategy——capabilities and processes——customer value——financial results

All the boards mainly discuss their strategy in their annual board retreats, the quarterly board meetings focus mostly on short term financial results as a result, words often fail to monitor its intermediate steps.... capability creation and delivering the customer proposition—on a routine basis. This failure can have serious consequences. Boards men make resource allocation decisions— including major acquisitions— without a deep connection to the overall strategy; it put pressure on management to deliver short-term financial results, rather than focus on long-term strategic success; and they may not ensure that the company's financial performance is communicated to investors in the contexts of the company's strategy, leading investors to focus on short term results.

One way to make sure that company's board integrates strategy into its monitoring function is to (1) use the annual board retreat to set the year's strategic agenda, (2) use about strategic information system to get regular information on the progress on this agenda and (3) design a quarterly meeting agenda to monitor and discuss it.

1. Use the annual board retreat to set the company's strategic agenda: annual board retreat can be a powerful mechanism through which a board can agree with management on the year's strategic agenda. Company's strategy,which by definition is a long-term vision to create value, is unlikely to change every year. However, even when a company's strategy is working well, it is useful to review it annually to see whether it needs to be modified in any way, given the industry changes.

Even when it was started it does not require any significant modification, there may be a need for strategic initiatives to execute the strategy better. Example there may be new challenges and opportunities facing the industry for the company, such as dealing with and emerging competitive with an innovative business model that threatens to disrupt the industry, an opportunity to expand to a new geographic market, any to improve the company's innovation capacity. These discussions would lead to identification of new strategic initiatives that need to be undertaken for accelerating the initiatives already in the place.

2. Include strategic information brief in every board book:

To monitor the strategic initiatives identified during a board literate, boards need to receive regular updates. One useful way to accomplish this is to create a strategic information brief for the company's board book.

Simple design of the following kind works very well—

A "one pager" providing brief answers today for strategic questions outlined earlier. This document essentially reiterates the company's agreed upon strategy and makes sure that both management and the board keep it in mind as they meet each quarter to discuss the company's progress and performance. The term 'one pager' is intended to remind everyone that brevity and simplicity are essential for effective communication at the board level.

*A 'One pager' on each of the strategic initiatives identifies that year's annual retreat as a part of the strategic agenda. This document provides a progress report. Using agreed upon metrics and milestones that track the initiative's implementation. The Matrix can either be financial or non-financial, qualitative or quantitative. Once again, the key requirements are brevity and simplicity.

*A 'one pager'a new development regarding the company's customers and competition. This document is intended to ensure that the body is constantly informed about any important industry development that might force strategic risks and need board attention. The boat book of contains very little information about customers and competition, so this document is meant to correct this bias.

3. Use the regular board meetings to update on strategic issues: the final piece in continual strategic engagement is to modify board agendas to create the space in every board meetings in which to discuss the strategic matters. In every board meeting, the agenda should allocate sufficient time to review and discuss the updates on strategic initiatives. In addition, it would be useful to create a boat calendar for discussing one aspect of the key strategic dimensions in each of the board meetings: customers, competition, key differentiation capabilities, and key strategic risks. This will ensure that the board is able to drill down into these key areas throughout the year and be ready for the following year's strategic engagement. Pre-scheduling these topics in the board's annual agenda in a predictable manner allows adequate preparation by the management and the board to discuss these topics without fail during the year.

It is common for goats to begin their meetings with a review and discussion of the latest financial statements and to schedule the business presentations for a letter type on the agenda. The board meeting must begin with a strategy update and discussion. This ensures that sufficient high quality time is spent on this important issue. It also allows the board to approach the financial discussion in the context of a strategic picture.

It is also important to integrate this strategic engagement with community work, as well as with making major board decisions. For example, CEO compensation and so annual evaluation should at least in part be tied to the accomplishment of the strategic agenda. When AC is to be replaced the board should use its strategic knowledge to find a candidate who best fits the strategic needs of the company. When major resource allocation decisions are to be made, the board should ask.

*The research shows that from a sample of 1800 transitions CEO's chosen from inside the organisation perform better than outsiders whether or not the company has been doing well, the difference is less dramatic when performance prior to succession has been good.

*Careful case by case analysis of succession suggest that the reasons for this difference in performance have to do with the insider CEO's knowledge of the company's technologies, operations, and competitors as well as his or her knowledge of company capabilities and culture.

*Despite the apparent superior performance of CEO appointed from the inside and importance of continuity, and in the face of the growing demands on leadership and the complexity of modern companies, CEO turnover is higher in this decade than in earlier times, as is the number of outsiders chosen as new CEOs. Data from booz Allen Hamilton's most recent study show outsiders replacing incumbents around 20% of the time, even though performance is consistently poorer and tenure shorter.

When the board makes the succession choice

We can begin to understand the problem the both face when it does put succession on its agenda. Let's summarise the problematic behaviours.

1. *attention to shorten performance has been all that counted for promotions.
2. *The organisation has been designed so that general management jobs are broken up into functional assignments, and candidates have never had their experience for running the whole business.
3. *General managers have not been developed with strategic assignments.
4. *CEO succession has been treated as an event and discussion of that event has been awkward or postponed.
5. *The incumbent CEO has managed in an imperial fashion so that the top management cohort has never really developed their capabilities.

Compensation system

Taken together, the assumptions,....which are still widely shared by directors, executives, and those who advise them—have created in ear universal set of beliefs about the components of effective compensation for senior executives, as a glance at the CD and A section in the 10-K of any public company will show. Those components include the base salary.

1. Salary-fixed income: except for the top 350 firms, usually a maximum of 1 US million. But, for 20 larger firms, salary is capped because of the IRS code.

2. Annual incentive—performance based: paid in cash or stock and usually paid as a percentage of basic salary. Based on individual and or company annual performance measures (financial, strategic and/or operational).
3. Long term incentive plan-performance-based: usually paid in stock and/or stock options. It is a reward for long term performance (usually defined as three years). Typical options vest based on the efflux of time (3-6 years). Performance based option grants vest based on EPS or stock performance.
4. Lump sum payments—unrelated to performance: make whole, golden parachutes, and change of control payments, as well as other contractually obligated payments.
5. Retirement benefits-and related to performance: it is defined benefit plans and/or deferred compensation plans. It also includes the use of company aircraft and cars.

The independent directors perspective

Serving as an independent director is a much more difficult task—and even more important—than most observers release. With new board governance regulations in place and rising expectations and criticism of corporate boards by outsiders, it is far more difficult to be an independent director now than it was in years past.

Many observers have worried that qualified people will not serve on boards. That has not been my experience. It's just that they won't serve on as many boards as in the past, which is appropriate given the time it takes to be an effective board member. There are valid reasons for directors not to spread themselves too thin.

The greatest challenge that independent directors face is to keep themselves fully informed about the company on whose board they serve. Independent directors typically engage with the company and its board 6 to 8 times a year—most frequently if they serve on the audit committee or other special committees. Given strict enforcement of director independence, directors generally lack the wealth of knowledge about the industry or the nature of the business that senior executives of the firms have. Thus, they are faced with a significant problem of information asymmetry because management has far more information than independent directors can ever observed.

The nine different boards on which I have served as an independent director include a wide range of industries, some financial services to oil and gas, pharmaceuticals, retail, outdoor lawn equipment, and large computers. In none of these instances did I have industry—specific knowledge, nor was it possible to learn the industry in great enough depth to contribute to the management discourse in a meaningful way.

Given the inherent limitations, what then should independent directors contribute? Beyond the legal requirements and fiduciary responsibilities that are inherent to board service, there are four principal areas where directors should provide leadership: 1. Providing management with sound judgements about difficult issues, and asking probing questions that cause management and the CEO to look at their challenges from a different perspective, 2. Being an advocate for Soundbot governance, 3. Helping to ensure the effectiveness of the company's leadership team and its leadership succession plans, and 4. Taking on leadership roles in crises.

Offering sound judgement and asking the right questions:

Given the problem of information asymmetry, how can directors keep informed of the vital information they need to perform these rolls? How can they provide management with sound judgements and ask probing questions? Here are a few fundamental ideas ensure that management provides a complete to board book so directors can properly prepare in advance for the meeting. This book should include copies of all presentations to be made at the upcoming board meeting, including confidential as well as non-confidential material. Abe directors should guard against management putting directors on "information overload" with more detailed information than they can reasonably be expected to absorb.

*The CEO should keep board members informed of important events between board meetings. This can be done with monthly progress reports, interim informational telephone meetings of the board, and individual telephone calls to all directors.

*Board meetings are most effective when they begin with an executive session with the CEO to update the board. Hindi Sachin the CEO should review the important events within the company and provide directors confidential opportunities to ask probing questions without having members of the management team present. The same objective can be accomplished by having a private dinner the night before the board meeting with the CEO, provided all directors are prepared to arrive early.

*directors can also be kept informed between meetings by providing them with copies of relevant press articles and analysts reports about the company.

A partial list of generally agreed upon best practices include the following:

- Board composition and size: boards of directors should be composed of members with a good mix of specialised expertise, including knowledge of the industry, customers, and important management functions. The board members should have diverse perspectives and opinions. The board should not be too large or too small. If board is too large it is more difficult for individual directors to become actively involved in the discussions. If the board is too small,it is difficult to have all the requisite knowledge and abilities at the hand, and the workload might be too great for directors to perform effectively. In the United States, the most common board size is 10 directors. Most board directors should be independent of management, as regulations now require.
- Board member behaviour: boards should be composed solely of members who are energetic, inquisitive, and attentive—which time to perform their duties. They should stay well informed about the developments in their company's industry. They should be willing to express their opinions in meetings in constructive ways.
- Board leadership: the independent board must control the agenda and conduct of the board meetings, not management. Depending on the situation, this can be done effectively either by an independent chair or a lead independent director. The leader should establish the orderly processes and encourage all the individual directors to stay properly engaged, contribute their knowledge and opinions freely, and work towards a consensus.
- Board committee: the board should delegate some discussions to the committee structure allowing for discussion of certain issues in more detail by both members the committee structure allows for discussion of certain issues in more detail by board members with specialised expertise. Care must be taken to ensure that communications between committees and the full both are effective.
- Role clarity: directors must understand and agree on their board's role, both legal and practical, particularly on issues involving relationships and separations of duties with management. The board members must also understand their individual responsibilities. They need to understand their areas of expertise that they bring to the board and the areas of expertise of the other

board members. They also need to understand when they should forcefully argue their positions rather than accede to others' judgements.

- Board evaluations: the board should evaluate itself and its individual members regularly. Feedback from the evaluation should be used to improve the board composition, structures, and processes as necessary.

Board tensions and trade offs

As boards enact these various best practices and try to achieve an effective group process, the first President of UN avoidable tensions are trade-offs. Leaders of all groups must contend with these tensions. Not managing them appropriately can lead to pathologies, aur problematic group functioning, in even the most perfectly designed boards. As will become clear, managing the tensions can be a fluid process and often more of an art than a clearly delineated set of tasks. Simply recognising the tensions is an important first step for any board leader. Extensions in haran in the functioning of every group that are particularly challenging and relevant for boards of directors are discussed in this section.

Social cohesion tension: one tension that boards face is between creating social cohesion and avoiding it. Social cohesion refers to the total field of forces that bind a group of individuals together and keep members wanting to be part of the group. Factors may include attraction, common interests, cultural similarity, and social ties, among many others. Strong social cohesion in the board allows it to function smoothly, keeps directors motivated, and helps the group cope with internal conflict and politicking.

However, social cohesion can also cause heights and pressures of conformity in the group. Groups are notoriously powerful in creating social pressures to conform even when group members are performing an easy task, but this is especially true when the task is difficult and ambiguous, as the most important work of the board is. The more socially cohesive the group, the greater the pressure for any member to confirm to the majority's point of view. Conformity can prevent useful bits of information and opinions from surfacing and, extreme, can lead to the very dangerous group dynamic called groupthink.

To avoid destructive conflict while simultaneously guarding against conformity and groupthink, boards must develop a degree of social cohesion, but not too much. The choice is not between cohesion and no cohesion. Rather, the questions are how much cohesion and of what types?

The definition tension

Yah second tension is the degree to which dissent should be allowed to exist or even be encouraged in board discussions. On the one hand, dissent or simply expressing an alternative view point is critical to avoiding conformity. Research shows that nearly having considered a minority viewpoint allows a group to think more creatively and make better decisions. Dissent can also prevent groups from falling into stultifying habitual routines that can both obscure problems and prevent effective responses. Rather than applying past behaviours to a current situation dissent can help the group reevaluate its course of action. Finally, discipline or forced dissent can force new information into the table that otherwise might not become available to the group.

However, too much dissent can create conflict, undermine the aforementioned social cohesion of the group, and simply stal meetings. Trying to find the appropriate balance and the right manner in which to encourage dissent are two of the most important tasks for any one leading a board discussion. Some tension in the boardroom is good; too much can lead to infighting and chaos. The goal should be to create friendly, constructive dissension.

Psychological safety tension

Group psychological safety is the shared belief that the group is a safe place for risk taking, sharing unpopular ideas and admitting errors. Some degree of psychological safety is essential. When a group provides psychological safety, members are more likely to speak up, to ask questions, and to admit mistakes, all of which are important to other group outcomes, such as decision making and learning. Having psychological safety contracts conformity pressures and groupthink, and can keep a group from following an unexamined habitual routine.

However, too much safety creates a tendency towards social loafing. Social loafing occurs when individuals engaged in a collective task exert less effort than they would if they were performing this task alone. It is a well documented phenomenon that occurs in both trivial and serious situations, with many different kinds of tasks. The causes of social loafing have to do with identifiability. Individual believes that his or her effort will not be noticed or rewarded if he or she is inclined to loaf.

D. Quantitative Techniques, Digitalisation Development and Management Studies

9

Quantitative Techniques (Q.T.)

Small Sample Tests

In large sample theory we assured that the sampling distribution of statistics following normal distribution i.e., as the sample size in large size n>30, we assured that the sampling distribution followed normal distribution. However, this assumption is not true if the sample size is small i.e. $n \leq 30$ the same does not follow normal distribution and hence normal tests cannot be applied.

In this situation the new techniques and test of significance such as exact sample test or small sample tests have been developed the methods of small sample tests and applicable to large sample tests that the methods of large samples cannot be applied to small sample tests. An inference drawn from a sample would be less precise that drawn from large samples. When sample is small the deviation is more from normal curve. When the sample is small, the means of different samples will vary largely.

Test for Sample Mean

If we want to test a random sample x_i ($i = 1, 2...n$) of size 'n' drawn from a normal population with sample mean ($\overline{x}$) and if the sample mean differs significantly from the hypothetical value μ_0 of the population men, then we set $H_0 = \overline{x} = \mu$ i.e., There is no significant difference between the sample mean and population sample. Then given the H_0 the test statistic 't' is given by

$$t = \frac{\overline{x} - \mu}{s/\sqrt{n}} \text{ where } \overline{x} = \frac{1}{n}\sum_{i=1}^{n} x_1 \Lambda ¿$$

$$s^2 = \frac{1}{(n-1)}\sum_{i=1}^{n}(x_1 - \overline{x})^2 \textit{ follows students}$$

't' – distribution with (n-1) degree of freedom we complete the test statistic 't' under H_0 and we compare it with the table value of 't' for (n-1) degrees of freedom at given level of significance (α).

If the calculated value $|t| <$ ¿ table 't', H_0 is accepted of the given level of significance 'α'. *If the calculated value of $|t| \geq$ table value of f, we reject H_0 and we say that there is no significant difference between sample mean and population mean.*

't' test for difference of Means

Let $x_1 x_2 \ldots x_{n_1}$ and $yx_1 y_2 \ldots y_{n2}$ are two independent random samples drawn from a normal populations.

Hence we test that the two samples have been drawn from normal populations with normal Means

i.e., $H_0 = \mu_n = \mu_y$

Under given H_0, the test statistic 't'.

$$|t| = \left| \frac{\bar{x} - \bar{y}}{s^2 \left(\frac{1}{n_1} + \frac{1}{n_2} \right)} \right| t_{n_1} + n_2 - 2$$

Where

$$\bar{x} = \frac{1}{n_1} \sum x_i \wedge \bar{y} = \frac{1}{n_2} \sum y_1$$

and $$s_1^2 = \frac{1}{n_1} \sum (x_1 - \bar{x})^2 \; s_2^2 = \frac{1}{n_2} \sum (y - \bar{y})^2$$

and

$$s^2 = \frac{n_1 s_1^2 + n_2 s_2^2}{(n_1 + n_2)}$$

and it follows students t-distribution with $(n_1 + n_1^{-2})$ degrees of freedom.

We compute $|t|$ under given H_0, if calculated $|t|$ is greater than table 't' we reject H_0 otherwise we accept H_0

If CV of $|t|$ we reject H_0 as the sample we are differ significances. Otherwise we conclude that the two samples have been drawn from one single with the other means

$$\mu_x \equiv \mu_y$$

1. Problems: *The average number of articles produce by two machines per day are 200 and 250 with standard deviations 20 and 25 respectively on the books of records of 25 days production. Can we say that with the machines equally efficient at 5% level of significance?*

2. Problems: *Two random samples of size 9 and 7 are 196.42 and 198.82 respectively. The sum of the squares of the deviation from the mean are 26.94 and 18.73 respectively. Can the samples we consider to have been drawn from the same normal population.*

Solution: *Samples of two types of electric bulbs were tested for length of life and the following data are obtained.*

Table 9.1

	Type-I	*Type-II*
Sample size	$n_1 = 8$	$n_2 = 7$
Sample means	$\overline{x}_1 = 1234$ *hours*	$\overline{x}_2 = 1036$ *hours*
Sample S.Ds.	$s_1 = 36$ *hours*	$s_2 = 40$ *hours*

Is the difference in the means sufficient to warrant and type I is superior to type II regarding length of life.

Solution: *Given that*

The sample size $n_1 = 8, n_2 = 7$

Sample Means $\overline{x}_1 = 1234 \wedge \overline{x}_2 = 1036$ hours

Simple S.Ds, $s_1 = 36 \wedge s_2 = 40$

Here we have to test the life types of two types and equal

i.e., $H_0 = \mu_x = \mu_y \; VsH_1 = \mu_x > \mu_y$

under $H_0 =$ *the test statistics is*

$$t = \frac{|\overline{x}_1 - \overline{x}_2|}{\sqrt{s^2\left(\frac{1}{n_1} + \frac{1}{n_2}\right)}} t_{n_{1m}} 2$$

$$s^2 = \frac{n_1 s_1^2 + n_2 s_2^2}{n_1 + n_2 - 2}$$

$$¿ \frac{8 \times (36)^2 + 7(40)^2}{8 + 7 - 2}$$

$$¿\frac{8\times1296+7\times1600}{13}$$

$$¿\frac{10368+11200}{13}$$

$$¿\frac{21568}{13}$$

$$s^2 = 1.659.08$$

$$\therefore \quad t=\frac{|1234-1036|}{\sqrt{1659.08\left(\frac{1}{8}+\frac{1}{7}\right)}}$$

$$¿\frac{198}{\sqrt{1659.08(0.1250+0.1429)}}$$

$$¿\frac{198}{\sqrt{1659.08\times0.2679}}$$

$$¿\frac{198}{\sqrt{444.3964}}$$

$$¿\frac{198}{21.0807}$$

$$(t) = 9.3925$$

The calcucated values $|t|=9.3925$ is greater than table values $|H|=77$. Hence we reject H_0 at 5% level of significance.

i.e., the life time of two electrical bulbs are not equal type I is superior to type II.

F – test for equality of Population variance

Let $x_1, x_2,.....,x_n$ be a random smaple of size n_1 from the first population with variance σ_1^2 and y_1, y_2 ....x_{n2} be a random variance of size n_2 from the second normal population with variance σ_1^2. Here we have to test whether the samples are independent.

Under H_0 the test statistic is

$$H_0 = \sigma_1^2 = \sigma_2^2 = \sigma^2$$

Under H_0 the test statistic is

$$F=\frac{s_1^2}{s_2^2}=(n_{1-1}, n_{2-1})$$

Where s_1^2 and s_2^2 are unbiased estimates of the common population variance σ^2 and are given by

$$s_1^2 = \frac{1}{(n_1 - 1)} \Sigma(x - \overline{x})^2$$

and

$$s_2^2 = \frac{1}{(n_2 - 1)} \Sigma(y - \overline{y})^2$$

Following 'F' distribution with (n_{1-1}, n_{2-1}) d.f.

We compute the test statistic under H_0 and compare it with tabulated value of F for (n_{1-1}, n_{2-1}) d.f. at given value of significance.

If calculated value of F is ≥ table value of then we conclude that there is a significant difference between two population variances. Hence we reject H_0.

If calculated value of F < table value of F we accept H_0 at the given level of significance.

Q: Using the following two random samples drawn from the normal populations test the null hypothesis that the variances of two populations are equal. Test at 5% level of significance.

Sample I: 10, 6, 17, 13, 12, 8, 14, 15, 9

Sample II: 7, 13, 22, 15, 12, 14, 18, 8, 21, 23, 10, 17

Solution: *Let N $(\mu_1 - \sigma_1^2)$, N $(\mu_2 - \sigma_2^2)$ are two populations from which the two samples are drawn.*

Let $x_1, x_2 \ldots\ldots x_{n1}, y_1, y_2 \ldots\ldots y_{n2}$ are two samples are drawn from two normal populations. Let s_1^2, s_2^2 are two variances of two drawn samples. Here we want to test

$$s_1^2 = \frac{1}{n} \sum_{i=1}^{n_i} (x_i - \overline{x})^2$$

$$s_2^2 = \frac{1}{n_2} \sum_{i=1}^{n_i} (y_i - \overline{y})^2$$

Let

$$F = \frac{n_1 s_1^2}{(n_{1-1})\sigma^2} / \frac{n_2 s_2^2}{(n_{2-1})\sigma_2^2}$$

In the test statistic and if follows normal distribution with (n_{1-1}) (n_{2-1}) *degrees of freedom.*

If the calculated value of F is less than the value F as 5% level of significance, we accept H_0 *otherwise reject* H_0.

Calculation: *We have two samples drawn from two normal populations.*

$x_1 = 10, 6, 16, 17, 13, 12, 8, 14, 15, 9$

$x_2 = 7, 13, 22, 15, 12, 14, 18, 8, 21, 23, 10, 17$

Table 9.2

x_i	y_i	x_i^2	y_i^2
10	7	100	49
6	13	36	169
16	22	256	484
17	15	289	225
13	12	169	144
12	14	144	196
8	18	64	324
14	8	196	81
15	21	225	441
9	23	81	529
	10		100
	17		289

Here

$$\bar{x} = \frac{1}{n}\Sigma x_1 = \frac{120}{10} = 12, \bar{y} = \frac{\Sigma y_i}{n} = \frac{180}{12} = 15$$

$$\Sigma x_1^2 = 1560, \Sigma y_1^2 = 1314$$

$$\therefore \quad s_1^2 = \frac{1}{n}\Sigma x_1^2 - x^{-2}$$

$$¿\frac{1560}{10} - (12)^2$$

$$s_1^2 = 156 - 144 = 12$$

$$s_2^2 = \frac{1}{n}\Sigma y_1^2 - y^{-2}$$

$$\frac{1}{12} \times 3014 - (15)^2$$

$$¿251.1666 - 225.000$$

¿46.1666

Note: Whenever 'F' is calculated, it must be always greater than 1 if F < 1, then take numerator as denominator and denominator as numerator with results F as > 1.

$$\therefore F = \frac{n_1 s_1^2 / (n_1 - 1)}{n_1 s_2^2 / (n_2 - 1)} = \frac{10 \times 12 \times 9}{10 \times 12 \times 11}$$

Here we take

$$F = \frac{n_2 s_2^2 / (n_2 - 1)}{n_1 s_1^2 / (n_1 - 1)} = \frac{12 \times 46.1666 \times 11}{10 \times 12 \times 9} = 2.1409$$

$\therefore$ *sure calculated value of F(11,9) is 2.1409 where is less than the table values of F (11,9) at 5% level of significance 3.105. Here we accept* H_0.

Z^2 – test for independence of attributes

Let us assume that the given population is of size N is divided into 'r' mutually exclusive and exhaustive classes A_1 A_2 ... A_r *with respect to the attribute 'A' and also the population is divided into s mutually exclusive classes* B_1 B_2 ... B_s *with respect to another attribute B.*

The frequency distribution of the items belonging to the classes A_1 A_2 .... A_r *and* B_1 B_2 .... B_s *can be arranged in the following r x s contingencies table.*

Table 9.3

A	B_1	B_2	B_i	B_s	*Total*
A_1	$(A_1 A_1)$	$(A_1 B_2)$	$(A_1 B_i)$	$(A_1 B_s)$	(A_1)
A_2	$(A_2 B_1)$	$(A_2 B_2)$	$(A_2 B_i)$	$(A_2 B_s)$	(A_2)
A_r	$(A_r B_1)$	$(A_r B_2)$	$(A_r B_s)$	$(A_r B_s)$	(A_r)
A_s	$(A_s A_1)$	$(A_s B_2)$	$(A_s B_j)$	$(A_s B_s)$	(A_s)
	(B_1)	(B_2)	(B_i)	(B_s)	N

Here (A_i) *is the frequency of the* i^{th} *attribute* A_i, *i.e., it is the number of members having the attribute* A_i, $i=1,2....r$; (B_j) *is the number of members having the attribute* B_j, $j = 1, 2 .....s$; *and* (A_i, B_j) *is the frequency of the number of members having the attributes.*

A_i *and* B_j; $(i=1, 2.....r, j=1, 2....s)$

If $(A_i, B_j)_0$ *denote the expected frequency of* (A_i, B_j) *then*

$$(A_iB_j) = \frac{(A_iB_j)}{N}, i-1,2...r; j=1,2...s$$

The expected frequencies are calculated for different values i and j for different class frequencies.

Here our aim is to test the independent of attributes, i.e.

H_0: the attributes and bare independent test the given H_0, we have the test statistic.

Simply $\chi^2 = \Sigma\left[\frac{(0_{iJ} - \in_{iJ})^2}{\in_{iJ}}\right]$ *as*

$$\chi^2 = \Sigma_{ij}\frac{\Sigma 0_{iJ}^{\ 2}}{\in_{iJ}} - N$$

This statistic χ^2 follows χ^2 distribution with (r-1)(s-1) degrees of freedom.

Problem: *The standard of education of 100 persons selected at random are as follows. Using the following data test the standard of education depends on the difference of men and women.*

Table 9.4 Standard of Education

	Middle School	*High School*	*College*	*Total*
Women	25	15	10	50
Men	25	10	15	50
Total	50	25	25	100

Solution: *Here we have two attributes say A and B. Where 'A' is Standard of Education and B is Sex i.e., Male and Female. Here we have to test the standard as education depends on the difference of Men and Women.*

i.e., H_0: the standard of education and sex of the people are independent.

H_0 : A and B are independent.

Vs

H_0: The Standard of Education depends on the difference of male and female.

Let 0_{ii} is its value of class of A and its value of B and is the observed freqeuency. Here i = 1, 2 ... r, and 1 = 1, 2 .... s.

0_{ii} is the given observed frequencies

Using these observed frequencies we obtain e_{ij}'s, which are expected frequencies.

$e_{iJ} \frac{n_i \times m_i}{N}$ *where N is the total frequency.*

To test given H_0 we use the following test. Statistic χ^2 as follows.

$$\chi^2 = \sum_i \sum_J \frac{(O_{iJ} - e_{iJ})^2}{e_{iJ}}$$

$$\chi^2 = \sum_i \sum_J \frac{O_{iJ}^2}{e_{iJ}} - N$$

This statistic χ^2 (r-1)(s-1) degrees of freedom.

If the calculated values of $\chi^2_{(r-1)(s-1)}$ is less than the table values of $\chi^2_{(r-1)(s-1)}$ we accept H_0 Λ $\chi^2_{(r-1)(s-1)}$ is greater than equal to table values of $\chi^2_{(r-1)(s-1)}$ we reject H_0.

Calculation: *Here we have to test H_0 such that*
H_0 : A and B are independent.

Table 9.5 Standard of Education

	Middle School	*High School*	*College*	*Total*
Women	25	15	10	50 n_1
Men	25	10	15	50 n_2
Total	50 m_1	25 m_2	25 m_3	100 N

Using the above observed frequencies (0_{ii}'s) we calculate (e_{ii}'s) expected frequencies by the following formula.

$$e_{i} = \frac{n_i \times m_i}{N}$$

$$e_{11} = \frac{n_1 \times m_1}{N} = \frac{50 \times 50}{100} = 25$$

$$e_{12} = \frac{n_1 \times m_2}{N} = \frac{50 \times 25}{100} = 12.5$$

$$e_{13} = \frac{n_1 \times m_3}{N} = \frac{50 \times 25}{100} = 12.5$$

$$e_{21} = \frac{n_2 \times m_1}{N} = \frac{50 \times 50}{100} = 25$$

$$e_{22} = \frac{n_2 \times m_2}{N} = \frac{50 \times 25}{100} = 12.5$$

$$e_{23} = \frac{n_2 \times m_3}{N} = \frac{50 \times 25}{100} = 12.5$$

Table 9.6 Standard of Education

	Middle School	*High School*	*College*	*Total*
Women	25	12.5	12.5	50
Men	25	12.5	12.5	50
Total	50	25	25	100

$$\chi^2_{(r-1)(s-1)} = \sum_i \sum_J \frac{O_{iJ}^{\ 2}}{e_{iJ}} - N$$

$$\chi^2_{(2-1)(3-1)} = \frac{25^2}{25} + \frac{15^2}{12.5} + \frac{10^2}{12.5} + \frac{25^2}{25} + \frac{10^2}{12.5} + \frac{15^2}{12.5} - 100$$

$$\chi^2_{\ 2} = 25 + \frac{15 \times 15}{12.5} + \frac{10 \times 10}{12.5} + 25\frac{10 \times 10}{12.5} + \frac{15 \times 15}{12.5} - 100$$

¿25+18+8+25+8+18 –100

¿102–100

$\chi^2_{\ 2}$= '2'

∴ *The calculated values of* $\chi_2^{\ 2}$ *at 5% level of significance is 5.99 since C.V.* $\chi_2^{\ 2}$ *is less than table values of* $\chi_2^{\ 2}$, *we accept* H_0. *That is the standard of education does not depend on the difference of men and women.*

Chi-square (χ^2-square) test of goodness of fit

Karl Pearson developed a test for testing the significance of the discrepancy between experimental values and the theoretical values obtained under some hypothesis. This test is known as χ^2 *– test of goodness of fit.*

Here we test the null hypothesis that there is no significance difference between the observation experimental values and the theoretical on hypothetical values.

For the given observed frequencies 0_i, i = *1, 2, ...n but there 'K' classes* 0_1, 0_2 .... *0k are the observed class frequencies and* $e_1 e_2$ *.....e are* *expected frequencies which are calculated from the prohibited.*

Here we have to test the difference between observed frequencies and expected frequencies. To test this we use the statistic χ^2 which is given by

$$\chi^2 = \sum \frac{(0_i - e_i)^2}{e_i}$$

This statistic follows $\chi^2_{(k-1)}$ distribution with (k-1) degrees of freedom.

To fit the Pearson distribution for the given data the parameter should know first. If parameter is not known then its estimate is to be found. Then the expected frequencies are calculated. When this parameter is estimated its degree of freedom reduced by 1.

If calculated values of χ^2 is less than the table value of χ^2 at given level of significance then we accept H_0. Then we can say that the experiment does not support them or there is significance between theory and experiment.

Problem: *In a town the various centers have got numbers as 0,1,2,3,4,5,6,7. In a particular day the numbers of cars passing through the above centers are given below.*

Table 9.7

Centers	*0*	*1*	*2*	*3*	*4*	*5*	*6*	*7*
No. of Cars	*364*	*376*	*218*	*89*	*33*	*13*	*2*	*1*

Solution: *First we have to fit the Poisson distribution for the given data. The following function of the Poisson distribution is*

$$P(X = x) = \frac{e^{-\lambda}\lambda^x}{x!} x = 0,1,...$$

Here the Mean of the distribution, is the parameter of the distribution and is not known, have we estimate this by

$$\lambda = \text{Mean} = \frac{\sum f_i x_i}{\sum f_i}$$

The given data is

Table 9.8

x_i	*0*	*1*	*2*	*3*	*4*	*5*	*6*	*7*	*Total*
f_i	364	376	218	89	33	13	2	1	1096
$f_i\,x_i$	0	376	436	267	132	65	12	7	1295

$$\lambda = \bar{x} = \frac{\sum f_i x_i}{\sum f_i} = \frac{1295}{1096} = 1.18$$

$\therefore\ \hat{\lambda} = 1.18$

$$P(X = x) = \frac{e^{-\lambda}\hat{\lambda}^{x}}{x!}$$

$$\text{¿}\ \frac{e^{-1.18}(1.18)^{x}}{x!}$$

$\therefore$ *To test the expected frequencies we have to substitute the values of x = 0,1,2, ... in the following*

$$P(X = x) = \frac{N.e^{-\hat{\lambda}}\left(\hat{\lambda}\right)^{x}}{x!}$$

$$\text{¿}\ \frac{1096e^{-1.18}(1.18)^{x}}{x!}$$

For x = 0,1,2,3,4,5,6,7, we get the expected frequencies as 3365, 397.1, 234.6, 92.5, 273, 6.5, 1.3, 0.2.

Table 9.9 Expected Frequencies

x_i	*0*	*1*	*2*	*3*	*4*	*5*	*6*	*7*
0_{ij}^{s}	364	376	218	89	33	13	2	1
e_{ij}^{s}	336.5	397.1	234.6	92.5	27.3	6.5	1.3	0.2

Table 10.10

x_i	*0*	*1*	*2*	*3*	*4*	*5*
0_{ij}	364	376	218	89	33	16
e_{ij}	336.5	397.1	234.6	92.5	27.3	8

$$\chi^2_{(4)} = \sum_{i=1}^{6}\left(\frac{0_i - e_i}{e_i}\right)^2$$

$$¿\frac{(364-336.5)^2}{e_i}$$

$$¿\frac{(89-92.5)^2}{92.5} +¿ \frac{(33-27.3)^2}{27.3} +¿ \frac{(16-8)^2}{8}$$

On simplification, we get

$$\chi^2_{(4)}=9.99$$

the calculated value of $\chi^2_{(4)}$ *is 9.99 is greater than the table value 9.49 at 5% level of significance, we reject* H_0. *Thus fitting of Poisson distribution is not a good fit.*

10

Management of Tribals Produce in Andhra Pradesh

By DR. A.Venkata Rayudu

"Management of Tribal's produce in Andhra Pradesh" entitled article is divided into two Parts. Part-I broadly deals with the general setting of tribal including their natural abode. The basic features of the tribal economy viz., its primitive nature, inheritance of indebtedness, inadequate institutional finance, the inevitable dependence of tribal on private traders as they are ever ready to extend credit to raise crops and for other purposes, the deceptive role played by private money lenders, middlemen and other traders in the transaction of tribal's produce, the economic, social and cultural functions of weekly markets and above all their impeccable qualities of honesty and reliability even if they are at disadvantageous position in monetary terms are presented. Part-II is exclusively devoted to the activities of Girijan Co-operative Corporation, which is a State level Tribal Development Co-operative Corporation, exclusively meant for the benefit of tribal in Andhra Pradesh.

PART-I

Tribal in India form the very segment of the weaker sections of the society. They have been living in remote, interior and inaccessible areas including on hill-tops and slopes. They depend, by and large, on agriculture and collection of minor forest produce for their livelihood. Higher priority is, therefore, required to be given to these twin spheres of activity in any programme of action for the development of tribes in India. The tribal economy, especially in the interior area, is still not fully monetized, and it is woven round the weekly markets or 'Haats', where a major portion of the transactions are being carried out under barter system. The money-lender-cum-traders still continues to occupy an inevitable place in tribal economy in many parts of the country. The tribals look to him for their needs; especially credit for agricultural and personal needs, supply of domestic requirements, marketing of agricultural and minor forest produce etc. Credit for social and religious Purposes, such as marriage, death, worship, etc., is also readily advanced by the money lenders. The standard of high rate of honesty and integrity amongst the tribal convinces the money lender fully to get back his money lent with assured interest at a pre-fixed time, that too, without any tangible security.

A. Dependence on Agriculture

In India, the tribal are at various stages of development ranging from food gathering to market economy and from living in compact villages to those living in scattered ones. Except for a handful of sophisticated tribal groups in plain areas, the tribal by and large are in abject poverty and high indebtedness. About 80 percent of the tribal in India are stated to have been engaged in agriculture. However, the production of agricultural crops is possible only in such areas where soil erosion is at minimum and on the gentle slope of the valley areas where just sufficient irrigation potential is available. It is an established fact that the agricultural practices in tribal areas are mostly of subsistence in nature and are characterised by the production of food grains and other millets just enough to meet their own requirements, generally at a low level of living. In addition, poor soils with little water-conservation, un-economic landholdings and low adoption of improved agricultural inputs also curb the agricultural production in the tribal areas to a considerable extent. Difficult hilly and undulated terrain, technological backwardness, lack of proper education, poor means of communication, lack of needed irrigation facilities, small and scattered size of land holding are the major constraints resulting in low income from agriculture. Thus, surplus agricultural produce for sale is minimal and not even sufficient to meet their own consumption needs and social purposes, leaving aside to clear their age old debts.

B. Dependence on Forest Produce

Next to agriculture, the tribals draw their sustenance largely from the forests. The forests not only provide them food, material to build houses, fuel for cooking, light and warmth, fodder for their cattle, but also satisfy the deep rooted sentiments. Also, forests are their last succor in times of distress like famine. Tribal economy is, therefore, closely connected with the forests. In fact, their folklore revolves around forest. It is also true to say that tribal life is closely connected in one way or other with forest right from birth to death. As forests are the natural abodes of various tribal groups in the country, they play a very significant role in their lives. The tribals are accustomed to collect various items of Minor Forest Produce (MFP) such as; gallnut, tamarind, honey, canes, seeds, spices, oilseeds, dry-fruits, lac, resins, Niger seeds, Karanj, Kusum Harra, Salseed, Dori, Gus, Chironji, Tasar cocoon, so ices, bamboos, roshya, medicinal items, pungam, Maua seeds etc., to supplement their meager earnings from agriculture and other allied sources as the forests are endowed with rich variety of minor forest items. Their life is, therefore, inextricably linked with the collection of MFP and is brought to the weekly markets/Haat Bazars, which are not merely market places but also Social Centers, around which most of the life of the tribals revolves.

C. Characteristic Features of Tribal Economy

(i) The tribal people of India living in the distant hills and forests for years together led a secluded life, which was generally uninfluenced and unperturbed by the plains' people. As stated above, the **tribal economy is mostly primitive in nature** and is based on the concept of subsistence. The technology adopted by the tribals is simple and is often in harmony with their ecological surrounding. Their economy shows endless variations from shifting cultivation to settled agriculture. Agriculture among the tribals is practiced on the poorest and rocky soils with little depths, minimum irrigation, and unscientific cropping pattern with the result of low yields.

(ii) Indebtedness is the bane of tribal economy. An altogether peculiar set of economic and social customs of the aborigines make indebtedness a chronic and endemic malady. The rate of indebtedness is exorbitant basically due to the peculiar characteristics of its economy. Agriculture which constitutes the occupation of 82 percent of the tribal's population is practiced on the poorest and ill-responsive soils. Periodic scarcities and famines, absence of subsidiary industries and non-existence of gainful employment opportunities still aggravate the problem. Expenditure on customs and traditions of the tribals at the time of marriage, death and religious ceremonies accentuate the extent of indebtedness. The consequences of improper trade practices adopted by the private traders and dishonest money-lenders from the plains have ultimately resulted in the passage of the hitherto cultivated land of the tribal to non-tribal and other erstwhile non-agriculturists. As a result, land alienations of the tribal are also at an alarmingly high rate. Although the country had experienced some tribal uprisings in the past, the political activity among the tribals is still at its rock bottom. The above situation necessarily brings to the conclusion that, in general, the economic activities of the tribal economy are at the lowest order.

(iii) **The institutional finance in tribal areas is grossly inadequate** to meet the just demands of the aborigines at reasonable rates. Hence, there is no other alternative for the tribal except to approach the money-lender, who is ever present and ready to extend them a pseudo - helping hand. This is one of the worst forms of exploitation, to which the tribals are very often exposed to the traditional money-lending system. It is a common feature in the tribal economy, for the debt to come down the hierarchy from father to son and also pass on to the third generation. One of the most pitiable things of the tribals is the faith and trust they have with the money-lenders although they exploit them to the core.

(iv) There are various forms by which the **private traders deprive the tribal** of their due share in various transactions. One such aspect which has widely attracted the attention of the government is that of bonded labour. This practice is called by different names in various States of India. In Rajasthan it is called as Sagri; in Andhra Pradesh, vetti; in Orissa, Gothi; in Karnataka, Jeetha; and in Madhya Pradesh as Naukri Nama.

The second practice of money lending is by persons called as Punjabi, Madrasi, or Kangal Bank, who lend small amounts of money at exorbitant rates of interest and resort to all sorts of means to recover their amounts.

The third category is the professional money-lender, who lends money for both productive and non-productive purposes at atrocious rates of interest. The rates of interest charged by the money-lenders at very exorbitant rates anywhere between 24 to 60 percent per month and if the loan is not repaid within the fixed time, it is followed by the interest being added to the principal amount.

(v) **The tribal normally sell their agricultural produce to non-institutional agencies i.e., private traders/merchants,** as this had been due to the fact that the private traders (showkars) extend the credit to the households to raise the crops and at the same time they enforce a binding over the farmers to sell their agricultural produce to them only or to re-pay the loan in terms of kind along with the vaddi or pechhulu (interest). It is in this context, the tribals had to sell the produce after the harvest at a certain pre-determined price which was agreed upon at the time of taking the loan. Therefore, this price will be invariably much lower than the price that prevails in the market. Further, the price will go down in the harvesting season for all crops and most of the farmers in general wish to sell the produce soon after the harvesting in order to purchase immediate necessities and to redeem the earlier debts that have been taken at the time of busy sowing season. Also, it is a fact that the traders never go for deferred payments.

(vi) Unfortunately, the **tribal are mostly guided by their social standing and social values** rather than narrow considerations of profit and loss or acquiring more assets. Under such social compulsions he gets into debt and the debt gets compounded with interest. His ignorance and the malpractices of the money lender place him at such a disadvantageous, where he is forced to alienate his land to the money-lenders. The traders by advancing their goods have fore-closed the crops at the harvest period. And the tribal has no other choice except to sell his harvested produce at the pre-determined price. Also, it appears the benefits extended to the tribal through the economic betterment activities of the government agencies are grabbed to a certain extent by the money-lenders.

D. Weekly markets/Haat Bazars

One of the basic characteristic features of tribal economy is the existence of weekly markets. The tribal's generally live in small villages inside or near the forest areas. Agriculture is their main occupation, but they also gather medicinal herbs, and other Non-Timber Forest Products (NTFPs) for selling in weekly markets locally called 'Shandies'. They also buy certain consumer goods or commodities of daily requirement not locally available, e.g., salt, spices, ready-made clothes, cloth, utensils, inexpensive cosmetics, as well as other items for body ornamentation.

In addition to the sale/purchase of plant, animal, or other products, the weekly market provides a meeting place for relatives and friends of neighbouring villages and an occasion for other social or religious events. The term market, as in the modern market, does not necessarily refer to a condition of mutual knowledge of buyers and sellers and the price situation in tribal areas. These markets are weekly, fortnightly or bi-weekly, though it is difficult to state their exact timings or hours as it all depends on local situations. They are locally known as 'Bazar', 'Haat', 'Pitia', 'shandies', 'Santha', etc., in various regions. The tribal villages mostly fall within a radius of about 5 to 12 kms, have a fixed separate market place. They can also be referred to as place markets, where buyers and sellers meet face to face. These markets are held in different places each day - one day in a village; the next in the forest; another day in an open meadow-but each time it's the same; hundreds of tribe's people from different villages, each specialising in a different craft or skill, converge in one spot to trade their wares. In short, the economic, social and cultural functions of tribal weekly markets may be summarised as follows:

- The tribal weekly markets serve not only economic but also social and cultural functions. These markets bring tribal together from within a radius of ten kilometers and facilitate the exchange of local goods and purchase of non-tribal goods.
- These markets serve as the most powerful channels of communication within a tribal region. Every market attracts the tribal from the villages. Every tribal makes himself or herself sure to attend the market. So, market becomes the best meeting place for the people. Local leaders make arrangements of community interests in the market place in order to get them relayed all over the region immediately.
- Local administrations, social workers, etc choose the market places to convey their messages, hold their meetings and plan their programmes.
- The tribal market maintains a network of socio-cultural ties among the people of its land and gives them a common base for regional ethnology. Discussion and settlement of disputes of tribal villages and marriage negotiations are done in the tribal markets. It also serves as a center of re-distribution of resources and material goods of occupationally reverse communities in the region.
- The markets serve as centers of recreation like screening of films, etc. They also serve as centers for selling the local liquors, and as centers for obtaining the services of palmists, astrologers etc.

It can be viewed from the above, that a tribal weekly market is a comprehensive one as it is the hub for many social and economic activities reflecting their day to day needs. In other words, the market caters practically for all the requirements and needs of the tribal, express or latent. In respect of articles they purchase, it was generally observed that they are getting attracted by the size and colour of the article rather than its quality. The bigger the object, the greater should be the price and the more colourful it is, the more expensive should be the price according to their assessment. In such a context, the simple tribesman with only the fruit of his hard and honest labour behind him, but without a developed power of bargaining, has to wage a silent struggle to meet his needs. How this artless tribal, unarmed with the knowledge of marketing and unaware of exploitation, fights this grim economic duel with the unscrupulous and economically stronger trader becomes, at times, a tense problem in tribal areas. Given the peculiar nature of difficulties associated with their place of living, the tribal still enjoy life with simplicity without compromising their impeccable qualities of honesty and reliability even if they are at disadvantageous position in monetary terms.

E. Categorisation of markets in Tribal Area

Against the above background, it may be pertinent to mention the categorisation of markets, depending upon participation of private and public agencies, in tribal areas into Non-institutional agencies such as private traders, money lenders, petty traders, middlemen and finally consumers, and Institutional Agencies such as Tribal Development Co-operative Corporations (TDCCs).

I. Non-Institutional Agencies

(a) Private Traders

The plains traders visit weekly shandies and purchase the produce. They establish long standing contacts with some tribal villages and visit these villages to purchase produce. Sometimes, they engage tribal agents in important villages, who take the sellers to the traders. This agent measures the commodity and arranges the payment. The agent is paid a fixed wage by the trader on the shandy day. They advance 40 to 50 percent of the value of the produce pledge to be sold to them by the tribal farmers or by those, who collect NTFPs. Sometimes, credit is advanced to them in agricultural season in lieu of the fixed quantity of specified produce/products.

The trader usually offers low prices to tribal except on occasions when he has to compete with a State owned Tribal Development Co-operative Corporation in the State. However, the tribal prefer to sell their produce to the established private traders because of their long standing acquaintance and personal touch in their transactions. The tribal seller is more satisfied by the usual fringe benefits like cigars, etc., which he gets free of cost, than the price he receives from the trader. This personal touch conceals the nature and extent of exploitation in the form of under weighment and under payment. The trader transports the produce to the nearby urban centres by carts or through some other means and sells it to the wholesale dealers. Sometimes, the traders advance loans to petty traders, who in turn sell their commodities to them. The money lenders and the middlemen also sell the produce to the traders in the shandy.

(b) Petty Traders

Some petty traders take loans either in cash or/and kind from the plain's traders in the shandy and advance them as credit to tribal people in the interior and inaccessible villages in lieu of repaying the such loans with the specified/fixed quantity agreed upon at the time of contracting the loan. The tribal treats repayment as an obligation to be honoured, made at the time of harvest. Some bidarulu transport essential commodities like salt, jiggery, tobacco, etc., to the interior villages and exchange them for commercial crops like turmeric, ginger, etc.

(c) Middlemen

It is also true that some tribal people act as middlemen. They purchase produce just a few yards away from the shandy and sometimes within the shandy and sell the same produce to the traders in the shandy. Sometimes they purchase produce from the fellow villagers at low prices and sell it in the shandy, because the tribal is completely ignorant of the market prices and the weights and measures used or he does not have adequate mechanism to transport the produce to the shandy or he needs to release the value immediately instead of waiting for the coming shandy. The middlemen who purchase the produce wait for the coming shandy to sell it to traders. The middle men are different from the Bidari traders as the latter advance' loans against commodities and purchase and sell commodities, whereas the middlemen only purchase commodities.

(d) Money-lenders

As banks do not provide assistance as and when the tribal's need, their dependence on either private traders or money-lenders is still high. They take advances from the latter on the condition of disposing off their produce at a lower price than market rate. Under the guise of indebtedness the whole yield of the tribal is taken away at a cheap price. Thus, the degree of exploitation by money-lenders was of a higher order. Money lenders normally offer petty loans for festivals, marriages and for purchase of cloths and collect at least three times of the original amount. They usually receive the repayment of loan in kind and normally sell the produce to the traders in the shandy itself instead of taking the trouble of transporting the same to the urban centres.

(e) **Bidari Traders**

These traders draw cash and kind loans from the traders in the plains on the shandy day and advance them as credit to tribal people in the interior and inaccessible villages' in lieu of a fixed quantity of specified produce in the harvesting season. Some of them carry essential commodities like salt, jiggery, tobacco, etc., to the interior villages and exchange them for commercial crops like turmeric, ginger, etc., while spending four to five days and return on the shandy day. The Bidari traders always sell the produce to the same trader who advanced them loan amount.

II. Institutional Agencies/ Tribal Development Co-operative Corporations (TDCCs)

Further, in view of the severe exploitation that had been perpetrated by the private and petty traders, the Government had taken up many remedial measures to extricate tribals from the clutches of money lenders and traders. Various State Governments had taken-up several protective measures in the form of establishing State level TDCCs or other state level Agencies for procurement of MFP from tribals to eliminate the private traders, petty traders, middlemen and Bidari traders from tribal areas and also to render services for the betterment of tribal households. The main objectives of establishing these TDCCs is to ban the activity of private traders in purchasing agricultural and forest produce from tribals at a low price; stop malpractices and cheating in the weighing, payment, quality grade, etc, and stop the exploitation by moneylenders who give loans in exchange for goods.

PART-II

In this context, it is proposed to present and analyse the economic activities undertaken by Girijan Co-operative Corporation Ltd (GCC), which is a dedicated organisation exclusively for the betterment of tribal in Andhra Pradesh. The GCC Head Quarters are located at Visakhapatnam. The Organogram depicting the hierarchical structure of the GCC is presented below:

HIERARCHICAL STRUCTURE OF GIRIJAN CO-OPERATIVE CORPORATION, ANDHRA PRADESH

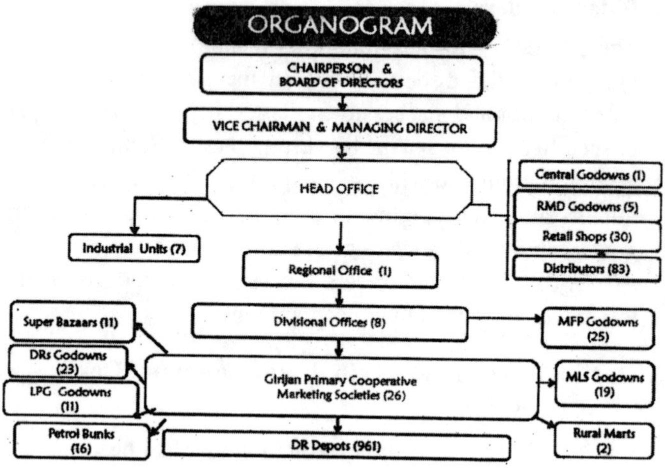

The above Organogram reveals that GCC is headed by a non-official Chairperson, usually nominated by Govt. He/She is assisted by Board of Directors and Vice Chairman cum Managing Director, who is normally a senior I.A.S Officer. It has one Regional Office, eight (08) Divisional Offices, 26 affiliated Girijan Primary Co-operative Marketing Societies (GPCMSs), 961 Daily Requirement (DR) Depots cum Purchase Centres, 73 Storage Godowns excluding 11 LPG Godowns and seven (07) Industrial Units for value addition purposes.

The major objectives of the GCC are:

- To procure Minor Forest Produce (MFP) from tribal families, who are dependent on forests for their livelihood, duly ensuring them remunerative prices through the network of affiliated Primary Societies.

- To procure surplus Agricultural Produce from the tribal farmers to the extent of assured market in competition with private traders.
- To take up value addition to the produce collected and sold by the tribal families so as to ensure realisation of better sale returns for such produce.
- To establish small scale Industrial Units in the tribal areas to develop consumer products and thereby to explore sale potential in the consumer market.
- To supply Essential Commodities (ECs) under PDS and also other daily requirements at competitive prices to the tribal consumers through a wide network of Daily Requirements (DR) sales Depots.
- To provide Credit-support to the tribal farmers for their agricultural activities with repayment facility by way of cash or produce.

PROCUREMENT OF MFP by GCC

- GCC was appointed as "Agent to Government" with monopoly rights for procurement and trade of MFP in scheduled areas of the State.
- As per A.P. Forest Act, 1967, Gum, Myrobolans, Addaleaf and other items whether found in or brought from a forest are declared as "forest produce".
- The A.P. Scheduled Areas MFP (Regulation of Trade) Regulation, 1979 further specifies MFP as any forest produce other than timber, trees and charcoal, as may be notified by the Government in this behalf.
- The MFP units leased out to GCC are thrown open to the tribal for collection of the produce.
- As stipulated in the Forest Act, 1967 and Regulation, 1979, the produce from the forests should be transported on prescribed "Permit". In pursuance of this stipulation, GCC is taking up transportation of MFP after obtaining "Form-I & Form-II Permits" from Forest department.
- The Pricing policy dictates that GCC should pass on the nearest whole sale market rate of MFP commodities to the tribal without making any deductions towards over heads and establishment costs.
- As many as 35 items were originally notified as MFP under the said Trade Regulation, 1979.

Procurement Methodology of MFP

The procurement activity is being monitored by the affiliated Girijan Primary Marketing Societies and the maintenance of Storage godowns is entrusted to MFP/SAP stocks.

- The procurement prices fixed are declared well in advance and wide publicity is being given in the tribal areas.
- Purchases are made in the Weekly Markets/shandies, notified Purchase Centers, D.R. Depots and also in the villages of the gatherers to suit the convenience of tribal.
- Minimum Support Price Scheme (MSP) of G.O.I, is being implemented.
- Entire range of produce collected by the tribal is being procured irrespective of its quantity and quality to mitigate hardship in this regard to tribal.
- Weighing of produce, billing and spot payment in cash to the MFP gatherers is ensured.

The purchase prices of MFP commodities by GCC during 2020-21 are presented in the following Table 10.1:

Tabie 10.1: Purchase Prices of MFP Commodities during 2020-21

Sl. No.	Name of the Commodity	Purchase Price Per Kg (Rs)	Sl. No.	Name of Commodity	Purchase Price Per Kg (Rs)
1.	Rock Bee Honey	170.00	11.	Adda leaf	7.00
2.	Apiary Honey	150.00	12.	Hill Brooms(Nos)	35-45
3.	Honey Wax	150.00	13.	Wild Brooms(Nos)	21.00
4.	Myrobalans	12.00	14.	Dry Amla	55.00
5.	Marking Nuts	10.00	15.	Cleaning Nuts	45.00
6.	Nuxvomica Seed	52.00	16.	Mohwa Flower	10.00
7.	Naramamidi Bark	22.00	17.	Terripods	NA
8.	Soap Nuts	25.00	18.	Raulphia serpentine Roots	100.00
9.	Sheekakai	50.00	19.	Sugandhipala	NA
10.	Maredugaddalu	350.00	20.	Kusum Oil Seed.	NA

As per the information furnished by the GCC, around one lakh tribal families benefited with MFP procurement activity during 2020-21. Under the Scheme of MSP for MFP, the Govt. of India released Rs 828.75 lakhs towards revolving fund since 2016-17. Against which, GCC had purchased MFP worth Rs 1286.12 lakhs during 2016-17 to 2020-21.

SUPPLY OF ESSENTIAL COMMODITIES (ECs) AND OTHER ITEMS TO TRIBALS

- In early 1950s, the tribal economy was non-monetized and "Barter system" was more prevalent. The tribal were subjected to exploitation of the unscrupulous petty traders in this barter system.
- In 1956, while forming GCC, the Government entrusted the responsibility of catering to the daily needs of the tribal through a specially designed network of "Domestic Requirements Sales Depots".
- In this background, GCC started opening of sales depots in the tribal areas together with a marketing network for MFP.
- Over the years, more number of D.R. Depots within the easy reach of the tribals were opened to avoid trekking long distances for fetching their daily needs.
- The Government institutionalised the distribution of Essential commodities such as Rice, Sugar, Kerosene, Palm oil etc. under PDS to the ration-card holders in the agency areas of the State through GCC.
- Pursuant to this directive the D.R. Depots of GCC are now functioning as Fair Price Shops. Besides essential commodities, other items such as pulses, edible oils, salt, dry fish, Jaggery, cloth items, Utensils etc. are also made available to the tribal consumers at competitive rates in these depots.
- GCC appointed local tribal youth as Salesmen in these depots to serve the card holders without any interruption.

ECs distribution process

- The ration cards of the tribal consumers are attached to the nearest D.R. Depot and supplying ECs through Home delivery by the Govt. mobile vehicles.
- The ECs under PDS are distributed to the card holders as per their eligibility and at the rates fixed by the Government.
- For uninterrupted distribution of ECs, maintenance of Mandal-level stock points and Stage-II transportation on behalf of A.P. Civil Supplies Corporation is also taken up.
- The entire activity is carried out by the GPCM Societies under the overall supervision of the Divisional Managers.

Supply of other Daily Requirements

- The daily needs such as Pulses, edible oils, Salt, Jaggery, Utensils, cloth items, fancy goods and cosmetics procured from open market are supplied to tribal consumers at competitive rates.
- "Girijan" brand value added products also are made available in the depots to the general public and tribal consumers.
- Separate storage godowns for ECs and other items have been opened under the control of GPCM Societies.

Supplies to T.W Educational Institutions

- GCC undertakes monthly supply of food provisions and cosmetics to about 3.25.
- Lakh inmates of Tribal Welfare Residential Junior Colleges, Residential Schools, Ashram Schools, Hostels, children of Anganwadi Centers and other Government Institutions on credit basis.

Retail marketing by GCC

Aims and Objectives

- Avoidance of bulk sale of raw produce collected by the tribal.
- Value addition to the MFP and Agricultural produce through processing to realise better sale returns.
- Retail marketing of products eliminating middle level market forces and reaching end-consumers direct.
- Exploring consumer-market potential to the maximum possible extent for the natural, pure and organic products of the tribal.
- Continuous efforts to bring out quality products and to pursue sale in competition with leading brands in consumer market.

Institutional arrangements made

- Small industrial units to take up value addition.
- Processing centers in tribal areas for cleaning and processing thereby generating income to the tribal women.
- Storage godowns exclusively for Value added Products.
- Distributors network in major towns for value added products.

Table 10.2: Industrial Units and Processinq Centers of GCC

S.No.	Name of the Unit	Location
1.	Honey processing unit	Rajahmundry
2.		Chittoor
3.	Soap making unit	Vizianagaram
4.		Araku valley
5.	Sheekakayi pulverizing unit	R. Chodavaram
6.	Turmeric Powdering Unit	V. Madugula
7.	Tamarind Processing Unit	Saluru

Table 10.3: Processing of MFP Commodities taken up by GCC

Sl. No	Name of MFP	Processing done	End product
1.	Honey	Pasteurisation & moisture reduction	Bottled Honey
2.	Tamarind	Deseeding, de-pulping and flower making	Pulp & Flower Tamarind
3.	Soap nuts	Deseeding, pulverizing and extraction	Pulp, Powder & Shampoo
4.	Sheekakai	Deseeding, pulverizing and extraction	Pulp, Powder & Shampoo
5.	Amla	Deseeding, pulverizing and extraction	Powder & Sherbet and in Triphala
6.	Maredugaddalu	Extraction	Sherbet
7.	Myrobolans	Pulverizing and extraction	Triphala powder & liquid concentrate
8.	Tanikaya	Pulverizing and extraction	Triphala powder & liquid concentrate
9.	Hill brooms	Grading & bundling	Packed Broom

Table 10.4: Processing of Agricultural Commodities by GCC, Visakhapatnam

Sl. No.	Agricultural Produce	Processing done	End product
1.	Turmeric	Drumming, polishing, pulverizing & packing	Turmeric Power packs of different sizes
2.	Rajmah	Cleaning & packing	Rajmah packs of different sizes
3.	Kattings		Kattings packs of different sizes
4.	White Beans		White bean packs of different sizes
5.	Dry Chillies	Pulverizing & packing	Chilli power packs of different sizes
6.	Ragi	Powdering & Packing	Powder Packs of different sizes

AGRO-CREDIT ACTIVITY by GCC

- Till 1990s, the tribal farmers were almost totally dependent on money lenders for their agricultural needs due to ineffective institutional credit flow and disinterest of the commercial banks on tribal areas owing to poor repayment capacity of the tribal farmers.

- GCC's loaning strategy emerged in the given background and after its recognition as a District Cooperative Central bank and its affiliated GPCM Societies as PACs by NABARD vide its Ref. No.NB.Hyd/3118/Plan/H.51/90-91 dt.28.05.1990.
- Thereafter GCC secured credit limit from NABARD and extended short-term, Medium-Term and also Long-term loans to the tribal farmers after the year 1990.
- Due to continuous drought conditions and crop failure tribal farmers remain as chronic defaulters in repayment of loans to GPCMS.
- At this stage the Interest relief and Debt waiver packages sanctioned by the G.O.I and State Government have reduced the burden on the tribal farmers to greater extent. But the repayments by the tribal farmers to the GPCMS are badly suffered.

Present loaning strategy

- To concentrate on interior tribal villages which are not effectively served by the commercial banks and other lending agencies.
- To extend crop loans at reasonable scale of finance suitable to the tribal farmers and thereby reducing the loan burden on them.
- To provide repayment facility to the tribal farmers in small amounts at their convenience in cash or through MFP/SAP.
- D.R. Depot to function as a single window for loan disbursement and its collection through cash or produce.

Coffee Plantation

This Project was sanctioned to Integrated Tribal Development Agency (ITDA), Paderu, which consists of 11 Agency Mandals in Visakhapatnam District of Andhra Pradesh. This agency/scheduled area are about 4500 ft. above the sea level with required tree shade and convenient for growing coffee plantation based on climatic conditions. As such, the Government have sanctioned a Comprehensive Coffee Development Project (CCDP) at an estimated outlay of Rs 56.00 Cr. covering ten year period from 2015-16 to 2024-25. The outlay was proposed to be met under State Tribal Sub-Plan (TSP) funds amounting to Rs 34.00 Cr and balance of Rs 22.00 Cr as subsidy from Coffee Board. The specific; features of this project include quality improvement through wet processing and organic certification.

This certification issue was entrusted to Girijana Vikas Swachanda Samstha & Girijan Vikas (NGO) @ Rs 1.00 lakh/per month for getting certification through M/S TQ Certfn. Services. Pvt Ltd., (A wholly owned subsidiary of Tata Projects Ltd.). Accordingly, the organic certification costs Rs 36.00 Cr for a period of three years.

The GCC offers marketing support by way of (a) pooling of coffee seeds from tribal coffee growers and (b) undertaking processing and marketing activities through auctions'. The tribal coffee growers, hitherto, are being paid sale proceeds from TSP funds/ Coffee Board subsidy. However, the APEX Committee decided to arrange payment to tribal coffee growers in single installment subject to necessary approval in this regard from the Govt.

Table 10.5: Procurement and Sale of Coffee Beans during 2015-16 to 2020-21

<table>
<tr><th rowspan="2">Season / Year</th><th rowspan="2">No. of farmers</th><th rowspan="2">Ar. Parchment (in MTs)</th><th rowspan="2">Ar. Cherry (in MTs)</th><th rowspan="2">Rob. Cherry (in MTs)</th><th rowspan="2">Total Quantity (in MTs)</th><th rowspan="2">Total Sale Value (In Rs. Lakhs)</th><th colspan="3">Sale Value paid to Farmers (In Rs. per kg)</th></tr>
<tr><th>Parchment</th><th>Cherry</th><th>Robusta</th></tr>
<tr><td>2015-16</td><td>4744</td><td>166.11</td><td>1237.84</td><td>0.00</td><td>1403.95</td><td>1121.66</td><td>155.78</td><td>69.71</td><td>0.00</td></tr>
<tr><td>2016-17</td><td>1444</td><td>143.45</td><td>170.99</td><td>13.35</td><td>327.79</td><td>368.22</td><td>151.07</td><td>81.72</td><td>60.62</td></tr>
<tr><td>2017-18</td><td>4203</td><td>203.34</td><td>672.76</td><td>2.52</td><td>878.62</td><td>802.83</td><td>139.68</td><td>78.12</td><td>60.62</td></tr>
<tr><td>2018-19</td><td>2747</td><td>187.46</td><td>867.19</td><td>10.26</td><td>1064.91</td><td>799.58</td><td>130.00</td><td>63.30</td><td>67.77</td></tr>
<tr><td>2019-20</td><td>929</td><td>42.00</td><td>145.22</td><td>13.30</td><td>200.52</td><td>166.04</td><td>156.92</td><td>67.93</td><td>66.80</td></tr>
<tr><td>2020-21</td><td>293</td><td>9.75</td><td>131.30</td><td>64.49</td><td>205.54</td><td>137.00</td><td>140.00</td><td>63.00</td><td>63.00</td></tr>
<tr><td>Total</td><td>14360</td><td>752.11</td><td>3225.30</td><td>103.92</td><td>4081.33</td><td>3395.33</td><td></td><td></td><td></td></tr>
</table>

It is evident from Table 10.5 that a total of 4081.33 metric tons of the three categories of coffee seeds were procured by GCC from a total of 14,360 tribal farmers during 2015-16 to 2020-21. It is also evident that the number of farmers and the quantity procured declined substantially during the period covered. Considering the years 2015-16 and 2017-18, it is true that there is no definite relation between the number of farmers and the quantity of coffee seeds procured. Therefore, the GCC need to step up its procurement activity of coffee seeds from tribal farmers so as to not to allow them to fall into the trap of private traders.

In this context, it is proposed to study the procurement of agricultural produce in respect of seven commodities by GCC, for which the data was made available. The same is presented in Table 10.6 below covering the five year period from 2016-17 to 2020-21. Since the commodity rajmah is split into three varieties, the total number comes to seven instead of five.

Table 10.6: COMMODITY-WISE PROCUREMENT OF AGRICUTURAL PRODUCE BY GIRIJAN CO-OPERATIVE CORPORATION LTD, VISAKHAPTNAM, ANDHRA PRADESH

(Qty in Qtls & Value in Rs Lakhs)

	2016-17		2017-18		2018-19		2019-20		2020-21		Total		% Qty	% Value
Items	**Qty**	**Value**	**Qty**	**Value**	**Qty**	**Value**	**Qty**	**Value**	**Qty**	**Value**	**Qty**	**Value**		
Turmeric	579.49	54.51	635.07	58.87	2579.9	229.4	15.3	1.38	0	0	3809.8	344.15	9.60	10.41
Chillies	1320.4	90.37	1498.2	118.6	1307.4	109.6	876.6	97	651.9	78.33	5654.5	493.91	14.26	14.95
Rajmah (Red)	309.94	14.6	728.45	32.75	343.26	16.35	787.3	37.56	261.7	17.01	2430.7	118.27	6.13	3.58
Rajmah (White)	0	0	0	0	80.94	5.67	0	0	0	0	80.94	5.67	0.20	0.17
Kattings	40.4	1.21	53.47	1.6	14.9	0.45	18.6	0.65	14.5	0.44	141.87	4.35	0.36	0.13
Annato Seeds	3.37	0.15	0	0	6.05	0.06	736.4	62.36	28.06	2.26	773.88	64.83	1.95	1.96
Coffee	3277.9	368.2	8786.2	802.8	10649	799.6	2005.2	166	2055	137	26774	2273.7	67.50	68.80
Total	5531.51	529.1	11701.4	1014.6	14982	1161	4439.4	365	3012	235	39665	3304.9	100.00	100.00
% in Total	**13.95**	**16.01**	**29.50**	**30.70**	**37.77**	**35.13**	**11.19**	**11.04**	**7.59**	**7.11**	**100.00**	**100.00**		

Source: GIRIJAN Co-operative Corporation Ltd, Vishakapatnam.

It is evident from the above Table 10.6 that the commodity 'coffee' dominated in procurement, both in quantity and value terms, to the extent of around 68 percent followed by chillies, turmeric, rajmah and annato seeds during the period covered. Prior to Covid-19 pandemic i.e., 2019-20, there was a definite trend of increase in procurement of the agricultural commodities considered, both in quantity and value terms. Also, it can be noticed that there is a significant fall in value of coffee during Covid-19 pandemic years, 2019-20 and 2020-21, though its procurement quantity-wise is above 2000 Metric Tons in each year. Therefore, the GCC need to secure better value to the agricultural commodities procured from tribal farmers in the post-Covid scenario. It may be pertinent to mention that the Government of India, represented by Tribal Co-operative Marketing Development Federation of India (TRIFED) conferred National Award, 2nd rank, to Andhra Pradesh and GCC for procuring highest total value of MFP procured worth Rs 4,50,74,000.

Conclusion

It is an established fact that tribal in India form the very segment of the weaker sections of the society. They have been living in remote, interior and inaccessible areas including on hill-tops and slopes. They depend, by and large, on agriculture and collection of minor forest produce for their livelihood. Higher priority is, therefore, required to be given to increase the productivity of agriculture in tribal area. Besides, procurement of agricultural produce and MFP to be stepped up and provision of better marketing facilities are required to these twin spheres of activity in any programme of action for the development of tribes in India. The tribal economy is woven round the weekly markets or 'Haats', where a considerable portion of the transactions are still being carried out under barter system. The weekly market is, therefore, happens to be the hub for many social and economic activities reflecting their day to day needs and caters practically for all the requirements and needs of the tribal, express or latent. In this context, the Andhra Pradesh State owned Girijan Co-operative Corporation Ltd, Visakhapatnam is playing a protective role between the innocent tribal and the private money lender cum trader, while procuring and selling agricultural and Minor Forest Produce (MFP) in order to pass on the benefit to tribal. Also, the GCC need to step up its marketing activity in order to access the national and regional markets for securing better price for tribal's produce.

References

1. Behera, H.C 2008. Weekly Market in Tribal Areas:A case study in Kadhamal District of Orissa, Man in India, 88(4):585-600.
2. Chakravarti, I and Verma, R.1991, Marketing of Minor Forest Produce (MFP) in Tribal Sub-Plan (TSP) Area through Co-operatives in Rajasthan, Indian Journal of Economics, 73(3): 311-320.
3. Chandra, R.1973. Market in Tribal Village: Its Socio-Economic Implications among the Bhils, Vanyajati, 21(2):52-59.
4. Dongre, Y. 2003. Role of Maharashtra State Co-operative Tribal Development Corporation in the Tribal Marketing. Co-operative Perspective, 38(1) 2003: 32-38.
5. Geil, A. 1982. The Market Wheel: Symbolic aspects of an Indian Tribal Market, MAN, 17(3): 470-491.
6. Maharashtra, S. 1989. Tribal Groups and Market Development in India, Journal of Rural Development, 8(2):135-145.
7. Mahalingam, S. 1993. Integrated Credit and Marketing Support to the Tribals through Co-operative Institutions in Arunachal Pradesh- A case Study. Land Bank journal, 31(4): 1-2.
8. Moharana, B.B 1977. A Weekly Tribal Market in Orissa, Journal of Social Research, 20(2): 41-53.
9. Rajgopal. 1988. Economics of periodic Markets and Cultural Integration in Tribal Areas: A Case Study, Tribal Research bulletin, 10(2):21-29.
10. Sharma, S. 2006. Dynamics of Tribal Market in India: With Special Reference to Jharkhand, Journal of Development and Management Studies, 4(1): 1745-1761.
11. Verma, R.R. 2004. Tribal Exploitation in Marketing System: A Case Study with reference to Sahibganj District (Santhal Paragana), Journal of Regional Studies, 14(30): 69-82.
12. Girijan Co-operative Corporation Ltd. Visakhapatnam- A note on its Activities, 2021.

11

Digitalisation Banking

Introduction

Banking is a service industry. The product manufactured by it is a service, which is multi-dimensional in nature. Banking institutions are no longer expected to act as traditional mobiliser and deployer of financial resources in a particular country. Now they have to act as catalyst of change in the service sector. On account of globalisation and liberalisation, several sweeping changes have taken place in the financial sector. Since mid-1991, in India, there have been many financial reforms like deregulation of interest rates, dismantling of direct credit, etc. These economic reforms have created ample opportunities and challenges to financial intermediaries. They present banks, besides devising a suitable package of services to the domestic users of services, have to face the challenges of formulating an appropriate package of financial services useful to both domestic and international users.

Present banks in future have to face stiff competition in the financial sector. They cannot sell services which are not user-specific. They would have to act as providers of services in buyers' market rather than sellers' market. The market driven banking is moving beyond the horizons of direct banking. In view of this, the banks have to adopt modern strategic marketing philosophy, besides, maintaining banks of operational management of their services. Modern bank management starts with the customers, live with customers and dies because of the customers. So, it is very important to know about the customer behaviour. The formulation of marketing mix is directly or indirectly influenced by changing behaviour of the users. A gradual change in the users' behaviour is a natural phenomenon as multi facet developments in the socio-economic condition affect their mental condition. Either the general users or the industrial users can not overlook the impact of socio-economic transformation on their needs and requirements. The growing rate of literacy, expanding avenues for job creation, changing environmental conditions, Governmental regulations, sophistication in communication, innovation in education and a number of allied factors govern the behaviour of users. It is essential that a marketer is aware of all these developments so as to make the marketing decisions productive or effective.

Banking Technology and Customers' Satisfaction

Technology in the banks is presently catching up with a high level of development around the world. The gaps between the Indian banks and their counterparts in the technologically advanced countries are gradually narrowing down. The world has witnessed an information and technological revolution of late. This revolution has touched every aspect of public life including banking. Since two decades, due to an increasingly competitive, saturated and dynamic business environment, retail banks in many countries have adopted customer-driven philosophies to address the rapid and changing needs of their customers (Walker *et al.*, 2008). Technological advances have changed the world radically, altering the manner in which individuals conduct their personal and business affairs. Over the past two decades in particular, the banking industry has invested substantial resources in bringing ICT to customers. The banking industry is undergoing through the significant technological changes; it has several impacts on customer satisfaction and loyalty. "It has revolutionised every industry including banking in the world by rendering faster and cost effective delivery of products and services to the customers. Core banking solution enables banks to extend the full benefits of ATM, tele-banking, mobile banking, internet banking, card banking and other multiple delivery channels to all customers allowing banks to offer a multitude of customer centric services on a 24x7 basis from a single location, supporting retail as well as corporate banking activities (Chakrabarty, 2010).

Technology is the surest and most appropriate way of bringing inclusion in respect of any product and/or service. The banking industry is a large and highly diverse service industry than other services. This industry covers all types of customers and their financial needs including deposit, lending and other banking services. It also makes a significant contribution in the economic development of the nation. Recent world wide technological revolution influenced the banking industry than other service sector in India.

Since 1980, Indian banking sector undergoing through technological advancement phase and most of the banks have countered their business as e-business. Technology and the internet have had a profound effect on service marketing including banking services. Banks today are increasingly providing customer service in support of relationship marketing strategic objectives, with the help of technology via e-service. With these developments, a new era of banking has emerged, which is known as "e-banking." E-banking encompasses an arrangement of financial transactions, once done through the tangible exchange of information, now are done electronically (Moutaz Abou-Robieh, 2005).

E-banking services are new services for Indian customers. As a result Indian banks are investing heavily in the technologies such as branch automation and computerisation, core banking, tele-banking, mobile banking (M-banking), internet banking, automated teller machine (ATMs), data warehousing etc. ICT innovations in the previous few years have changed the landscape of banks in India (Mittal and Dhingra, 2007). Today public sector and private sector banks are offering online banking services. Various alternative channels to provide easy and anywhere banking are properly thought of. The process of bank computerisation was stated since 1985 in public sector banks in India. However, some private sector banks have started computerisation prior to the public sector banks in India. The banks in India are using ICT not only to improve their own internal processes but also to increase facilities and services to their customers. The Reserve Bank is playing an important role in bringing the technology based banking, which has resulted in large scale computerisation of the banking sector in India. The Financial Sector Technology (FST) vision serves as a lighthouse for the banks to make their own IT initiatives based on the broad approach as envisioned by the Reserve Bank. With the efforts of the RBI today most of public sector banks are fully computerised as on 2010. Now, there are various alternative banking services available to bank customers in India e.g. core banking, ATM, credit card, debit card, NEFT, RTGS, SWIFT, internet banking, mobile banking, MICR clearing, speed clearing, cheque truncation etc.

A customer satisfaction is an ambiguous and abstract concept. Actual manifestation of the state of satisfaction will vary from person to person, product to product and service to service. The state of satisfaction depends on a number of factors which consolidate as psychological, economic and physical factors. The quality of service is one of the major determinants of the customer satisfaction, which can be enhanced by using ICT available to survive. The banks in India are using Information Technology (IT) not only to improve their own internal processes but also to increase facilities and services to their customers. Particularly, in the banking sector ICT is one of the most important tools, because it provides many suitable alternative banking channels to the customers. It brings connivance, customer centricity, enhance service quality and cost effectiveness in the banking services. Even now, customers are evaluating their banks based on availability of high-tech services. Therefore, implementation of ICT in the banking business continues to improve the banking service. Many researchers from USA, UK, Finland, Malaysia, Taiwan, etc. have proved that the use of technology positively affects the customers satisfaction in banking industry. But some researches evidence that, technology based banking service can't satisfy the each and every need of the customers "and each type of customers". There are may be some possibilities of gaps between customers "expectations and actual services perception in ICT based banking service, which leads to customer dissatisfaction. Hence, there is a need to assess the impact of alternative banking services on customers" satisfaction in India context to study the level of satisfaction, problems and areas of further improvements.

Adoption of Core Banking Values

At many banks the implementation of core banking has consumed significant resources and management attention over last five years. Following the RBI mandate on core banking, banks move forward with large core banking transformation programmes. The focus was on automation and significant progress was made in reducing manual processes specifically at the branch. Customer data was centralised, teller operations were streamlined and networks were established to connect branches to a common platform.

However, this initiative has also been inwardly focused. Many banks have adopted a "lift and shift" approach of moving processes as is with "workarounds" rather than a holistic business process reengineering approach. In many cases, this has resulted in sub-optimal implementations with dubious business cases. In the current scenario, most banks use their core banking system as a "transaction platform" without getting the full benefit of enterprise customer insight and process integration. There is a significant opportunity to reduce redundant steps in processes, optimize core banking functionality to reduce revenue leakage and speed up customer service processes.

The establishment of a core banking platform has, however, given banks a strong launch pad to offer various services across alternate channels such as the web, mobile, call centers, ATMs, kiosks, and other systems, such as point of sale. It has also helped to build a robust repository of data, both static as well as transactional, which could potentially be leveraged to analyze and offer business solutions targeted at specific customer segments. The implementation of core banking therefore, narrowed the technology gap that was very apparent between private banks and public sector banks.

Core banking has also spawned multiple initiatives in the areas of IT governance, infrastructure, performance improvement, upgrade of data center, real time alerts on security incidents, bolstering business continuity planning and disaster recovery, virtualisation of servers among others. Overall this has been a big step forward for the industry and has increased maturity levels across the board.

Customer Satisfaction Index

Indian Customer Satisfaction Index (ICSI), unveiled the first-of-its-kind Customer Satisfaction Industry Benchmarking Report, highlighting the score of Indian Banking Industry at 69. The report used ACSI methodology to successfully measure customer satisfaction and related consumer perceptions within twelve of the largest commercial banks in India.

ICSI analysed customer data that was collected in the last months of financial year, 2015 and early 2016. It measured customer's cumulative satisfaction based on their anticipation of the quality of goods and services.

Bank Names	Customer Satisfaction Scores
Axis Bank	68
Bank of Baroda	68
Bank of India	65
Canara Bank	66
Citibank	73
HDFC Bank	68
HSBC Bank	76
ICICI Bank	70
Kotak Mahindra Bank	71
Pubjab National Bank	67
Standard Chartered Bank	74
State Bank of India	62

Source: www.icsi.org.in

The nationwide research, conducted on 12 commercial banks across length and breadth of India included Axis Bank, Bank of Baroda, Bank of India (BOI), Canara Bank, Citibank, HDFC, HSBC, ICICI, Kotak Mahindra Bank, Punjab National Bank, State Bank of India and Standard Chartered Bank.

Revamping the Digital Agenda

By 2020 the average age of India will be 29 years. This new age consumer based is technology savvy, always connected and looking for a personalised, contextual experience with real-time online information. Cell phone penetration has reached almost 85 percent and the rise of the middle class has increased the number of households with internet connectivity.

Banks are acknowledging this change and almost all banks are in the process of rolling out online, mobile and social banking extensions to their core offerings in an effort to respond to this changing consumer demographic. Several banks have deployed best in class online and mobile banking feature including personalisation, bank wide customer relationship views and cross channel integration.

However, branches continue to remain the primary service delivery channel for all banks. In many banks, we see very low customer migration to alternate delivery channels. There are several reasons for low adoption rates. The key issue is consumer behaviour many banks have large customer segments who are not computer savvy and still do not have access to the internet. This segment has grown up with a deep rooted faith in paper transactions and the belief that the branch is the place to conduct all banking transaction. Added to this is the fear of transacting online. While measures such as 3-factor authentication and one-time passwords are starting to make a difference, online security is still a very big concern, especially for the older generation of banking customers. Banks are therefore, undertaking channel migration initiatives to increase enrolment of new customers and increase usage across customers who have already enrolled for the internet banking service. In order to increase enrolment and activation, banks are integrating the opening of an online account along with the basic account opening process so that a new customer receives her online banking credentials along with the welcome kit. Once the customer has been enrolled there is a need to create an ecosystem that drives the channel usage for enrolled customers.

Indian banks need to aspire high and move toward implementing world-class digital capabilities. Digital transformation involves delivering new consumer propositions that are engaging, comprehensible, intuitive, personalised and contextual to customers by leveraging underlying digital technologies such as the internet, mobile, social cloud and analytics. To do this banks need to start thinking differently about their digital channels and deliver capabilities that are not a mere replica of basic banking transactions but those that provide customers a strong handle on their current and prospective future financial health along with intuitive information dissemination to make better financial decisions — be it for transacting, saving or shopping through the web.

Digital Transformation

One of the major advantages offered by digital technologies is that they enable enterprises to modify business process to attain operational and financial excellence. In addition, they can improve customer experience substantially.

The banking sector has been at the forefront of digital adoption-both in business as well as technology. In the past six to seven years, banks in India have evolved to provide digital avenues from Internet banking to mobile banking to more recently, social application banking. Banking will continue to go digital in a wider manner, as Digital India government policies to enable mass financial inlusion across the country will gain steam.

According to a CII report, the banking sector in India is currently worth INR 81 trillion, and is expected to become the fifth largest in the world by 2020. The BFSI sector contributes about 40 percent of the revenue for major IT companies. As digital technologies evolve around the concept of data sharing over public networks on a number of devices, ensuring privacy and security related with banks are the major concerns at all levels. Hence, adoption of digital technologies will impact the core processes of a bank at a much deeper level, requiring them to revisit their legacy IT infrastructure and workflows.

A major differentiator among banks is the speed in customer query resolution, the response time, and the extent of omni channel support. A service oriented industry; there is growing expectation that customer service and response is instantaneous as well as appropriate in tone. It is a daunting task to ensure such services when responses and notifications are triggered through non-human interactions. For example, when and how should an alert be sent to a credit card holder if the credit limit is reached, has to be carefully devised in order to expect quick action from the customer without sounding negative.

The other challenge is that use of various channels for financial transactions requires that the transactions are ubiquitous and migrate seamlessly between channels. For example, if a transaction is initiated in one device, the user should be able to complete the transaction in another device, even if on another network.

These are but a small percentage of challenges that are shaping the contours of new-age banking. Digital transformation initiatives in this vast industry are gaining momentum due to the increase in consumerisation of IT. The use of digital technologies in the sector has enabled banks provide differentiation in terms of services and solution and hence attract new customers as well as retain existing customers. Two major challenges of the Indian banking sector are presence of huge unbanked population heterogeneous economic and social conditions of the existing customers. These challenges can become opportunities for banks, if strategies are framed by banks to address pain points of all the people.

Banks have two approaches with respect to adopting digital transformation.

The first one is to upgrade back office systems to address demands of the new age technologies. This will involve modification in the current IT systems to be compatible with analytics and mobility tools, revamping the data centers to move into service based offering, improving the usability of application interface (API), and developing a suitable enterprise architecture framework with service oriented architecture enabled core system.

The second approach, digital banking, is the key to improve banking experience of the consumers. It includes all services from missed call banking to mobile phone banking to address the requirements of various set of customers. Banks have utilised digital technologies not only to improve internal processes and address the digitally-aware population, but also to reach the unbanked population.

For example, HDFC bank has the facility of missed call banking, wherein the rural population can give a missed call and get a call back from the call center in the local language to address their query. At the same time banks are catering to the highly techno savvy customer as well. For example, even before the introduction of Google watch in India, HDFC had launched mobile banking Apps for Google watch.

Many initiatives adopted by Indian banks are within the social, mobility, analytics and cloud (SMAC) framework and related technologies. While some of these initiatives are still conservative, they have enabled banks to look at newer ways of customer and employee engagement and empowerment.

Social: Indian banks are not only using public social networks for consumer interaction, understanding customer sentiments, and personal branding, but also offering real time money transfers. Banks such as Kotak Mahindra (KayPay on Facebook) and ICICI (icici bankpay on Twitter and Pockets by ICICI Bank on Facebook) have enabled a number of banking services such as fund transfers, account balance and transaction checking, and even recharging prepaid mobile phones.

Mobility: Banks in India are considering the mobile first approach for launching new application, as more than half of the total transactions that happened in 2014 were on mobile phones. Besides improved penetration of smart phones, the mobile first approach can be attributed to the development of user friendly application and increased awareness among consumers for using mobile applications due to the emergence of e-Commerce.

Analytics: In early 2000, banks like HDFC and ICICI set up their data warehousing centers and invested in the technology to analyze the huge data available. With advancement in technology and reduction in cost of its application, man power, computing and analysis, banks are trying to integrate high end analytics tools to the existing big data warehouse and the bank's core operations to gain valuable insights on customers. The insights generated would help banks to generate additional revenue and at the same time, lower the risk of being exposed to fraudulent activities.

Cloud: Banks in India are using public cloud to move applications such as lead management, e-mail services, and human capital management which tend to fluctuate in volume. Though public cloud platforms provide the advantages of decreased total cost of ownership, increased flexibility and agility, relief from software licensing management, and reduced cost for hardware maintenance and IT talent, concerns of security, regulations and interoperability are preventing banks from adopting public cloud platforms for mission critical applications.

Security and privacy issues are the major barriers for digital technology adoption in banks. Banks fear insecure application programme interface, confidential data leakage, and malicious attacks. The lack of proper mechanism that decides on issues of ownership, accountability, and risks is also acting as an inhibitor. Moreover, there is lack of regulatory standards such as compliance with laws and regulations and legal liability.

In the next five years, the adoption of digital technologies in the banking sector will be driven by improvement in regulations pertaining to data sharing and ownership, sector specific solutions that address issues related with security and privacy, and improvement in solutions and services to suit rapidly changing new age consumer preferences. Private and public sector banks should concentrate on improving their legacy infrastructure to make them compatible to new age tools. Rural banks and credit cooperatives need to leverage the advantages of mobility and analytics to facilitate financial inclusion.

Need for the Study

The IT (Information Technology) revolution is entirely changing the way the banking business transaction which leads in widened the range of product and services as well as demands and expectations level of the customers. For the systematic improvement of software process, knowledge and experience of its employees and customers cannot be overlooked in an organisation. The majority of the population in India opting bank deposits as a good investment option though majority of them still are unbanked. There is a huge scope for the expansion of the banking operations in India. The banks are serving wide range of services to the customers with technology and able reach even in rural market.

In this scenario there is a desperate need to identify how public and private sector banks are learning and adopting Digitalisation in this competitive environment and there is a need to study that digitalisation practices in public and private sector banks are catering to the needs of the customers and employees as well or not.

Significance of the Study

After independence India planned economic growth for efficient financial system to meet the many multifarious requirements of credit and development. To formulate this objective they adopted a mixed pattern of economic development and analysed effective the financial system. Banks had adopted various core banking technology to enhance customer relationships and expand the market for banking services. The technology ought to help the banks achieve cost-effective scalability in the services they render which indicates in productivity enhancing through total factor productivity growth in the banking industry. The impact of digitalisation in Indian banking sector has been discussed. This project deals various issue of digitalisation adoption among the employee and customers.

The factors to be understood in understanding the digitalisation requirements shall be elucidated along with the inter-relationship between the technologies and workplace transformation. Exploring the impact of digitalisation the research also examines other aspects such as digitalisation practices, adaptability of digitalisation and implementation of digital solution in the banking sectors.

Problem Statement

Computer are getting more sophisticated will indicates rises in banks potential and have given bank customer high expectations. Convergence of computing, communications, information and knowledge in radically changing the way Indian banks operate. RBI notified that there is lack of vision among banks in providing the effective user friendly technology. Regulatory and policy compliance are need to be implemented properly. To overcome for this kind of issues most of the banks in India are using information technology to meet core needs. The central bank said despite technology, bank penetration and productivity had not risen as desired. In turn, customers who visit the bank for high value transactions and other important business can be given more attention and better service. But concerted efforts are required to make the customers, especially the elderly and the not so tech-savy, who may not be comfortable and reluctant to use the machines. With the development of information technology, the world has become a global village and it has brought a revolution in the banking industry. The banks appear to be on fast track for IT based products and services. Bank customers are becoming very demanding and it is the extensive use of technology that enables banks to satisfy adequately the requirement of customers. Further the banking sector reforms and introduction of e-banking has made very structural changes in service quality, managerial decisions, operational performance, profitability and productivity of the banks. E-banking is one of the emerging trends in the Indian banking and is playing a unique role in strengthening the banking sector and improving service quality. Hence digitalisation in Indian banking sector have to learn the technology to cater the needs of the customers. Digital solution should be learnt, embraced and implemented in Indian banking sectors to enhance the customer expectations than as regulatory or policy compliance. By effective utilisation of digitalisation in banking sector help to reduce delays in rendering services, workload and overcome from many frauds aspects.

Review of Literature

Nagar, Nirupma and Mishra, Jitendra Kumar (2002): - The present study is confined to State Bank of Indore which has large spread of branches in most of the parts of Madhya Pradesh. The bank lengthy judicial process, time and costs overrun in project implementation, shortage of raw materials etc. the state banks is trending low with regard to NPAs year by year basis so as to reduce this particular situation it can be tackled through better selection of borrowers, more scientific credit appraisal and supervision.

Aparna, T (2002):- This study focuses that SBI is the largest and traditional public-sector banks of India. As to trigger the changes in this competitive world SBI felt the need to restructure itself. SBI is planning for technology upgradation which has shifted its focus from traditional banking to retail finance and housing finance. The financial performance of banks has been satisfactory over a period of time. SBI has automated 80 percent of its business operations and is possessing high number of ATM's in the country. SBI should continue its restructuring process as to merge to the user satisfaction.

Kumar, Pramod (2006):- The study attempts to explore the broad structure of banking system in India, to analyze the overall efficiency of the system in terms of various financial parameters, technical efficiency and allocation efficiency. The analysis has been carried out at the banks group pertaining to overall economic efficiency, the public-sector banks are only performers whereas private banks are slightly lower than the foreign banks level.

Mittal, R.K. and Dhingra, Sanjay (2007):- The paper evaluates the impact of computerisation on the performance of Indian banks in terms of their profitability and productivity. The findings result show that ICICI Bank is found to be efficient in all indicators. Only two public sector banks, Oriental Bank of Commerce and Corporation Bank were in top ten. The output indicates that private banks are much better than public banks in productivity and profitability indicators with resisting technological advancements.

Kumar, Sunil (2008):- The study explored the relationship between technical efficiency in the Indian public sector banks. This implies that public sector banks can produce efficiency frontier with performance variance and relative efficiencies of 19 public sector banks excluding State Bank group operating in India.

Bodla, B S and Verma, Richa (2008-09):- The study attempted to analyze the earning quality of Indian banks with regard to operating profit, net profit, fund based and fee based income of banks. Profitability of Scheduled Commercial banks is growing continuously due to increasing feebased income and operating expense.

Ram Mohan, TT (2010):- The article highlighted the automation status of banks which depicts the customer and employer adoption as well participation in the financial crisis of the century, Indian banking sector. All these indicators place banking sector among most profitable banks in the world today. It is suggested that banks need more sophisticated to meet the challenges of financial inclusion.

RESEARCH GAP

As per Literature study, it is observed that many research studies in India have performed research and analytical studies on variety of parameters viz., the Technology adoption model being followed by the Indian banks vis-à-vis. the Global models. Also, some research studies have focused on Issues such as technology impact on the banking service level Performance, Digital banking impact on the growth of the Market Value, and Shareholders wealth etc. The above studies have focused on the various areas such as:

- Few studies have emphasised on the Rural sector ignorance.
- Many studies reflect the comparison of private and public sector banks digital services.
- Lack of infrastructure as the main problem in growth of banking technology.
- Many studied on the digital revolution and its impact on various sectors including the banking sector.
- The security issues were also studied in the previous studies in transacting the business through e-banking.
- Few studies have attempted to study the attitude of the employees on the digital operations in the banking sector.
- The high penetration of internet impact on the banking delivery system of services through the digitalisation.
- The authors have examined the role and its importance of technology in the present banking growth.
- The few research papers have studied the impact of technology on the growth of wide variety of services provided by the Indian banks.

Hence, keeping in view of the above considerations there is a need to undertake a study which could study the adoption and usability of ICT (digitalisation) in the banking sector from the employee and customer perspective.

Objectives of the Study

1. To study the nature and extent of digitalisation practices in the Banking Sector in India.
2. To study the perception of the banking employees and customers on the digitalisation of banking services.
3. To study the customers and employees adoptability of digitalisation of selected banking in Hyderabad.
4. To study the perceived level of satisfaction of employees and citizen with the usability of ICT in the banking sector of study area.
5. To identify the challenges and suggests the measures to improve the digital services in the banking.

Hypothesis

In order to attain the objectives, the following hypothesies have been set for the tests conducted in the respective chapters and are specified below in Table.

Hypothesis	*Test Conducted*
H0: The selected employees' demographic factors will not have the association with digital attributes of banking	Chi Square.
H0: The selected Customers' demographic factors will not have the association with digital attributes of banking	Chi Square.
H0: There is no influence of digital banking attributes on the customer's service satisfaction of banking	Linear regression.
H0: There is no influence of banking digital attributes on employee's operational satisfaction of banking	Linear regression
H0: Measures of digitalization will not improve the digital banking services.	Factor analysis.

The following is the list of primary and secondary data related variables used for the hypotheses:

Demographic Factors

Age

Gender

Education

Occupation

Income

Determinants of Digitalisation

Performance expectancy

Effort expectancy

Social Influence

Dependent variables

Behavioural Intension to use

Employee Involvement

Customer satisfaction

Adaption of Technology

Scope of the Study

The study covers the e-services of the banks to the customers and the banking employees' effective participation in adapting the new technological changes in their day to day operations.

The study mainly focuses on the following aspects:

- Role of Digitalisation in the banking sector.
- Extent of IT adaption process in Indian public and private sector banks.
- The changing strategies in the management of digitalisation in the Public and Private Sector Banks.
- The various IT Services in the Public Sector Banks and their impact on employee and the customer satisfaction.
- The practical difficulties faced by the employees and the customers while using the various IT applications.

Period of Study

The survey is conducted with primary data collection during the period 2015 to 2017 for Hyderabad districts in Telangana state. The period of study is constructed as two years.

Sources of Data

Primary data has been collected from 530 respondents of public and private sector banks in Hyderabad district of Telangana state. Simple random methodology has been applied to collect the primary data from the respondents. In the study 172 sample data has been collected from the banking employees.

Selection of E-Banks: The sample data has been collected for adaption of Digitalisation by the various banks of public and private sector located in Hyderabad district. These banks were selected based on the Indian Customer satisfaction Index of banking. The list of the banks are as follows:

Public Sector Banks – SBI, Canara Bank, PNB, Bank of India and Bank of Baroda.

Private Sector Banks – HDFC Bank, ICICI Bank, Axis Bank, CITI Bank and Kotak Mahindra Bank were considered for the study.

Selection of Employees

The present study has considered the branch banking employees who are interacting with the customers on day to day basis in providing the services. The primary data has been collected from branch manager and the call centers of these banks that interact with the banking customers. The top level and middle level employee's responses have been considered who had experience in formulating the different e-channels in their respective banks.

Methodology

The statistical tools were used to find the reliability of the sample data which has been collected from 530 respondents of five public sector banks and five private sector banks (**Public Sector Bank** – SBI, Canara Bank, PNB, Andhra Bank and Syndicate Bank, **Private Sector Bank** – HDFC Bank, ICICI Bank, Axis Bank, Yes Bank and Kotak Mahindra Bank) in Hyderabad of Telangana state has been considered for the study and sample data has been collected from the customers and employees of these banks.

Sampling Methodology

Customer Sample Determination: In the present study primary data has been collected from the banking customers by using the simple random methodology. In the study 530 samples has been collected from 10 banks customers in Hyderabad district.

Sample Determination Formula

Sample size (n) = $\frac{Z^2 Npq}{Nd^{2+} Z^2 pq}$

Z= 1.96(5% level of significance)

P=0.5

Q=0.5

D=0.05 (Confident level)

N=1856490 (holding customer in selected banks)

=4.7416* (1856490*0.5*0.5)/((1856490* 0.0025) + (4.7416*0.5*0.5))

=530.125 (Approximately 530 sample)

Employee Sample Determination: In the present study the primary data has been collected from the banking employees with the help of simple random technique, in the study 172 samples has been collected from the 10 banks employees in Hyderabad district. The following is the sample determination formula has been mentioned.

Sample size (n) = $\frac{Z^2 Npq}{Nd^{2+} Z^2 pq}$

Z=1.535025

P=0.5

Q=0.5

D=0.05 (Confident level)

N=14600 (Employees in selected banks)

=1.535025*(14600*0.5*0.5)/((14600*0.0025) + (1.535025*0.5*0.5))

=171.6008 (Approximate 172)

Statistical Tools

- The Pearson chi-square test has been used to know the association between the various variables with the demographic factors. The Lambda and Goodman & Kruskal Tau are used to know the association strength between the demographic factors with sample data variables.
- The perception of the banking employees and customers on the digitalisation of banking implications has been examined with the help of t-test and applied the discriminant analysis.

- The various factors were analyzed using Multiple Linear Regression, Beta coefficient values to identify the digitalisation changes influence on the customer's satisfaction.
- The factor analysis has been applied to identify the high load factor from the sample data variables. The high load factors are extracted by using the verimax method and applied t-test to know the change impact on the employee participation. Anova test has been applied to know the overall extracted load factors changes impact on the employee participation.
- Technology Adoption model has been developed based on the primary data in relation to the customer satisfaction which using the different banking IT applications. This quantification of customers satisfaction by the banks Technology adaption in Hyderabad of Telangana state along with the employee participation made possible comparison of different aspects of different variables. In addition, results are also presented in the form of tables and graphs.

Limitations of the Study

Every study is subjected to certain limitation and this study is not an exception in the banking area. The following are the limitations to the study:

1. The present study is confined to Hyderabad city only. The other parts of the country customer's expectations may differ from the Hyderabad city customer's expectation.
2. The study mainly focuses on one particular segment i.e., digitalisation of banking. The customers and employees some of the needs may not require the technological support.
3. The customers and the employees who have participated in the survey may not aware of the digital technological changes in the banking sector. They may be unaware of the functionality and technicality of it.
4. The present study has not considered the organisational and regulatory factors to assess the influence on employee involvement in e-bankng operations.
5. No availability of the required data and non-responsive banks are major limitations of this study. The banks don't maintain the data with regard to the issues while implementing the technologies pertaining to employees and the customers. Hence the study mainly

relies on the web portals of the banks for analyzing the extent of technological learning of banking employees.

6. Finally, the present study results mainly depend on the data collected from the primary and secondary sources. Therefore, accuracy of the study results depends upon the accuracy of the data.

CHAPTER PLAN OF THE STUDY

Chapter I Introduction.

Chapter II Review of Literature.

Chapter III Progress of Digitalisation Banking in India.

Chapter IV Digitalisation Practices in the Banking Sector in India.

Chapter V Perception of Employees' and Customers' on the Digitalisation of the Banking Sector.

Chapter VI Employees and Customers Satisfaction.

Chapter VII Challenges and Measures to Improve the Digitalisation Services in the banking sector.

Chapter VIII Summary Conclusions and Suggestions.

Findings of the Study

The findings of the study have been framed based on the five objectives. The following are the findings which are derived on the primary data with the help of statistical tools. The objective based findings are as follows:

1. The chi-square analysis result depicts at five percent significant value as there is an association between the demographic factor Age and the digital banking attributes. The study found that the 31 years to 40 years employees' participation in the adoption and implementation of the digitalisation in the banks. The 32.6 percent of the employees participation indicated that the Improves efficiency and productivity in the operations of the banking.
2. The chi-square analysis result depicts at five percent significant value as there is an association between the demographic factor, employee age and the accounting services. The frequency table indicated that the 40.7 percent of the employees felt that the nature of the accounting services will have the positive impact in the banking operations.
3. The study depicted that the digital investments services of the banking will not have the impact of the digitalisation. The frequency table reflects that the 29.1 percent of the responses are

indicating neutral opinion. The chi-square result reveals that at 5 percent significant value as there is an association between the demographic factor employee age and the investment services offered by the banking.

4. It has been observed that the digitalisation require maintenance cost. The primary data responses indicated that 26.7 percent of them given opinion that cost to the banking will increase in short-run.
5. The chi-square analysis result depicts at five percent significant value as there is an association between the demographic factor employee age and the nature of the accounting services. The frequency table reflected that banking employees observed that the ATM usage (25.6%) and Smart Cards (43%) have increased after digitalisation implementation.
6. The chi-square analysis result depicts at five percent significant value as there is an association between the demographic factor employee gender and increase of banking activities through digitalisation. The study observed that banking employee gender factor analysis primary data frequency table reflected that the production on cost reduction (38%) and followed by increase in the message speed (16.3%).
7. The chi-square analysis result depicts at five percent significant value as there is an association between the demographic factor employee gender and the activities improved in the banking through digitalisation. The study found that the 33.7 percent of the respondents of them had given neutral opinion on lack of information security. The employees of the banking of 32.6 percent are disagreed with the lack of security of the banking information.
8. The chi-square analysis result depicts at five percent significant value as there is an association between the demographic factor employee Monthly income and the activities improved in the banking investment services. The study indicated that the 54.4 percent of the employees reflected that the banking transaction will minimize from the operations perspective.
9. The chi-square analysis result depicts at five percent significant value as there is an association between the demographic factor employee education and the preference of digitalisation in the banking sector. The study observes that 32.6 percent of the banking respondents state that improves the efficiency and productivity of the banking operations.

10. The chi-square analysis result depicts at five percent significant value as there is an association between the demographic factor employee education and the problems experienced düe to digitalisation. The study observes that the 26.7 percent of the employees indicated the maintenance cost will increase due to digitalisation.
11. The study of strengthen of association of the demographic factors of employees of the bank has been measured by the kruskal-wallis and lambda. The result reveals that the demographic factors age (0.525 and 0.469) and gender (0.379 and 0.438) of the banking employees association with the digital attributes of the banks strength is found to be moderate. The education (0.736 and 0.704), Monthly income (0.604 and 0.676) association strength is observed to be strong.
12. The chi-square analysis result depicts at five percent significant value as there is an association between the demographic factor "Age" of the banking customers with digital service increases the customers satisfaction. The study found through the primary data that the total respondent (530) in which respondent felt Convenient time (102 respondent) is the major factor that influencing digital services followed by reduced cost of transactions (89 respondent), variety of services (85 respondent) and confidentially is preserve (80 respondent).
13. The chi-square analysis result depicts at five percent significant value as there is an association between the demographic factor Gender of the banking customers with awareness level of digital services offered by the banks. The female customers (28.68) are strongly agreed that they are aware about the services through the digital banking.
14. The study observed through the primary data the most of the banking customers are giving the preference to the money transfer and ATM usage with the help of digitalisation.
15. The chi-square analysis result depicts at five percent significant value as there is an association between the demographic factor Gender and the opinion on the reasons for not using the e-banking services. The majority of the banking customers indicated for the fear of insecure transaction.
16. The chi-square analysis result depicts at five percent significant value as there is an association between the demographic factor education and the digital services increases the satisfaction of the banking

customers. The majority of the educated customers are indicated that they are satisfied by the services offered by the bank.

17. The chi-square analysis result depicts at five percent significant value as there is a association between the demographic factors. Monthly income with in which bank customer would like to have the account. The primary data indicated that most of the customers like to have the account with the foreign bank. The foreign banks are serving the customsers with digital services.
18. The study of strengthen of association of the demographic factors of customers of the bank has been measured by the Phi and Cramer's V with digital banking attributes. The result reveals that demographic factors age (0.551 and 0.676) and gender (0.376 and 0.425) of the banking customers' association with the digital attributes of the banks strength is found to be moderate. The education (0.729 and 0.767) association is found to be strong, Monthly income (0551. and 0.543) association strength is observed to be moderate. Occupation demographic factors association (0.702 and 0.694) with the digital attributes of the banks.
19. The study observed that the employee perception on the digital banking operations is found to be significant at five percent level under T test. The mean score of the Operational reliability (0.543) is found to be high.
20. It has been observed that the employee perception on the digital banking operations attribute mean score "Chance of data lose" (0.501) found to be second highest among the eight attributes.
21. The study found with the help of primary data that the mean score of the employee perception on the digital banking operations inference attribute "Inadequate information" (0.154) mean score is lowest compared to other attributes.
22. The discriminant analysis has been applied and with the help of relative total discriminant score employee perception level has been examined. The analysis result reveals that the "Operational reliability" found to be highest discriminant score (17.55%).
23. It has been found that the employee perception on the digital operations in banking sector inference has been analysed with the relative total discriminant score and it has indicated that the "Chance of data loss" is observed to be the second highest relative TDS (15.63), followed by the attribute of "Lacks information security" with the third highest relative total discriminant score (14.95%).

24. The study observed that the lowest discriminant score has been found for the attribute of "Website". The analysis depicted the relative total discriminant score (6.64%), which is lowest among the eight attributes.
25. The study observed that the customer perception on the digital banking services is found to be significant at five percent level under T test. The mean score of the "Convenient Time" (0.585) is found to be high.
26. It has been observed that the customer perception on the digital banking services attribute mean score "Quick Transaction" (0.571) found to be second highest among the eight attributes.
27. The study found with the help of primary data that the mean score of the customer perception on the digital banking services inference attribute "Variety of services" (0.122) mean score is lowest compared to other attributes.
28. The discriminant analysis has been applied and with the help of relative total discriminant score customer perception level has been examined. The analysis result reveals that the "Conveninet Time" found to be highest discriminant score (26.27%).
29. It has been found that the customers' perception on the digital services of banking sector inference has been analysed with the relative total discriminant score and it has indicated that the "Quick Transaction" is observed to be the second highest relative TDS (18.34), followed by the attribute of "Easy to do banking activities" with the third highest relative total discriminant score (15.18%).
30. The study observed that the lowest discriminant score has been found for the attribute of "Variety of services". The analysis depicted the relative total discriminant score (6.15%), which is lowest among the eight attributes.
31. The study found that the citizen validating factors influence at five percent significance on the behavioural intension of digital banking services. The beta coefficient values of performance expectancy and social influence (0.631 and 0.371) had influenced the behavioural intension of the citizen in adoption of digital banking services.
32. The independent variable effort expectancy is having high influence (0.793) on the citizen behavioural intension to use digital banking services. The R^2 value for three independent variables found to be above slab value of 60 percent. The linear regression result reveals

that citizen constructs are having influence on intensions of citizen behviour for adaption of digital banking services.

33. The linear regression beta coefficient values reflect that the demographic variables influence at five percent of district, age, gender, education and profession influence is observed on citizen's behavioural intension in adopting the e-banking. The gender influence (0.204) is having the least influence on the behavioural intension.
34. The study found that the banking customers demographic factor education influence (0.712) has been observed on the banking customer's digital banking services behavioural intension. The education demographic factor influence is found to be highest among all the demographic factors.
35. The present study found that the demographic factors occupation of the banking customer positive influence (0.361) along with the annual income influence (0.525) has been observed with the help of linear regression beta coefficient values.
36. The study found that the beta coefficient value of behavioural intension influence at five percent on the citizen's adaption of digital banking services. The citizen's behavioural intension is having the influencing the adaption of digital banking services. The R^2 value is observed to be above 60 percent base value i.e., 81.3 percent.
37. The study found that the employee's validating factors influence at five percent significance on the behavioural intension of involving in the operations of digital banking. The beta coefficient values of linear regression indicated that the performance expectancy (0.582) influence has been observed on the behavioural intension of the banking employees on adoption of digitalisation in banking.
38. The independent variable effort expectancy is having high influence (0.831) on the citizen behavioural intension to involve in the operations of digital banking. The R^2 value for three independent variables found to be above slab value of 60 percent. The linear regression result reveals that employee constructs (performance expectancy and effort expectancy) are having influence on intensions of employee behaviour for adaption of digital banking in day to day operations in the branch.
39. The linear regression beta coefficient values of demographic variables employees influence at five percent of age, gender, education and annual income is observed on employee's

behavioural intension in adopting the digital or e-banking in day to day operations. The gender influence (0.015) is having the least influence but education influence (0.473) is observed high on behavioural intension in adoption of digital banking.

40. The study found that the beta coefficient value (0.642) of behavioural intension influence has been observed at five percent on the employee's adaption of digitalisation of banking. The employee's behavioural intension is having the influence on the adaption of digitalisation in banking. The R^2 value is observed to be above 60 percent base value i.e., 884 percent.
41. The study observed that the employee statisfaction on the usage of ICT in banking services is found to be significant at five percent level under T test. The mean score of the increases operational efficiency (1.56977) is found to be high.
42. It has been observed that the employee satisfaction on the usage of ICT in banking services attribute mean score "improves service quality" (0.94186) found to be second highest among the nine attributes.
43. The study found with the help of primary data that the mean score of the employee satisfaction on the usage of ICT in banking services attribute "facilitates quick response" (0.02326) mean score is lowest compared to other attributes.
44. The discriminant analysis has been applied and with the help of relative total discriminant score employee satisfaction level has been examined. The analysis result reveals that the "Increases operational efficiency" found to be highest discriminant score (22.85%).
45. It has been found that the employee satisfaction on the digital operations in banking sector inference has been analysed with the relative total discriminant score and it has indicated that the "Facilitates quick response" is observed to be the second highest relative TDS (17.63), followed by the attribute of "Improves service quality" with the third highest relative total discriminant score (15.62%).
46. The study observed that the lowest discriminant score has been found for the attribute of "Minimizes inconvenience". The analysis depicted the relative total discriminant score (4.52%), which is lowest among the nine attributes.

47. The study observed that the customer satisfaction on the usage of ICT in banking services is found to be significant at five percent level under T test. The mean score of the "Confidentiality is preserved" (1.43019) is found to be high.
48. It has been observed that the customer satisfaction on the usage of ICT in banking services is found to attribute mean score "Quick Transaction" (1.00189) found to be second highest among the nine attributes.
49. The study found with the help of primary data that the mean score of the customer satisfaction on the digital banking services inference attribute "Reduced cost of transactions" (0.0943) mean score is lowest compared to other attributes.
50. The discriminant analysis has been applied and with the help of relative total discriminant score customer satisfaction level has been examined. The analysis result reveals that the "Quick Transaction" found to be highest discriminant score (31.52%).
51. It has been found that the customers' satisfaction on the usage of ICT in banking services has been analysed with the relative total discriminant score and it has indicated that the "Convenient Time" is observed to be the second highest relative TDS (24.61%), followed by the attribute of "Information regarding existing services" with the third highest relative total discriminant score (14.15%).
52. The study observed that the lowest discriminant score has been found for the attribute of "Variety of Services". The analysis depicted the relative total discriminant score (3.82%), which is lowest among the nine attributes.
53. The study found that problem encounter among the public and private banks employees regarding problems faced by the employee in using the digital based network in the bank. The significant difference among the both banks employees have been identified in all case of problems since their 't' statistics are significant at five percent level except in resistance in UPS. Among the various problems maintenance is observed to be the major problem as the private banks mean score 4.618 and public sector mean score 4.175.
54. The factor analysis has been applied and principle component method had extracted high load factors among the 14 highly viewed problems which were considered by the banking employees of private and public sector. Among them three factors from hardware, three factors from internet segment, two factors from maintenance

and four factors from the security were extracted. The cumulative percentage of the variables considered as 57.93.

55. The significant mean difference is found in all the issue like Hardware issue, internet issue, Maintenance issue and Security issues among the public and private bank employee and their respective t-statistics are significant at five percent level. The higher mean difference is noticed high in security issues (0.1435).
56. The higher discriminate coefficient is observed in security and Internet issue and their respective coefficient values are 0.2495 and 0.2359. The relative contribution in TDS observes to be higher in Maintenance issue with 41.12 percent followed by 28.67 percent in security issue.
57. The study found that problem experienced among the public and private banks customers, regarding problems faced by the customers in using the digital based services by the bank. The significant difference among the both banks customers have been identified in all case of problems since their 't' statistics are significant at five percent level in public and private sector, digital based services problems are high in factors i.e., Satisfied with the security system of e-banking, debit/credit card delivery delay if misplaced, Privacy factors influence the adaption of e-banking services and their mean score values are 4.652-4.628, 4.425 – 4.152 and 3.724-3.274 as their significant value is five percent.
58. The factor analysis has been applied and principle component method had extracted high load factors among the 13 highly viewed problems which were considered by the banking customers of private and public sector. Problems regarding time are seemed to be high and its percent of variance explained value is 31.264 and consists of three variables, whereas security also consists of three variables but the percent of variance explained with 22.624. Transactions issues consist of four variables with percent of variance explained of 16.274 and lowest percent of variance explained in cards with 8.573 which consisting of three variables.
59. The significant mean difference is found in all the issue like time, security, transaction and cards among the public and private bank customers and their respective t-statistics are significant at five percent level. The higher mean difference is noticed high in cards delivery delay (0.143).
60. The higher discriminate coefficient is observed in time and security issues and their respective coefficient values are 0.273 and 0.168.

This analysis indicates that two major issues (time and security) mentioned are more specific discriminate co-efficient. The relative contribution in TDS observes to be higher in time issue with 33.52 percent followed by 28.85 percent in cards delay in delivery. Further it reveals that Internet and security problem are the core issue faced by both the public and private bank customers.

Hypothesis of the Study

The following hypothesis has been framed in the objectives of 2nd, 3rd, 4th and 5th by applying the various statistical tools and based on the significance level indicated the acceptance or rejection of hypothesis.

Table 11.0

Hypothesis	*Test Conducted*	*Accepted Or Rejected H0*
H0: The sample data is not reliable	Reliability test (Cronbach's Alpha)	Rejected
H0: The sample data is not adequate	KMO test	Rejected
H0: There is no association between the employee demographic factor Age with the attributes of "why do you prefer computerization in Banks".	Chi-Square test	Rejected
H0: There is no association between the employee demographic factor Age with the attributes of "what is the nature of impact on use of digitalization in your banks".	Chi-Square test	Rejected
H0: There is an association between the employee demographic factor Age with the attributes of "what is the nature of various investment services impact on use of digitalization in your banks".	Chi-Square test	Accepted
H0: There is no association between the employee demographic factor Age with the attribute of "What are the problems you faced in using computer based network in your banks"	Chi-Square test	Rejected
H0: There is no association between the employee demographic factor Age with the attributes of "Bankers' Perceptions of the nature risk associated with digitalization in Banking"	Chi-Square test	Rejected
H0: There is no association between the employee demographic factor Gender with the attributes of "why do you prefer computerization in Banks".	Chi-Square test	Rejected
H0: There is no association between the employee demographic factor Gender with the attributes of "what is the nature of impact on use of digitalization in your banks".	Chi-Square test	Rejected

Contd...

H0: There is no association between the employee demographic factor Gender with the attribute of "What are the problems you faced in using computer based network in your banks".	Chi-Square test	Rejected
H0: There is no association between the employee demographic factor Education with the attributes of "why do you prefer computerization in Banks".	Chi-Square test	Rejected
H0: There is no association between the employee demographic factor Education with the attributes of "what is the nature of impact on use of digitalization in your banks".		
H0: There is no association between the employee demographic factor Education with the attributes of "what is the nature of impact on use of digitalization in your banks".	Chi-Square test	Rejected
H0: There is no association between the employee demographic factor Education with the attribute of "What are the problems you faced in using computer based network in your banks".	Chi-Square test	Rejected
H0: There is an association between the Customer demographic factor Education with the attributes of "what is probable adoption rate of digitalization in the bank across the city"	Chi-Square test	Accepted
H0: There is no association between the employee demographic factor Education with the attributes of "Bankers' Perceptions of the nature risk associated with digitalization in Banking"	Chi-Square test	Rejected
H0: There is no association between the employee demographic factor Annual income with the attribute of "What is the estimated percentage of your customers using each technology"	Chi-Square test	Rejected
H0: There is no association between the employee demographic factor Annual income with the attribute of "Bankers' Perceptions of the nature risk associated with digitalization in Banking"	Chi-Square test	Rejected
H0: There is no association between the employee demographic factor Employees with the attributes of "why do you prefer computerization in Banks".	Chi-Square test	Rejected
H0: There is no association between the employee demographic factor Employees with the attributes of "what is the nature of impact on use of digitalization in your banks".	Chi-Square test	Rejected
H0: There is no association between the employee demographic factor Employee with the attributes of "What are the problems you faced in using computer based network in your banks".	Chi-Square test	Rejected
H0: There is no association between the employee demographic factor Employee with the attributes of "Bankers' Perceptions of the nature risk associated with digitalization in Banking".	Chi-Square test	Rejected
H0: There is no association between the Customer demographic factor Age with the attributes of "Awareness level of Digital services offered by the banks".	Chi-Square test	Rejected

Contd...

H0: There is no association between the Customer demographic factor Age with the attributes of "Do you agree Digital services increase customer satisfaction".	Chi-Square test	Rejected
H0: There is no association between the Customer demographic factor Age with the attributes of "Factors influence you the most for using Digital services".	Chi-Square test	Rejected
H0: There is no association between the Customer demographic factor Age with the attributes of "Bankers' Perceptions of the nature risk associated with digitalization in Banking".	Chi-Square test	Rejected
H0: There is no association between the Customer demographic factor Age with the attributes of "State the frequently faced problem by customers while using the digital services"	Chi-Square test	Rejected
H0: There is no association between the Customer demographic factor Gender with the attributes of "Awareness level of Digital services offered by the banks".	Chi-Square test	Rejected
H0: There is no association between the Customer demographic factor Gender with the attributes of "Factors influence you the most for using Digital services".	Chi-Square test	Rejected
H0: There is no association between the Customer demographic factor Age with the attributes of "Awareness level of Digital services offered by the banks".	Chi-Square test	Rejected
H0: There is no association between the Customer demographic factor Education with the attributes of "Do you agree Digital services increase customer satisfaction".	Chi-Square test	Rejected
H0: There is no association between the Customer demographic factor Education with the attributes of "Factors influence you the most for using Digital services".	Chi-Square test	Rejected
H0: There is no association between the Customer demographic factor Education with the attribute of "Bankers' Perceptoins of the nature risk associated with digitalization in Banking".	Chi-Square test	Rejected
H0: There is no association between the Customer demographic factor Education with the attributes of "State the frequently faced problem by customers while using the digital services".	Chi-Square test	Rejected
H0: There is no association between the Customer demographic factor Education with the attributes of "Factors influence you the most for using Digital services".	Chi-Square test	Rejected
H0: There is no association between the Customer demographic factor Annual Income with the attributes of "State the frequently faced problem by customers while using the digital services".	Chi-Square test	Rejected

Contd...

H0: There is no association between the Customer demographic factors Annual Income with the attributes of "Factors influence you the most for using Digital services".	Chi-Square test	Rejected
H0: There is no association between the Cusomer demographic factor occuptations with the attributes of "Do you agree Digital services increase customer satisfaction".	Chi-Square test	Rejected
H0: There is no association between the Customer demographic factor Occupations with the attributes of "Factors influence you the most for using Digital services".	Chi-Square test	Rejected
H0: There is no association between the Customer demographic factor Occupation with the attributes of "Bankers' Perception of the nature risk associated with digitalization in Banking".	Chi-Square Test	Rejected
H0: There is no association between the Customer demographic factor Occupation with the attributes of "State the frequently faced problem by customers while using the digital services".	Chi-Square test	Rejected
H0: There is no association between the Customer demographic factor Occupation with the attributes of "Factors influence you the most for using Digital services".	Chi-Square test	Rejected
H0: Performance expectancy will not have influence on behavioural intension of the employee	Linear Regression	Rejected
H0: Effort expectancy will not have influence on behavioural intension of the employee	Linear Regression	Rejected
H0: Behavioral intension of the employee will not have influence on Digitalization adaption	Linear Regression	Rejected
H0: Demographic factor age of the employee will not have influence on Digitalization adaption	Linear Regression	Rejected
H0: Demographic factor gender of the employee will not have infleunce on Digitalization adaption	Linear Regression	Rejected
H0: Demographic factor education of the employee will not have influence on Digitalization adaption	Linear Regression	Rejected
H0: Demographic factor Annual Income of the employee will not have influence on Digitalization adaption	Linear Regression	Rejected
H0: There is mean difference of banking service benefit's attribute "Minimizes the cost of transaction"	T-test	Accepted
H0: There is mean difference of banking service benefit's attribute "Saves times"	T-test	Accepted
H0: There is mean difference of banking service benefit "Minimizes inconvenience"	T-test	Accepted
H0: There is mean difference of banking service benefit "Provides up-to-date information"	T-test	Accepted
H0: There is mean difference of banking service benefit "Increases operational efficiency"	T-test	Accepted

Contd...

H0: There is mean difference of banking service benefit "Reduces HR requirements"	T-test	Accepted
H0: There is mean difference of banking service benefit "Facilitates quick response"	T-test	Accepted
H0: There is mean difference of banking service benefit "Improves service quality"	T-test	Accepted
H0: There is mean difference of banking service benefit "Improves service quality"	T-test	Accepted
H0: There is a mean difference of factor "Convenient time" which influence the digital services	T-test	Accepted
H0: There is a mean difference factor "Quick Transaction" which influence the digital services	T-test	Accepted
H0: There is a mean difference of factor "Information regarding existing serices" which influence the digital services	T-test	Accepted
H0: There is a mean difference of factor "Easy to do banking activities" which influence the digital services	T-test	Accepted
H0: There is a mean difference of factor "Reduced cost of transactions" which influence the digital services	T-test	Accepted
H0: There is a mean difference of factor "Variety of services" which influence the digital services	T-test	Accepted
H0: There is a mean difference of factor "User Friendly Interface" which influence the digital services	T-test	Accepted
H0: There is a mean difference of factor "Confidentiality is preserved" which influence the digital services	T-test	Rejected

Suggestions of the Study

Based on the findings and conclusions that emerged from the study, the following suggestions may be worth considering vis-á-vis. titled Digitalisation in the banking sector with reference to employees and customers in Hyderabad.

1. The study found that the 33.7 percent of the respondents of them had given neutral opinion on lack of information on security. The employees of the banking of 32.6 percent are disagreed with the lack of security of the banking information. Hence it is suggested to increase the security level for the online banking transactions, so that customers' safety concerns will be addressed effectively.
2. The study observes that 32.6 percent of the banking respondents state that improves the efficiency and productivity of the banking operations. Hence it is advised to the banking management to increase the spending on the technology to remain competitive by increasing the productivity and efficiency of the banking.

3. The analysis of employee perception level has been depicted through the relative total discriminant score (6.64%), which is lowest among the eight attributes for the "website". Hence it is suggested to increase the awareness among the customers about the website through which the customers can do online transactions and also can lodge the complaints and track the status of it.
4. The analysis of customers' perception level has been depicted through the relative total discriminant score (6.15%), which is lowest among the eight attributes for the "Variety of services". Hence the study suggests that there is need to increase the awareness level of the customers on the digital services. The variety of services the banks are providing at door step to the customers.
5. The study observes that the digitalisation in the banking has got the lowest relative total discriminant score (4.52%) for the attribute of "minimize the inconvenience" of day to day operations of the employees. Hence it is advised to conduct the regular training sessions to the employees for the latest technological upgradations.
6. The study observed that the growth of the e-commerce business in India is tremendous, therefore online banking transactions will increase accordingly. Hence it is advised to increase the variety of services with banking platform, in order to tackle the competition which is coming through the e-commerce and other segments.
7. In India, rural population is still remained as unbanked area. The banks by the usage of digital technology with low cost they can reach the masses and cover the unbanked areas.
8. The mobile application based banking is poised to be the next big thing in the evolution of banking. There is a need to generate the awareness on the mobile banking so that more customers use it for their benefit.
9. The present banks have to realise that they have to provide the service to the tech-savvy generation in near future. Hence innovative and tailor made services are to be designed accordingly. As the market conditions are very dynamic and customers needs ever changing, banks need to invest in advanced analytical tools for the timely introduction of new and variety of products, which will give the banks early mover advantage.
10. The customers will give importance to the banks which will have more number of ATMs. Increased number of ATMs network, bank can increase the revenue from the use of ATM by non-customers, also benefit of reduction of operating cost.

Conclusion of the Study

The adoption of latest technological changes by the banks across the world has raised many challenges to the banks in India and it is important for the Indian banks to tackle these challenges effectively in order to survive in the globalisation era. In the present highly competitive world the success of the banks depends on the efficient, prompt and on time customer service, which calls for the appropriate customers friendly procedures and schemes.

The study observed that the perception of the employees and the customers are positive on the digital services of the banking sector. The perceived level of satisfaction of the employees and the customers influenced positively through the usage of information and communication technology in delivering the banking services through digitalisation. The banks must absorb the technological changes and upgrade their services constantly in order to be competitive.

The present study is confined to the Hyderabad district, where educated citizen, who can use the information and communication technology in their day to day banking transactions. At the same time application of the technology in India where there is the predominance of illiterate, poor and even rural areas is not an easy affair to be done effectively since they are least concern in level of efficiency of services and automation.

The study observed that the present banking system is adopting the latest technology and they are more concerned with ease of services without much complications and safer transactions. The present banking is focused on the urban areas and only mandal level banking is available in the rural area. The digitalisation will play crucial role in future to reach the citizen even in rural areas and expand to the unbanked markets. Therefore, there is a long way to go for the Indian banks by making these classes aware of the various services and train the employees and the customers in transaction using these latest technologies, along with ensuring safety. In spite of the many challenges, it is stated that the banks in India will play effective role in the economic development in the coming days.

Scope for Further Research

The banking technology is not a single or stand-alone discipline, but a combination of several disparate fields such as information technology, communication, computers, finance and marketing. Therefore, there exists greater scope for further research in this area. As an extension of present study, the researcher felt the possibilities for further research in the following fields:

1. The usage of smart phones has increase in India. The mobile banking is popularised in the urban areas but in rural areas it is popularised much. The customers are still waiting for some more time for the extensive use of mobile banking. Hence it has been suggested by focusing exclusively on mobile banking.
2. The demonetisation in India had influenced the digitalisation growth tremendously. The growth of e-commerce also influenced the digital transactions through banks. Hence it has been suggested to do a research on the corporate banking.
3. The study also suggested of examining the adoption of digital banking by the public sector, private sector, foreign and rural banks and impact on their customers' growth and reduction of employee cost.
4. The study suggested of examining the behaviour and attitude of the employees of the banking in adoption of digitalisation in delivering the services to the customers.

References

1. **Agarwal, R N, 1993,** "Analysis of Profitability of Public Sector Banks: A Case for Financial Sector Reforms", Journal of Income and Wealth, Vol. 15, No. 2, pp. 123-131.
2. **Athma Prashant, March 2000,** "Performance of Public Sector Commercial Banks – A Case Study of State Bank of Hyderabad", Finance India, Indian Institute of Finance, Vol. 14, Issue No. 1, pp. 183-186.
3. **Altunbas Yener, Lynne Evans, Philip Molyneux, 2001**, "Bank Ownership and Efficiency", Journal of Money, Credit and Banking, Vol. 33, No. 4, pp. 45-49.
4. **Aparna, T, September 2002,** "State Bank of India: Flying High", Chartered Financial Analyst, Vol. 8, Issue. 9, pp. 60-61.
5. **Birla Institute of Scientific Research 1981,** "Banks Since Nationalisation", Economic Research Division, Allied Publishers, New Delhi, Vol. 29, p. 2.
6. **Bhalla (2002),** February "Customer satisfaction and retail banking". www.emeraldinsight.com/doi/abs/10.1108/02652320210432936. Vol. 54, No. 2, pp. 47-50.
7. **Bhide, MG, Prasad, A, Ghosh, Saibal, February 2, 2002,** "Banking Sector Reforms: A Critical Overview", Economic & Political Weekly, Vol. XXXVII, No. 5, pp. 399-408.
8. **Bhasin, Niti, January 2006,** "Banking Developments in India 1947 to 2007 Growth, Reforms and Outlook", New Century Publications, New Delhi.
9. **Bodla, B S & Verma, Richa, 2008-09,** "Earning Quality of Scheduled Commercial Banks in India: Bank-wise and Sector-wise Analysis", Prajnan, Vol. XXXVII, No. 4, pp. 257-283.

10. **Chaudhari, Saumitra, June, 2002,** "Some Issues of Growth and Profitability in Indian Public Sector Banks", Economic & Political Weekly.

11. **Chellasamy, P & Sumathi, N, December, 2004,** "Role of Banking System in India", Journal of Global Economy, Vol. 2, No. 4, pp. 289-295.

12. **Chakrabarti, Rajesh & Chawla, Gaurav, 2005,** "Money and Finance-Banking Efficiency in India since the Reforms – An Assessment", Money and Finance, Vol. 2, Issues, pp. 22-23.

13. **Das, Abhiman, June-September, 1997,** "Technical, Allocative and Scale Efficiency of Public Sector Banks in India", RBI Occasional Papers Vol. 18, Issue No. 2 & 3, pp. 23-29.

14. **Das, Abhiman, 1999,** "Profitability of Public Sector Banks: A Decomposition Model", Reserve Bank of India Occasional Paper.

15. **Dasgupta, Debajyoti, September 2001,** "Profitability of Indian public sector banks in the light of liberalisation of Indian economy-An overview", The Management Accountant, Vol. 36, No. 9, pp. 693-699.

16. **Das, Abhiman, February 2, 2002,** "Risk and Productivity Change of Public Sector Banks", Economic & Political Weekly, Issue 5, pp. 15-17.

17. **Dey, SK & Kumar, Pradeep, 2007,** " Relevance of Social Lending in Indian Banking" in Mohan Prasad Shrivastava, Pradeep Kumar Pandey, V P Vidyarthi (ed.) 'Banking Reforms and Globalisation', APH Publishing Corporation, New Delhi, pp. 297-304.

18. **Dhade, Aruna, December 2009,** "Impact of New Private Sector Banks on State Bank of India Special reference to Madhya Pradesh State" Abstract of Doctoral Dissertation, Finance India, Indian Institute of Finance, Vol. XXIII No. 4, pp. 1357-1363.

19. **Gopinath, Shyamala, April, 6, 2007,** "Special Features of Financial Sector Reforms in India", Deputy governor, RBI delivered at the 18th Annual National Conference for Forex Association at Bangkok.

20. **Gupta, Sumeet & Verma, Renu, June, 2008,** "Comparative Analysis of Financial Performance of Private Sector Banks in India: Application of CAMEL Model", Journal of Global Economy, Vol. 4, No. 2, pp. 144-158.

21. **Gulati, Rachita & Kumar, Sunil, December 2009,** "Efficiency-Profitability Relationship in Indian Domestic Banks: A Disaggregate Analysis", Asian Economic Review, Journal of the Indian Institute of Economics, Vol. 51, Issue No. 3, pp. 411-433.

22. **Herring and Litan (2003),** 'Trends in Risk Integration and Aggregation' Banking and Finance, Vol. 30, pp. 717-42.

23. **Janaki, J, 2001,** "Impact of Liberalisation on Banking", in S. Gurusamy (ed.) 'Banking Challenges and Strategies', Kanishka Publishers, New Delhi, pp. 109-117.

24. **Kumar, Parmod, 2006,** "Banking Sector Efficiency in globalised Economy", Deep and Deep Publications, New Delhi.

25. **Kumar, Vishal & Savita, 2007**, "Banking in the New Millennium: Challenges and Strategies", in R K Uppal & Rimpi Kaur (ed.) 'Banking in the New

Millennium: Issues, Challenges and Strategies", Mahamaya Publishing House, New Delhi, pp. 155-172.

26. **Kapoor, Seema, 2007,** "Reforms in Indian Banking Sector: Agenda for Future" in R K Uppal & Rimpi Kaur (ed.) 'Banking in the New Millennium: Issues, Challenges and Strategies', Mahamaya Publishing House, New Delhi, pp. 379-394.

27. **Kalluru Siva Reddy & K Bhat Sham 2008,** "An Empirical Analysis of Profitability Determinants in India Commercial Banks during Post Reform Period", The ICFAI University Journal of Industrial Economics, Vol. V, No. 4.

28. **Kumar, Sunil, 2008,** "An Analysis of Efficiency-Profitability Relationship in Indian Public Sector Banks", Global Business Review, Vol. 9, No. 1, pp. 115-129.

29. **Kalluru Siva Reddy & Sham Bhat K, November, 2009.** "Does Foreign Bank Entry Affect Operations of Domestic Banks? A Study of Indian Public sector Banks", The ICFAI University Journal of Managerial Economics, Vol. VII, Nos. 3 & 4, p. 98.

30. **Kumar, Sunil & Gulati, Rachita, June 2009,** "Income-Generating Efficiency of Public Sector Banks in India: An Application of Data Envelopment Analysis", Arth Vijnana, Vol. 11, No. 2, pp. 103-126.

31. **Kodian, Narender, Kumar, Shalinder & Kodan, Anand Singh, February, 2010,** "Scheduled Commercial Banks: Growth Trends", Yojana, Vol. 54, No. 2, pp. 47-50.

32. **Kumar, Sunil & Gulati, Rachita, 2010,** "Measuring efficiency, effectiveness and performance of Indian public sector banks", International Journal of Productivity and Performance Management", Vol. 59, Issue. 1, pp. 51-74.

33. **Kumar, Sunil & Gulati Rachita, March, 2010.** "Dynamics of Cost Efficiency in Indian Public Sector Banks: A post-Deregulation Experience" Paper submitted for presentation in the Twelfth Annual Conference on Money and Finance in The Indian Economy, Vol. 59, Issue 6, pp. 65-69.

34. **Khan, MY, 1 October, 2010,** "A U-turn Banking" The Economic Times, Vol. 98, Issue 9, pp. 55-57.

35. **Leela Dhar, (2006),** Perspective of Technology in Achieving Financial Inclusion in Rural Areas, Vol. IV, No. 1, 2007, pp. 20-36.

36. **Malhotra, R N 1986,** "Banking Enter a New Phase", The Journal of the Institute of Bankers, Special Number: Bank Economists Conference, April-June 1986, Vol. 57, Issue 2, pp. 94-103.

37. **Mathur, K B L, June 8, 2002,** "Public Sector Banks in India – Should They Be Privatized", Economic & Political Weekly, Vol. XXXVII, No. 23.

38. **Mohan, Rakesh December, 2005,** Address delivered at the 21st Annual General Meeting and conference of the Pakistan Society of Development Economists at Islamabad.

39. **Mittal, R K & Dhingra Sanjay, June, 2007,** "Assessing the impact of computerisation on productivity and profitability of Indian banks – An Application of Data Envelopment Analysis", Delhi Business Review, Vol. 8, No. 1.

40. **Mittal, Manish & Dhade, Aruna, May 2007,** "Profitability and Productivity in Indian Banks: A comparative Study", AIMS International, Vol. 1, No. 2, pp. 137-152.
41. **Monterio Mohan, N.J & Ananthan, B R, June 2007,** "NPA in Public Sector Banks: Causes and Cures", The Indian Journal of Commerce, Vol. 60, No. 2, pp. 1-11.
42. **Moffat Boitumelo & Narayana, N, 2010**, "The Performance of Financial Institutions in Botswana: A Study of Selected Banking and Non-Banking Financial Institutions", Asian-African Journal of Economics and Econometrics, Vol. 10, No. 1.
43. **Nagar, Nirupma & Mishra, Jitendra Kumar, 2002,** "Non-Performing Assets of Commercial Banks – A Case Study of State Bank of Indore", Madhya Pradesh Journal of Social Sciences, Vol. 7, No. 1, pp. 102-112.
44. **Pandey, Rajendra & Bandyopadhyaya, Sanjiban, June 2003,** "Cost-Volume-Profit analysis and Banks Performance: A Case Study of Public Sector Banks", The Management Accountant, Vol. 38, No. 6, pp. 40-43.
45. **Prasad, A. & Ghosh, Saibal, July, 2005,** "Competition in Indian Banking" IMF working Paper, WP/05/141.
46. **Patnaik, U C & Patnaik, Manoj, 2005,** "Profitability in Public Sector Banks", Sonali Publications, New Delhi.
47. **Pal, Ved, Bishnoi, N.K, April 2009,** "Productivity Analysis of Commercial Banks in India", Decision, Indian Institute of Management, Kolkata, Vol. 36, No. 1, pp. 131-157.
48. **Robert, M, 1991,** "Profitability in Public Sector Banks in India" Thesis Abstract, The Journal of Institute of Public Enterprises, Vol. 14, issue no. (4), pp. 315-321.
49. **Ram Mohan, TT, February 2, 2002,** "Deregulation and Performance of Public Sector Banks", Economic & Political Weekly, Vol. XXXVII, No. 5, pp. 393-397.
50. **Rao Srinivasa, K S & Prasad Chowdari, December 2003,** "Can Public Sector Banks Compete with Foreign/Private Banks? A Statistical Analysis", Paper submitted to the International Conference on "Business & Finance" to be held during at ICFAI Business School, Hyderabad. Vol. 92, No. 16, pp. 140-143.
51. **Ram Mohan, TT & C Ray, Subhash, March 20, 2004,** "Comparing Performance of Public and Private Sector Banks – A Revenue Maximisation Effeciency Approach", Economic & Political Weekly.
52. **Rao Ramachandra, KS, Das, Abhiman, Singh, Arvind Kumar, March 2006,** "Commercial Bank Lending to Small-scale Industry", Economic & Political Weekly, Vol. XLI, No. 11, pp. 1025-1033.
53. **Rangarajan, C, July 31, 2007,** "The Indian Banking System – Challenges Ahead", Indian Institute of Banking and Finance, First R. K. Talwar Memorial Lecture.
54. **Rao, D Suryachandra, 2008,** "Banking Reforms in India: An Evaluative Study of the Performance of Commercial Banks, Regal Publications, New Delhi.

55. **Raju, D NM, September, 2009,** "Evaluation of the Performance of State Bank of India with special reference to Nonperforming Assets (NPAs)", Abstract of Doctoral Dissertation, Finance India, Indian Institute of Finance, Vol. XXIII, Issue no. 3, pp. 985-989.

56. **Rao, Nageshwar & Tiwari, Shefali 2009,** "Efficiency Indicators of Commercial Banks in Liberalised Environment in India", Abhigyan, Vol. XXVII, No. 1, pp. 10-19.

57. **Ram Mohan, TT, March 2010,** "A Crisis Proof Banking Sector", The Economic Times. Vol. 18, pp. 962-965.

58. **Ram Mohan, TT, 4 February, 2010,** "At last, the remaking of banks", The Economic Times, Vol. 16, pp. 963-969.

59. **Sarkar, 1990,** Banking, Finance, and Accounting Concepts, Methodologies, Tools, Vol. 14, pp. 424-438.

60. **Singh, Jagwanth, 1993,** "Indian Banking Industry – Growth and Trends in Productivity", Deep and Deep Publications, New Delhi, Vol. 87, issue 32, pp. 225-229.

61. **Shanjahan, K M, 1998,** "Priority Sector Bank Lending – Some Important Issues", Economic & Political Weekly, pp. 17-24.

62. **Saha, Gurudas, May 2001,** "Financials of Indian Banking Industry and the Competitive Viability of the Public-Sector Banks", The Management Accountant, Vol. 36, No. 5, pp. 373-386.

63. **Subramani & Raghav, June 2001,** "Operational Efficiency of Banks" in S. Gurusamy (ed.) ' Banking in the New Millennium – Issues, Challenges and Strategies', Kanishka Publishers, New Delhi. Vol. 10, issue 15, pp. 65-69.

64. **Singh, Kunal, 2003** "State Bank of India: Aggressive Game Plans", Chartered Financial Analyst, Vol. 9, No. 5, pp. 27-28.

65. **Sisodiya, Amit Singh & Rao, N Janardhan, 2004,** "Spotlight: State Bank of India", Chartered Financial Analyst, Vol. 10, No. 11.

66. **Sooden, Meenakshi & Bali, October 2004,** "Profitability in Public Sector Banks in India in the pre and post reform period", India Management Studies Journal, Vol. 8, No. 2, pp. 69-80.

67. **Singh, Bhupinder Pal, 2004,** "Banking Reforms and Productive Efficiency of Indian Public Sector Banks", Dissertation, Master of Philosophy in Economics, Punjab University, Patiala, pp. 51-56.

68. **Sensaram Rudra, July 2006,** "Are foreign banks always the best? Comparison of state-owned, private and foreign banks in India", Economic Modelling, Vol. 23, Issue, 4, pp. 717-735.

69. **Sahu, Bihari Gagan & Rajasekhar, D, Jan, 2005-06,** "Banking Sector Reform and Credit Flow to Indian Agriculture", Economic & Political Weekly, Vol. XL, No. 53, pp. 5550-5559.

70. **Samanta, Amitava, 2006,** "Impact of NPA on Working of Commercial Banks in India", Journal of Economic and Social Development, Vol. 11, No. 1, pp. 87-95.

71. **Sharma, Neeraj, 2006,** "Performance of Punjab National Bank in Competitive Environment: A Case Study of Haryana", Ph. D. Thesis, Punjabi University, Patiala.

72. **Sufian Fadzlan, 2007,** "Productivity Growth in the Malaysian Islamic Banking Industry: A Nonparametric Malmquist Productivity Index Approach", The ICFAI Journal of Industrial Economics, Vol. IV, No. 1, pp. 20-36.

73. **Singh, Sultan, 2007,** "Banking Sector Reforms in India", Kanishka Publishers, New Delhi. Vol. 124, Issue 65, pp. 45-49.

74. **Sharma and Vashishtha (2007),** Non Performing Assets have been substantially reduced since regulations. Vol. 16, pp. 963-969.

75. **Shankar, Daya, Wadud, IKM Mohtarul, Singh, Harminder, December, 2009,** "A Comparative Study of Banking in China and India – Non-Performing Loans and the Level Playing Field", The Indian Economic Journal, Vol. 57(3), pp. 118-138.

76. **Sinha, Ram Pratap & Chatterjee, Biswajit, 2009-10,** "Bank ownership and Deposit Mobilisation: A Nonparametric Approach", Prajnan, Vol. XXXVIII, No. 3.

77. **Sen Mittal, 2010,** "Liability Structure of Indian Commercial Banks", Northern Book Centre, New Delhi.

78. **Tandon, Deepak, Ahuja, Kanahaiya & Tandon, Neelam, July 2009,** "Relative Performance of Banks – A Study", The Indian Banker, Vol. IV, No. 7.

79. **Uppal, RK & Kaur, Rimpi, 2007,** "Banking Sector Reforms: Their Efficacy and Future Agenda" 'Banking in the New Millennium: Issues, Challenges and Strategies', Mahamaya Publishing House, New Delhi, Vol. 52, issue 12, pp. 1-21.

80. **Uppal, R K, 2008,** "Indian Banking in the Globalised World", New Century Publications, New Delhi. Issue 9, pp. 65-69.

81 **Uwafio Jeremaiah, Idialu & Yomere O Gabriel, 2010,** "Stochastic Frontier Analysis of the Efficiency of Nigerian Banks", Indian Journal of Economics and Business, Vol. 9, No. 1, pp. 75-86, Serial Publications, New Delhi.

82. **Varadi, Kumar Vijay, Kumar, Pradeep & Boppana, Nagarjuna (2006),** "Measurement of Efficiency of Banks in India, MRPA Paper No. 17350, posted 17, September 2009, Online at http://mpra.ub.unimuenchen.de/17350.

83. **Verma, Amitabh, 2009,** "The impact of Technology on Productivity and Profitability of Indian Bank in Post Liberalised Period", Abhigyan, Vol. XXVII, No. 2.

84. **Varshney, Chanchal, June 2009,** "Role of State Bank of India in Financing the Priority Sector: Case Study of Aligarh District" Abstract of Doctoral Dissertation, Finance India, Indian Institute of Finance, Vol. XXIII, No. 2, pp. 634-636.

85. **Zacharias Thomas, 1997,** "Performance effectiveness of Nationalised Banks – A case study of Syndicate Bank", Ph.D. thesis, Cochin University, Kochi, Finance India, Vol. XIV, pp. 187-193.

12.1

Analysis

An attempt has been made to analyse the entire work from chapter one to twelve. The entitled work is "Current Research Trends in Commerce and Management". Exclusively this chapter and the total work is devoted to Management. The following are potential and most important chapters for the readers as well as for active researchers:

1. Introduction.
2. Evolving scenario for commerce and management.
3. Corporate survival struggle during pandemic era.
4. Impact of sustainability dimension of corporate governance on select companies.
5. Gender Responsive Budgeting - Emerging paradigm in Management.
6. Geospatial Technology Applications in Disaster Management.
7. Role of Blockchain-Technology in Asia- A relook at China and India in Banking sector.
8. Role of Board of Directors in Policy formulation and decision making.
9. Quantitative Techniques in Management research (Research Methodology).
10. Digitalisation Banking and
11. Marketing (M), Management (M2) and Men (Human resource interations)(M3)factors in Tribal development: A case study for immediate and interaction by governance.

Finaly, 12th chapter has been devoted to four aspects which are quite essential to practice by the researchers they are: (1) Collection of data (2) Correction of data (3) Analysis (4) Problem identification and selection

(5) Funding the projected work as a project by financial agencies and (6) Reporting the material for proper action either by any social organisation or by the governance.

Commerce, Management and environment are quite important subjects for carrying out inter-disciplinary and multidisciplinary research in the current environmental scenario. Business environment, environmental management and Management of commercial activity relating to commercial activities at one place/point/centre/mal/Hub. These operations are being conducted at one place. Corporate social responsibility and its role for development is strongly and positively associated with environmental factorial phenomenon.

In the 2nd chapter, Dr. Rao has made an attempt to provide an overview of the four key components which are going to impact commerce and management for present decade and decades to come.

According to Rao, that, "the data gathering collection reports, from qualitative to quantitative, Covid-19 impacted communities, utilisation of risk communication messages from pandemic managing agencies; social and economic hardships faced by the migrant labour and displaced population and various aspects of human rights of pandemic response stakeholders".

Governanace activity has also been brought out by Dr. Rao such as, "Digital cashless payments, and Aadhar and pin-based transactions with tax compliance and GST, is transforming India from an informal to the formal economy, in the normal scenario. Primarily the state and G.O.I, provide all fund flows digitally with direct benefit transfer to eligible common citizen under different categories, on real time mode, with Dash Board and pop up monitoring and tracking".

(1) New Normal, (2) Circular economy, (3) Industry and (4) Artificial Intelligence are four important steps for improving the people over a period of time with normal functioning, keeping in view of Covid-19 pandemic.

S. Nagamani has identified the aspects of corporate survival struggle during pandemic era in her paper, in Chapter 3, she has analysed dataset sequentially step by step. They are:

1. Breaking the "Doom Loop", 2. Long term, "Scars" for consumer, 3. Planning for the next catastrophe, 4. Three keys to living in a crisis and 5. Debt stress.

She has further presented that, "however, further worsening of the economic environment could spell trouble for the giants too!"

6. Assets scales to the rescue, 7. Sheet downs and exists, 8. Fix fighting and Big lessons.

Keeping in view of the above aspects, finally concluded that, "only a steadfast focus on economic growth and adequate liquidity can get India Inc. out of mischief".

The author has attempted to present every aspect in the paper relating to economic growth and stress and it is doubtlessly created loss due to Covid-19 pandemic. The growth has been arrested to a zero point and the pertinent question is how to eke out the square meals by the population living such an environment and how long?"

Dr. K. Anjaneyulu has presented the entitled papers "Impact of sustainability dimension of corporate governance on select companies" and has further identified analytically step by step. They are:

1. Corporate Governance, 2. Sustainability and sustainable Development (SP); 3. Catalysing sustainability through corporate governance; 4. The governance of sustainability; 5. Sustainability governance best practices; 6. Factoring corporate governance in sustainability efforts and 7. Corporate Governance and sustainability; Action Agenda; and three ques-tions were presented.

Finally, suggested one and only one criteria for the progress is "Top down integration", besides 1. sustainable practices, 2. Sustainability reporting and 3. Total thoughts on corporate governance sustainability. Two important case studies such as 1. Hindustan Unilever (HUL) and 2) HDFC Ltd.

Finally, he has presented the Digital leverage, HDFC bank has effectively used digital payments to eke out distribution efficiency and cost to income ratio has been decreasing from financial year FY18 to Q2 FY21.

We conclude that it is an exemplary paper representing on Financial Management and efficiency measures during Covid-19.

Comment

The author of an excellent paper need not be praised because of its flow of excellency could be visible more in its run with more compound, complex sentences, and some times with simple sentences. The author must be thanked once again in this context. Many more people should have to follow to bring excellent papers in future by many researchers". (K.L. Narasimha Murthy) The methodology adopted in this regard is excellent.

"Gender Responsive budgeting - emerging paradigm in Management is a best paper in the field of planning and management subfield presented by Sri G.E. Lesilie. Tools & Methods of Gender budgeting and he has suggested for the future researchers to adopt either one tool or a combination of two or more tools at a time. It is understood that unimethod of variable is less better than multi-tool adoption for analysis (single to multiple method at a time). This is more praiseworthy while making use of the tools necessary, scholars may adopt six types of tools are given them at an analysis stage. They are:

1. Gender - Aware budget statement.
2. Sex-disaggregated beneficiary assessment of public service delivery and budget practices.
3. Sex-disaggregated Public expenditure benefit incidence analysis.
4. Sex-disaggregated Revenue incidence analysis.
5. Gender-Aware medium economic level and to incorporate gender variables into model.
6. Sex-disaggregated analysis of the impact of the budget or times use.
7. Gender-Aware policy/programme appraisal and impact analysis.

"Analysis of gender relations in a specific area of related policies and budget allocations, development of gender sensitive policies and their transaction into budgetory allocation, examination of impact of gender sensitive policy, analysis of impact of specific revenues on gender relations: development of a gender sensitive revenue policy and its implications and examination of the impact of gender sensitive revenue policy".

"The budget analysis is related to 9th, 10th, 11th and 12th plan and out of total budgetary support, a large chunk of amount has been earmarked for children, besides the allocation of revenues for new schemes have been introducted in the plan for women empowerment".

The analysis is quite excellent and apt to enable the researchers for the analysis for the future plan periods also. Ho doubt this is a new paradigm in Management studies and research. This is an additive model to the current knowledge in the field of management.

Comment

It must be a very good tool for empowering women by incorporating gender perspective for prospective gender and concerns at various stages and levels of development planning, policy, programmes and delivery dynamics.

The researcher has also presented important issues for women development and women empowerment.

Comment on paper 6

Professor V. Madhav Rao's research paper relating to "Geospatial Technology applications in Disaster Management" is highly scientific both for the researcher, administrator and to the managers of event management. Event Management is considered as a typical and topical subject of any discipline but the aptness and the quickness of the operator as well as operation of the machine mode approach to solve the problem oriented issues of the urgency precisely and certain measures have to be adopted for its clearance.

According to him Disaster and Disaster Risk Reduction are quite important to mitigate and manage it accurately Disaster, "a serious discription of the functioning of a community or a society causing wide spread human, material, economic and environmental losses which exceed the ability of the affected community society to cope using its own resources". The following phases, which consist the cycle 1. Disaster preparedness, 2. Disaster event, 3. Rescue and Relief, 4. Rehabilitation 5. Reconstruction and Mitigation.

"Remote sensing and GNSS Geospatial tools are important. The frequency, character and magnitude of disasters have an important spatial component. They are maps, aerial photograph, satellite imagery, GPS data and the allied etc. with different projection and co-ordinate system, to be brought out to a common map basis to overlay and generate inferences".

This paper is highly scientific and also important to operate them in the event management hierarchy. The costs and benefits are quite important for the governance to adopt (C&B Analysis).

In chapter 7, Ch.Kishore Kumar has presented the entitled paper, "Role of Blockchain Technology in Asia - A relook at China and India in Banking Sector". According to this study he has identified that, "but for all of the digital yuan's consequences, it is a toe peeking out from a giant red curtain.

Behind is an ambitives and largely invisible infrastructure programme to revise the country and its economy with a disturbed ledger technology known as Blockchain. China has moved deliberately to secure first mover and — advantage in what it believes is the future of the internet. If the digital Yuan is Beijings tender for the digital frontier; its blockchain initiative is its bid to build the railroads".

He has considered and analyzed theme based on 1. A new money 2. The West internet and also identified the benefits of blockchain.

He concludes that, "blockchain technology has the potential to create new industries and transform existing ones in a way we cannot imagine. For instance it has the capacity to facilitate nano-payments proportionate to an individuals contribution and value creation in the Internet, making it an ideal wealth redistribution tool for our digital age".

Comments

Finally, he has presented the future of cloud computing in India. This is essentially a descriptive research paper than an innovative methodological base for the basis of this paper. Any way, it is an exemplary paper in its own befitting status and structure without any statistical methodology.

Ms. M. Sangeetha has presented, "The role of Board of Directors in policy formulation and decision" and it is a good paper to the present knowledge. In her paper, she has identified and listed the ten most critical mistakes besides failed leadership. She has raised important questions such as, 1. How was the Board recruited? 2. How is the board used? 3. What is the attitude of management toward corporate governance 4. Why are they different to one of the most powerful tools available to management today? The above mistakes are the indicators of a failed board and perhaps a failing company and also has identified key reasons. They are 1. Perceived intent to independence, 2. Focus on tactics, 3. Makes extra work, 4. Resistance to change, 5. Ego and 6. Insecurity.

Nine steps to strategic recruiting has been indicated and also using objective recruiters, directors check test, independence decision making by Board and also their inter-related issues are stated. They are 1. Board role is level of involvement, 2. Time commitment Activities: (i) Strategy (ii) Management (iii) Development or succession (iv) Risk management (v) compliance.

2. Boards and standing of the company (i) From management (ii) from outside sources (iii) from prior experience; and

iii. Board management relationship i. Balance challenge and support ii. open and candid two way communication. i. A frame work for strategic engagement 2. Potential pay off and implementation 3. When the board makes the succession choice as the independent directors perspective; 5. Board tensions and trade offs in future by be new researchers in this field.

Comment

The above points are kept in mind for the smooth running of good policy formulation and decision. It is a good attempted paper and should be examined in some case studies of a company.

In Chapter 10, Dr. A. Venkata Rayudu has presented a paper on "Management of Tribal's produce in Andhra Pradesh". He has dealt with these aspects such as 1. Dependence on Agriculture 2. Dependence on Forest produce 3. Characteristic features of tribal economy - Economy is mostly primitive in nature - indebtedness is the both of tribal economy, the institutional finance in tribal areas private traders deprive the tribal - Role of non-institutional agencies i.e. private traders/merchants - weekly markets - categorisation of markets in tribal areas - non-institutional agencies - private traders - petty traders - middlemen -many leaders - bidern traders -

Institutional agencies/tribal development co-operative corporation (TDGCS) - were presented in part I of the chapter.

The second part has been dealt with 1. structure of Girijan Co-operative Corporation, Andhra Pradesh - Major objectives - procurement of MFP by GCC, procurement methodology, supply of essential commodities (ECs) and other items to tribals - ECs distribution process - supply of other daily requirements - supplies of TW Educational institutions - retail marketing by GEC - Institutional arrangements - processing of MFP commodities taken up by GCC - processing of agricultural commodities by GCC, Visakhapatnam Agro-credit activity by GCC - present loaning strategy - coffee plantation - Trade patterns - 2015-2020-21; commodity with procurement of Agro produce by GCC and conclusions were presented.

Comment

The above titled paper occupies a predominant position in the marketing of tribal produce and it is aptly presented by Dr. A. Venkatarayudu, and it helps further for the furtherence of the tribal society of the total population of Andhra Pradeh, G.O.A.P. should have to takeup welfare measures in this regard to Girijans.

In Chapter 9, Dr. Rao has presented the quantitative techniques (Q.T) in management studies for achieving analytical framework and good results. In this chapter, he has carried-out tests such as small sample tests, where in he has tested the following. They are 1. Test for sample mean, 2. 't' test for difference of means.

For the above, he has solved two problems 'f' test for equality of population variance. It is a good test. 'Z' test for independence of attributes.

Chi - square (χ^2-square) test of goodness of fit, Poisson distribution for the given data has also been tested. Quantitative techniques are quite important in order to identify the statistical soundness and results of the analyzed data.

Comment

This is an exemplary paper for new researchers to follow for carrying out the statistical analysis.

In Chapter 11, P. Padmamalini has submitted a thesis on "Digitalisation Banking" for the award of Ph.D. in Management. It is an outstanding and excellent thesis. She has dealt with the following aspects.

1. Introduction
2. Banking technology and customers satisfaction
3. Adoption of Core Banking values
4. Customer satisfaction index
5. Revamping of Digital agenda
6. Digital transformation
7. Need of the study
8. Significance of the study
9. Problem statement
10. Review of literature
11. Research Gap
12. Objectives of the study
13. Hypothesis Demographic factors
14. Determinants of Digitalisation
15. Dependent variables
16. Scope of the study
17. Period of study
18. Objectives of the study

19. Hypothesis
20. Sources of data
21. Methodology
22. Sampling methodology
23. Sample size
24. Employee sample determination
25. Statistical tools; and
26. Limitations of the study are important aspects of the study.

Important tests such as:

1. The chi - square analysis results.
2. The study has strengthened the association of the demographic factors of customers of the bank has been measured by the Phi and eramess with digital banking attributes.
3. The study observed that the employee perception on the digital banking operations is found to be significant at five percent level under 'T' test. The mean scope of the operational reliability (0.543) is found to be high.
4. The discriminant analysis has been carried out and with the help of relative threshold discriminant, score employee perception level has been examined. The analysis and its result reveals that the "operational reliability" found to be highest discriminant score (17.55%).
5. The factor analysis has been applied and the principle component method had extracted high load factors among the 13 highly viewed problems which are considered by the banking customers of private and public sector.

Comment

This work is highly sophisticated and statistically well presented. It is the best thesis and suits the order of the current scenario of Banking services.

12.2

New Areas of Research

Keeping in view of the current research scenario, there is every need to identify and recognise the potential areas of research in Management for the future research scholars which facilitates them to be on the right track and direction. The following are the new areas of research broadly. They are:

1. Corporate social responsibility; Retrospect and prospect.
2. Community Development through five year plans - A case study of the Indian Union.
3. Role of NGO's in Community Development : A state level study.
4. Banking Development in India 1969 to 2021. - A case study of Andhra Bank.
5. Impact of New private Life Insurance Companies on Life Insurance Corporation of India - A strategic appraisal.
6. Role of LIC Business abroad and India: A comparative study.
7. Globalisation, privatisation and liberalisation: A strategy of Development.
8. The Covid-19 Pandemic : Indian Experience.
9. Artificial Intelligence based healthcare: A strategy.
10. Healthcare market in India: a case study.
11. MDG - a critical evaluation (Management).
12. Disaster Management: An appraisal.
13. Flood and Disaster impact: A study of Micro and Macro Level.
14. Drought impact on society: An evaluation.
15. Time series analysis: An Analytic view (agniculture Sector)
16. Special Development strategy and management of healthcare system: A Study in a newly formed Telangana State, India.

17. Cost-Benefit analysis - A case study of a cement manufacturing industry.
18. Input and output analysis: Hindustan Steels Ltd.
19. Corporate sector and Development strategy.
20. Public sector banks and private sector banks (Changing roles and functions).
21. Integrated Tribal Development Agency - Its role and functional operation, Andhra Pradesh.
22. Integrated Tribal Development Agency: A case study of Telangana State, India.
23. Bank operation after Merger: Employee & Employer Relations.
24. Operations Research in Management studies: Andhra Bank.
25. Digitalisation Banking - Public sector Banks:
    A critical Note and Analysis.

Emerging Research Areas in Commerce and Management

1. India's Growth Strategy: Strengths and Challenges in Globalising World.
2. Rethinking India's Growth Strategy; Career building through Technical Education in the era of globalisation.
3. India's success in achieving balanced Regional Development in the wake of Liberalisation.
4. Growth Strategies- old and new economy models.
5. Development :A never ending process.
6. Transition in Indian Growth models.
7. Economic reforms, growth and structural change in India: State level Time series analysis.
8. Sectoral disparities in India
9. Sectoral shift in India's Economic growth and reflections from HR perspective.
10. Trends in Employment intensity of economic growth in the post-reform era across Indian states.
11. Manufacturing competitiveness and Indian Economic development: Some strategic imperatives.
12. Better strategies - Better management control systems in manufacturing area.

13. Development of pharmaceutical sector in India: trends, opportunities and challenges.
14. Competitive advantages of India incorporations.
15. Entrepreneurship skill development for inclusive growth.
16. Structural changes in Indian economy -Role of service sector.
17. Sectoral shift: service sector impact on South Indian states with special reference to knowledge economy.
18. BPO to KPO - Opportunities and challenges.
19. Modes, phrases and challenges in personalisation of World Wide Web.
20. Service driven Indian economy: a healthy trust towards brighter tomorrow.
21. Contribution of business services to India's economic growth.
22. Output and employment growth in service sector: The Indian experience.
23. Open policies in service sector growth in India: Does service sector promote economic growth of India.
24. Impact of EDI capital on accountants and auditors; a study of Indian automobile industry.
25. Rethinking growth strategy and tribal health in India.
26. A tripartite model for Rural development through vendor development project.
27. Post Liberalisation experience of agriculture growth, poverty, employment and rural indebtedness in different states.
28. Economic reforms and agrarian crisis in India.
29. Cropping pattern changes and performance of agriculture in different states.
30. Rural indebtedness: special reference to sugar cane growers.
31. Impact of double taxation agreements on international trade and flow of foreign capital.
32. Impact of Quota restrictions on marketing of Yarn in India.
33. From import substitution to export promotion: the changing contours of economic policy.
34. Challenges in International trade: efforts to regain the lost position.
35. Dynamics of foreign Trade : challenges and opportunities.
36. Trade and development in India: forging new linkages and strategic alliances.

37. The announcement impact of bank rate on certificate of deposit rates in India.
38. Financing secondary education: opportunities and challenges.
39. Corporate bank strategies : significance.
40. Eradicating Rural indebtedness through microfinance.
41. Central bank autonomy and financial deregulation in India.
42. Rethinking India's growth strategy in the light of financial sector reforms with particular reference to credit guarantee trust for micro and small industries.
43. Financial liberalisation in India: challenges and policy implications.
44. Infrastructure development for sustaining India's economic growth across manufacturing and service sectors.
45. Rule based fiscal control and public service spending : an analysis of state level FRBM legislation in India.
46. Disinvestment in India- a stakeholders' management perspective.
47. Public financing of elementary education under economic liberalisation.
48. Insurance - driven by innovative distribution channels.
49. Global outsourcing in service industries: experience of developed and developing countries.
50. Trade and development in India: gorging new linkages and strategic alliances.
51. Financing human development: policies and strategies in select states.
52. Reduction of poverty and unemployment in rural areas : an analysis.
53. Labour law reform in India: issues and concerns.
54. Industrial promotion policy and employment.
55. Sustaining business for development : a study of women.
56. Health management - a key driver to growth : stress factors amongst call centre employees.
57. Gender inequalities and deprivations.
58. Reforms in public sector and public private partnership

12.3

UGC Major Research Project Proposal

Healthcare Infrastructure in Telangana state (Newly formed state in India)

(A case Study using PCM and Cost Benefits Analysis

Introduction

'Protection of Health' is an important norm for any governance and proves that there is no exception to any State/Nation. Health is a fundamental human right and occupies a central point in health and health sector of any country. The quantity of life depends upon the quantity of health infractructure. Generally, the spatial inequality in healthcare infrastructure play an important role in the total health condition of the population. Besides this, 'Environment' leads to an active impact on human being residing in a Nation/State/District etc. or for example a micro level unit such as "Mandal". There exists a wide spread inequality in the distribution of healthcare facilities (health-infra) and this study is quite important and thus help to identify the inequality in health-infra particularly in the Newly formed Telangana state, India. According to Joseph and Phillips, 1984 that knowledge and understanding of healthcare infra is necessary for health resource allocation and planning. Healthcare is a social determination as it influences the socio-economic policies.

The basic objective of eleventh Five Year Plan was to achieve goal i.e. "health" for all, specially related to poor and the underprivileged. Keeping in view of the above scenario in mind, the department of Health and Family Welfare has concern and primary health services by channelising sufficient financial sources and many resources to provide healthcare service more possible and affordable particularly to poor in the hierarchy of society.

2. **Earlier studies:** The variations in different indicators of development in various regions may be attributed to the variations in policy

perspectives, critical background and uneven distribution of the resources. (Dadi Bhavi at 2006) A union of studies have been conducted dealing with regional disparities and level of development at macro levels using a number of development in bisectors. Debapriya and Mohanty (2000), analyses variation in the level of development and found growing disparities in Socio-economic sector at inter and intra regions. Wang (2007) has used the method of composite index and various social and economic indicators to measure the level of development. Sheban and Bhole (1999) used the principal component method (PCM) to assess the level of development in different districts of Maharashtra, using different indicators and variables. Amit Kumar Singh and V.K. Kumar, 'spatial inequality of healthcare Infrastructure in Allahabad district: A Geographical study' chol. 62(3) September: 2016 (pp. 283-284), important.

3. **Importance of the study project (Major Research Project) contribution:** The present research project attempts to investigate micro level (Mandal) disparities in the availability of healthcare facilities in the state and Micro regions. This study is likely to be helpful for administrators, Policy makers and planners to find solution to the existing problem and promote for the balanced development particularly at the micro level.

4. **Review of literature:** Aich, M, Mahizebin, Mend Fahria Subarna N, and Hassan, A (2014): A study on socio-economic condition and Nutritional profile of women workers in Shrimp and agriculture sectors in selected two districts of Bangladesh, Int. Res. J. Socisl Sc. 2. Barm, R. Acharya, A, Acharya S. Siva in India. Caste, class and Regime Economics and Political Weekly, 65(38)[2] Chouber, K (2008)[3] Healthcare/delivery in Madhya Pradesh, India. Healthcare Patterns and Planning, edited by Aichtar, R, ABH Publishing Corporation, New Delhi, Rajeshwari and Sinha, S. (2004)[4], spatial inequalities in the development of Public Healthcare facilities in Rural Haryana, India, Healthcare patterns and planning edited by Akthar, R, APH. Publishing Corporation, New Delhi, and W.H.O., 1978, Alma-Ata 1978 primary Healthcare: Health for All, Sr. No. 1, World Health Organisation, Geneva are important studies in this field.

5. **Study Area:** The newly formed state, Telangana state, and the main stay of Economy is primarily agriculture and Urban structural/ pockets. The state is characterised by fast growing population,

lack of appropriate transportation, adequate healthcare deliver and education.

6. **Objectives:** The following are the main ojectives of the present study:
   1. To evaluate the existing infrastructure for healthcare services in Telangana state/Sub-state regions.
   2. To assess the inter-Mandal variations in healthcare facilities in the study region i.e. Telangana state, and
   3. To find out the regional pattern in the distribution of healthcare infrastructure in Telangana state.
7. **Data Base and Methodology:** The present research work is based entirely on primary as well as secondary source of data available, @ Census of India, 2011 and Bureau of Economics and Statistics, Government of Telangana State, India. The present study relates to 12 indicators of physical infrastructure services will be considered to find out the Healthcare Infrastructure Index for Telangana state.
   1. Availability of Healthcare facilities
   2. Performance of Public healthcare Centre, and
   3. Accessibility to healthare facilities.
8. **Methodology:** To find out the level of development of healthcare infrastructure, Healthcare Infrastructure Index (HII) has to be computed. It will be calculated by taking a simple average of the chosen indicators. It may be algebraically expressed as

$$\frac{\mathrm{H}ii = \Sigma^{n}{}_{i} = \mathrm{I}i\mathrm{J}}{N}$$

Where 'N' represents total number of selected indicators for healthcare infrastructure and H*ii* denotes the Healthcare infrastructure Index for jth block. The high values of H*ii*, indicate high level of development and vice versa.

Selected indicators of healthcare Infrastructure

1. Availability of	X_1 Doctors population Ratio
Healthcare	X_2 Population Served per Primary Healthcare Centre (PHC)
Infrastructure	X_3 Population served per Centre

	X_4 Number of Medical institutions per 1,00,000 population
	X_5 Number of Beds for 1,00,000 population
2. Performance of	X_6 Percentage of indoor patients to total patients of the unit (Dist)
Public Healthcare centres	X_7 Percentage of Outdoor patients to total outdoor patients of the Unit (Dist)
	X_8 Percentage of immunisation to total immunisation of the Unit (Dist)
	X_9 Percentage of institutional delivery to total institutional delivery of the Unit (Dist)
3 Accessibility to	X_{10} Number of Medical institutions per 100 sq. Km
Healthcare	X_{11} Number of Sub Centers per 100 sq. Km
Infrastructure	X_{12} Percentage of villages with nearest PHC with in 5 Km (If not available within the village)

The above variables may be considered for undertaking this study, using PC. Methodology and cost benefit analysis for infra elements.

9. **Conclusion:** The present study focuses on infrastructural facilities of healthcare system in a unit (Dist). This study provides valuable information about present state of healthcare in the Dist. and also it focuses an extreme shortage of healthcare institution and manpower in the Public health system. The most important thing is to recruit the required no. of doctors and staff for public health institutions.

Access to services is an important determinant in meeting the healthcare needs of the people, especially living in remote areas, Ambulance service to transport serious cases to referred centers is very important.

There is every need to emphasise the process of strengthening the infrastructural facilities at CHC/PHCs level to utilise their full potential. To reduce the gap between existing and required analysis which facilitates there will be a need to propose the healthinfra with cost-benefit analysis to the governance to implement some of the recommendations of the planner in a phased manner during the plan period, keeping in view of the population increase. Another point to be considered here is the ongoing efforts of the government to buildup private public partnership (PPP) and involve the lower units more effectively in Participation Management of healthcare services are quite expected to ensure better healthcare services.

10. **Significance of the study:** This survey, analysis and result would definitely be useful to the dist/state machinery to enable them to implement some of the recommendations/ suggestions which may be incorporated in planning and development of the dist/state/plan.
11. **Relevance to the present day problems and needs of the society and country:**

    Step 1: The collected data should have to be analyzed in relation to its service and administrative functions. All the services (healthcare are to be arranged in a descending order of its population and also to establish the hierarchy).

    Step 2: The urgency warrants the project investigator to survey, identity, analyse and interpret the existing problems of the study area and also to find out possible solutions to overcome the situation. It is the primary duty of the individual or researcher to identify the most important needs of the society belonging to the existing environment.
12. **Likely Contribution to Knowledge:** This knowledge contributes at large for solving some of the needs of society and country. If we consider district as a micro unit, the maso unit is state and the Macro Unit is Nation. Though this work appears to be applied in nature the basis of planning at the grassroots level is much felt by the society. The strategy of the governance is that government has been trying to involve people to contribute their share for achieving the overall development as well as special stress on sectoral development. It is necessary for people to interact with the governments policies to achieve special development strategy through the management of healthcare system to an optimum level.

12.4

SUMMARY and CONCLUSIONS

The present work, "Current Research Trends in Commerce and Management (B. Management" have been divided into 12 chapters. They are: 1. Introduction, 2. Evolving scenerio for Commerce and management in India, 3. Corporate survival struggle during pandemic era, 4. Impact of sustainability dimension of corporate governance on select companies and 5. Gender Responsive budgeting - emerging paradigm in management.

Geospatial technology applications in disaster Management (6), (7) Role of Block chain technology in Asia, A relook at China and India in Banking sector, 8. Role of Board of Directors in Policy formulation and decision making, 9. Quantitative techniques in Management Research, 10. Digitalisation Banking and 11. Marketing Management.

In Chapter one, K.L. Narasimha Murthy has presented lucidy the relationship of 'search' and 'research' and further identified that active, reactive and interactive processes and its role to the maximum possible extent in the entire study. Interdisciplinary and multi-disciplinary approach is the order of the current research and environmental factors have its influence on human society, corporate social responsibility (CSR) and its role in community development. Nine gaps have been identified in the present literature survey and the same were answered serially and sequentially in the proceeding chapters and research work progressed step by step totally.

V. Madhava Rao has presented and provided an overview of the four key components which have an impact on commerce and management for present decade and decades to come in Chapter 2.

In chapter 3, S. Nagamani has presented the corporate survival struggle during pandemic era and the great depression caused real GDP decline for 43 months long, as a result it eventually reduced by 30 percent, she has further attributed that most of important indicators to watch are not only economic but also were the weekly trends in new Covid-19 cases number of deaths and governors making isolation orders but also more stringent or lenient.

K. Anjaneyulu has recognised and identified "the impact of sustainability dimension of corporate governance on select companies" in the present paper, in chapter 4. He has categorically stated that, the mindset of the business leaders of the people with money has begun to change and getting profits and more money is no longer the only leading principle in the corporate governance world. The sustainable development ideas have entered as well and have the potential to improve this world for the better".

Gender responsive budgeting - emerging paradigm in management keeping in view of MDG (Millenium Development Goals) has presented in 5th chapter including some problems relating to Gender ma ins t reaming in Urban sector by G.E. Lesilee.

"Geospatial Technology applications in Disaster Management" has been presented in Chapter 6, by V. Madhava Rao and found that technology, adaptability, mitigation measures, assessment, prediction, decision support and modern technologies have reduced the impact of disaster to a reasonable level.

Ch. Kishore Kumar has presented, "The Role of Blockchain Technology in Asia-A Relook at China and India in Banking Sector" in the 7th chapter and further recognised that, "during two decades of historic economic growth, clime has had a mixed record on high tederologies. It has struggle to attain self sufficiency, never mind dominace in the production of semi-conductors and chips. It was a head of the curve on 56 Broadband but lags behind the West in field of argually greater strategic value such as artificial intelligence".

Ms. M. Sangeetha categorically presented the, "Role of Board of Directors in Policy formulation and decision making" in the 8th chapter and further opind that, "Of course what drives the value of any board is the quality of the directors and their willingness and ability assume the tremendous obligations inherent in board membership. No set of systems and no check list can ever ensure good governance. Only good people can the magic comes when outstanding directors combine with best practices".

C.S.S.S.L. Hanumantha Rao in his paper presented in Chapter 9, the Quantitative Techniques (Q.T) in Management Research, play an important and pivotal role entirely. He has noted that the sampling distribution of statistics following normal distribution (i.e.) as the sample size in large size No. 30, we assured that the sampling distribution followed normal distribution.

In Chapter 11, P. Padmamalini has presented a good thesis, "Digitalisation Banking" and stressed that the banks have to adopt modern strategic marketing philosophy, besides, maintaining banks of operational management of their services. Further identified that, the formulation of marketing mix is directly or indirectly influenced by changing behaviour of the users. It is a good thesis during 2010-2021 period.

Annexure-I

71st All India
Commerce Conference of ICA
20–22 December, 2018

Conference theme:
Innovations,
Entrepreneurship &
Sustainable Development

Organised by:
Department of Commerce, Osmania University
Hyderabad, Telangana State

In Collaboration with:
Telangana State Council of Higher Education
Institute of Public Enterprise

Suman Kalyan Chaudhary
Faculty Member, P.G. Department of
Business Administration, Berhampur
University, Berhampur, Odisha;
PN: 760007

Corporate Social Responsibility: A Brief Study
Authors
Dr. Jyotindra Kumar Pathak
Assistant Professor, Tapeshwar Singh
Teachers Training College, Kayamnagar

Dr. S.P. Jain
Assistant Professor, Deptt. of BBA &
B. Com., D.K. College, Dumraon

Managing Talent Through Corporate Social Responsibility

Author
Prof. Dr. Suresh Ravjibhai Savani
Head & Dean, Faculty of Commerce,
Department of Commerce, Maharaja
Krishna Kumar Sinhji Bhavnagar
University, Bhavnagar-364002 (Gujarat)

Corporate Social Responsibility and Its Role in Community Development: An Indian Perspective

Author
Dr. Hetal Jyotkumar Mehta
Principal, Swami Sahajanand College of
Commerce & Management, (Affiliated to
M.K. Bhavnagar University), ISCON
Mega City, Bhavnagar-364002 (Gujarat)

Corporate Social Responsibility Initiatives by IOCI: A Case Study of Guwahati

Authors
Chandana Kashyap
Research Scholar, Department of
Commerce, Gauhati University
Guwahati – 781014, Assam
Dr. Amrit Pal Singh
Professor, Department of Commerce,
Gauhati University, Guwahati-781014,
Assam.

Dr. Ashima Sharma Borah
Associate Professor, Department of
Management, KC Das Commerce
College, Guwahati-781008, Assam.

Corporate Social Responsibility: Challenges And Opportunities
Author

Dr. Morage Prakash V.
Associate Professor, Govt. Women's
First Grade College Jewargi
Colony, Gulbarga. (Karnataka-India)

Implementing of CSR in India: Issues and Challenges

Author

Dr. Ambanna Malkappa
Assistant Professor, Govt. First Grade
College Farahatabad, Tq. &
Dist. Kalaburagi-585308

CSR Expenditure in Education Sector of Odisha: An Empirical Study

Authors

Dr. Kishore Kumar Das
(Second Author) Head, Department of
Business Administration, Ravenshaw
University, Cuttack

Ms Ananya Mitra (First Author)
Research Scholar in Utkal University,
Bhubaneswar

Dr. Shradhanjali Panda
(Third Author) Assistant Professor
(Finance) in Department of Business
Administration. Ravenshaw University

ROLE OF NGO'S IN CORPORATE SOCIAL RESPONSILITY (CSR)
Author

Dr. Md Imteyaz Hasan
H.O.D. Department of Commerce,
College of Commerce, Arts & Science.
Patna

Dr. Saad Bin Hamid
Associate Professor, Department of Commerce, Soghra College, Biharsharif
Dr. Tanvir Ahsan Nizami
Assistant Professor, Department of Economics, Oriental College, Patna City

INNOVATION ENTREPRENEURSHIP AND SUSTAINABLE DEVELOPMENT

Author
Dr. Anil V. Surkar
Lok Maha Vidyalay, Wardha, Maharashtra

CORPORATE SOCIAL RESPONSIBILITY: POLICY AND PRACTICES

Authors
Kundan Kumar Singh
Research Scholar, B.R.A.B.U. Muzaffarpur (Bihar)
Dr. Md. Firoj Alam
Research Fellow in Commerce, B.R.A.B.U. Muzaffarpur (Bihar)

Dr. Anish Chandra Mishra
Research Fellow in Commerce, B.R.A.B.U. Muzaffarpur (Bihar)

EVALUATING PRADHAN MANTRI GRAMIN DIGITAL SAKSHARTA ABHIYAN
(PMGDISHA) FOR SUSTAINABLE EXPANSION

Authors

Dr. Ravindra Gharpure
Assistant Professor, Central Institute of Business Management, Research and Development, Nagpur.
Dr. Rahul Mohare
Assistant Professor, Shri Ramdeobab College of Engineering and Management, Nagpur.
Prof. Tanmary Gupta
Assistant Professor, Shri Ramdeobab College of Engineering and Management, Nagpur.

CORPORATE SOCIAL RESPONSIBILITY : POLICIES AND PRACTICES

Authors
Bharat Bhushan
Research Scholar, Management
B.R.A.B.U., Muzaffarpur, Bihar
Amrendra Kumar
Research Scholar, Commerce
B.R.A.B.U., Muzaffarpur, Bihar

Index

C

Q

R

S